PRAISE FOR *VIBRANT VOICES*

So many forces in our hypermodern culture have denied the ancient triad of women, art, and the sacred that we can barely grasp all that has been lost to us. *Vibrant Voices* makes an insightful and deeply beautiful contribution to the recovery, as well as inspiration for creative new directions.

— Charlene Spretnak, author of *The Spiritual Dynamic in Modern Art, 1800 to the Present*

A stunning testimony to the importance of the path-breaking, boundary-crossing work of the Association for the study of Women and Mythology.

— Carol P. Christ, author of *Goddess and God in the World and A Serpentine Path*

This stunning volume reveals and celebrates the female divine through artistry, poesy, and superb scholarship. The thorough integration of historical, experiential, and visionary voices is a pivotal achievement. *Vibrant Voices* is an essential guide and touchstone for all future work on women and mythology.

— Miranda Shaw, author of *Passionate Enlightenment: Women in Tantric Buddhism* and *Buddhist Goddesses of India*

This collection of wisdom of foremothers of women's spirituality is indispensable for understanding the possibilities today in the midst of converging environmental, political, gender, and spiritual crises - - and to birthing a new civilization where nobody is 'othered' everybody creates a society of love and justice.

— Lucia Chiavola Birnbaum, author of *Dark Mother* and *Future Has an Ancient Heart*

This Anthology is an amazing amalgam of art, vision and scholarship by women dedicated to bringing Goddess consciousness to light in whatever form She is experienced and expressed. That Her presence has prevailed across cultures throughout time attests to the power of women spirit rising now to create Mother World in Her image. Her powerful presence across cultures throughout time gives hope that this troubled world can yet be re-created in Her image, as attested to by the power of women rising today! That She continues to emerge across cultures throughout time is a balm to the soul in today's troubled world.

— Musawa, founder of *We'Moon Gaia Rhythms for Womyn*

This is a rich and beautiful volume, presenting a vivid conversation among goddess scholars and artists working in many genres. In many of the chapters the text offers important insights into the artists' own journeys. In addition, the book takes seriously issues of indigenization and decolonialization in order to further a practice of transformational multiculturalism. Congratulations to all who brought this book into being. I am moved and inspired by this work.

— Mary Jo Neitz, Professor Emerita, Women's and Gender Studies, University of Missouri

This is an engaging and fascinating volume with a broad array of offerings. It features interdisciplinary and embodied research from diverse perspectives — those of emerging voices as well as familiar voices of established scholars and foremothers in the women's spirituality movement. The narrative, enriched with poetry, art images, and photographs, ensures that *Vibrant Voices: Women, Myth, and the Arts* is aptly titled. Anyone interested in mythological and archaeomythological studies, ritual studies, iconography, art and creative processes, women's studies, women's spirituality, and goddess spirituality will find a rich selection from which to gain inspiration, to explore and savor.

— Susan G. Carter, Ph.D.

VIBRANT VOICES:
Women, Myth, and the Arts

PROCEEDINGS OF THE ASSOCIATION
FOR THE STUDY OF WOMEN AND MYTHOLOGY
VOLUME II

Edited by
Sid Reger and Marna Hauk

Printed in the United States of America

ISBN: 978-0-9969617-8-3

Published by

Women and Myth Press
www.womenandmyth.org
Interior and cover designed by Rebekkah Dreskin
www.blameitonrebekkah.com
Front cover art "Bee Goddess of Rhodes Banner" by Lydia Ruyle
Bee goddess logo by Sid Reger

Excerpts from Miriam Robbins Dexter and Victor H. Mair, *Sacred Display: Divine and Magical Female Figures of Eurasia* (New York: Cambria Press, 2010), reprinted by permission.

"Blessing on the Poets" from Annie Finch, *A Poet's Craft: A Comprehensive Guide to Making and Sharing Your Poetry* (Ann Arbor, MI: University of Michigan Press, 2012), reprinted by permission.

"Dreams of Earth: Earth Dreaming as Eco-Resilience Practice for the Long Emergency" previously published in a slightly different version from Marna Hauk, *Ecopsychology* (Rochelle, NY: Mary Ann Liebert, Inc., 2015). Reprinted by permission.

"O Great Mother of Creation" from Marna Hauk, *At the Crossroads We'Moon 09* (Wolf Creek, OR: Mother Tongue Ink) and Arise, Movie, directed by Lori Joyce and Candice Orlando (2012; Idanha Films/ Mist Productions), reprinted by permission.

"Litha" from Patricia Monaghan, *Seasons of the Witch: Poetry and Songs to the Goddess*, (Cottage Grove, WI: Creatrix Books, 2004), reprinted by permission.

Excerpt from "Embodied Maps of Multicultural 'Integrative Solidarity': A Mestiza (Xicana, Filipina, and Euroamerican) Approach to Creative Texts" from Cristina Rose Smith, was previously published in *El Mundo Zurdo 4: Selected Works from the 2013 Meeting of the Society for the Study of Gloria Anzaldua* (San Francisco: Aunt Lute Books, 2013), pages 127-138. Reprinted by permission.

"Storytelling and Goddess Scholarship" by Nancy Vedder-Shults was previously published in *SageWoman*, Volume 83, Winter 2012, pp. 63-65. Reprinted by permission.

DEDICATION

This volume is dedicated to Mary B. Kelly and Lydia Ruyle, foremothers in art and research. Each of them brought to life images and symbols of goddesses in world cultures, inspired countless artists, scholars, and students, and shared their wisdom with our founders.

We also dedicate this book to our personal foremothers, who gave us our love of words and images:

> Carol Ashby Reger, artist and lover of nature and folklore, whose generosity and enthusiasm inspired many to find the art forms of their lives.

> Barbara Louise Hauk, artist and poet, who authored multiple volumes of poetry and co-edited the poetry magazine Pearl for more than twenty years with two other amazing women.

May these women's works spark future explorations of the arts and mythology.

—

CONTENTS

FOREWORD   i

INTRODUCTION   iii

SECTION 1
From the Beginning: Research into Images of the Female Divine

---

POEM: A GEOLOGY LESSON   2
Judy Grahn

ART, MYTH AND THE SACRED FEMININE   3
Arisika Razak

SACRED DISPLAY: DIVINE AND MAGICAL FEMALE   27
FIGURES OF ANCIENT EURASIA
Miriam Robbins Dexter

THE GODDESS SRI SPIRIT IN JAVANESE MITONI   59
PREGNANCY RITUAL: TRADITIONAL LURIK WOVEN
CLOTHS IN INSTALLATION ART
Aprina Murwanti

TONANTZIN COATLICUE GUADALUPE: CHRISTIAN   78
SYMBOLISM, COLONIZATION AND SOCIAL JUSTICE
Yuria Celidwen

SECTION 2
Inquiry into the Art of Experiencing the Goddess

POEM: LITHA   104
Patricia Monaghan

ABUNDANT EMBODIMENT IN AN ANICONIC TRADITION: 105
NATURE, TRANCE AND ART IN YORUBA RELIGIONS
Mei-Mei Sanford

SANCTUARY: FEMININE CENTERED DWELLINGS AS   116
AREAS OF SACRED PROTECTION
Toni Truesdale

DREAMS OF EARTH: MYTH AND PLANETARY PRESENCE
WHILE CONVENING A VIRTUAL HYGEIAN DREAM TEMPLE   129
Marna Hauk

SECTION 3
Honoring Our Artist-Scholar Foremothers

POEM: I GIVE YOU TO THE ANCESTORS   150
Gina Belton

LYDIA RUYLE: A PERSONALIZED BIOGRAPHY (1935 - 2016)   151
Joan M. Cichon

AN APPRECIATION OF MARY B. KELLY (1936-2016),   157
WITH PUBLICATIONS LIST
Joan Marler

SECTION 4
Artists, Their Work and Their Words

POEM: BLESSING ON THE POETS   174
Annie Finch

COLORS AND FORMS SHIFTING INTO TIME AND PLACE   175
Laura Fragua-Cota

IN THE EYES OF MEDUSA   188
Cristina Biaggi

SPLASH: MERMAIDS   197
Lydia Ruyle

SEEKING THE HOLY WIND: ARTISTS AT WORK   209

   FIRE GODDESS AND WATER GODDESS FROM
   THE YURT ~ Rae Atira-Soncea

   SHE CALLS TO THE SOUL SEEDS DANCING AT
   THE EDGE OF THE UNIVERSE ~ Denise Kester

   MEDUSA RE-MEMBERED ~ Helen Klebesadel

   PRAYING MANTIS & BUTTERFLY GODDESS ~ Louie Laskowski

   SHERAWALI ~ Lisa Levart

   HONORING LYDIA: A DOUBLE GODDESS ALTAR ~ Barb Lutz

   ARTEMIS BEE LABYRINTH ~ Lisa Noble

   I AM CRONE ~ Merry Grant Norris

   THE MASKS OF THE GODDESS PROJECT ~ Lauren Raine

   WISDOM HARVEST ~ Sid Reger

   LA GOLONDRINA IBON ~ Cristina Rose Smith

   A GRANDMOTHER'S LOVE ~ Carmen R. Sonnes

SECTION 5
Herstories and Solidarities

POEM: CALLING YOU--WHO!   236
Ann Filemyr

THE REPRESENTATION OF GODDESS IMAGERY   237
IN FEMINIST ART
Simone Clunie

STORYTELLING AND GODDESS SCHOLARSHIP   265
Nancy Vedder-Shults

STORIES OF MULTICULTURAL INTEGRATIVE SOLIDARITY: 275
A MESTIZA (XICANA, FILIPINA, AND EUROAMERICAN)
APPROACH TO CREATIVE TEXTS
Cristina Rose Smith

RESPECTFUL ENGAGEMENT WITH LIVING TRADITIONS   289
Kathryn Henderson

POEM: O GREAT MOTHER OF CREATION: A PRAYER FOR   308
SHEALING THE MATRILINEAL LINE
Marna Hauk

AFTERWORD   309

ACKNOWLEDGMENTS   311

APPENDIX: SCHOLARLY PUBLICATIONS BY MARY B. KELLY   313

CONTRIBUTORS   317

LIST OF ILLUSTRATIONS   327

FOREWORD

JUDY GRAHN

Art has always a major part of the development and wisdom teach-
ings of women's spirituality, from the earliest known stone goddess
icons to the sometimes controversial and often political art shows in
contemporary times. Judy Chicago's installations, including *The Dinner
Party*, are only the best known of what has been a continual outpouring
of visual interpretations of the sacred feminine since the resurgence of
women's spirituality in conjunction with waves of feminism and women's
activism, especially since the late 1960s. These early movement images
were skillfully contextualized by art critics such as Lucy Lippard, Gloria
Feman Orenstein, and Elinor Gadon and by works by artists as various
in approach as Yolanda Lopez, Mayumi Oda and Monica Sjöö. It is no
surprise, then, but sheer delight to find that this book is primarily an art
volume, with plenty of reflection and a plethora of color images accompanied by explanatory essays and representing contemporary artists from
many traditions. The essays add to our sensual experiences as well as to
our ever-expanding knowledge base of exactly what qualities goddess
practices and beliefs bring to the human table, and they address how we
can more effectively learn to call on the spirit powers that can help to guide
us and unite us in the current crisis-ridden times.

The art does not simply illustrate a concept. It actually *is* the concept.
It also is a knowledge-endowing text, in part because of the historic layer
that is always present and in part because the artists frequently use their
art to imaginatively replicate possible deeper cultural, spiritual, communal
and psychological meanings from the past or present. Such an artist in
this volume is Aprina Murwanti, who defines herself as an Asian Javanese
Muslim woman artist and whose installation art was created for the goddess
Sri, uses *lurik* cloth to portray the pregnancy safety ritual *Mitoni*, which the

artist experienced firsthand during her own pregnancy. Murwanti closely describes her use of bricolage—mixed media of nontraditional materials—in creating sewn-cloth soft sculpture figures at floor level that cast dramatic shadows high on the wall, implying a goddess with powers that fill the space both subjectively and objectively, an immanent goddess who occupies one's body while simultaneously watching from overhead. In Murwanti's essay, one experiences the art, even flat on the page, and simultaneously learns and feels something about the culture and character of the goddess.

This simultaneous combination of the subjective and the objective is what artist Laura Fragua-Cota calls her voice through "many languages of art." Her Pueblo Indian village scenes depict dances, sculpted and painted faces of members of the community, masked men dressed in deer antlers and dancing a blessing for the animals, and Mother Earth dressed in dark blue and pouring out water and abundance. Fragua-Cota herself has participated in Pueblo dances, and her art offering, like others in this volume, conveys the seamless fluidity between human lives and other earth lives, held together by spirit.

The invitational qualities and broad diversity of origin and expression of the selections in this volume—including an essay on the impossibility of depicting the Yoruba goddess Oshun, because she is a divine energy—are balanced by histories of the colonization that the foremothers and preservers of indigenous religions and community have had to endure. This historic truth, which continues to this day, is further balanced by thoughtful essays by Christina Rose Smith, about decolonizing the self, and by Kathryn Henderson, about ways that a seeker of current goddess knowledge from living traditions not her own can avoid the pitfalls of appropriation and misuse of partially learned practices. Inclusion is crucial at this time, and "the door is opening," she says. Walk through it.

An optimism pervades this volume, perhaps in part because, as Joan Marler says, making art is itself a form of praying but also because, I feel, these artists and authors are pointing us toward the future, toward what is possible.

INTRODUCTION: VIBRANT VOICES: WOMEN, MYTH, AND THE ARTS

Sid Reger, Marna Hauk and Cristina Biaggi

Paints fly out across sacred texts, forming words. Strings, flutes, and tambourine delight and ripple out: Music, in a welcome, echoes in the constellations. Women and goddesses awaken and converge. A bridgework forms from our world to this exceptional convergence. These sentinels—the wisdom carriers, path blazers, summoners, stokers of powers, old friends, world makers, heart tenders and catalysts of gifts—turn to welcome us and crowd the bridge from their realm to ours.

There is an old proverb that states that when you stand to do good in the world everyone who has ever done the same stands with you. From the beginning of humanity, art has been the sacred and necessary work of women. When we celebrate women's creativity and scholarship, we can feel the presence of all of those who came before us in creating art for the good of individuals and community. In this spirit, we have collected these articles and artworks.

We make space for voices and ideas that represent the emergent cresting wave of the field of women and mythology. We include bold voices, tender voices, voices at the front of the frothing wave of academic research in the field and voices from the margins.

As the Association for the Study of Women and Mythology (ASWM) has gathered in large conferences alternating with regional symposia, so too these articles are the gifts of convergence dedicated to women and myth. This book represents the same values, the same variety of offerings and the same balance between academic and personal ways of knowing that we encourage in ASWM's events. We invite women's curiosity, creativity and conversation.

> *This book, this text and the offerings within it are the hymns, tunes, susurrations, and insights of this gathering of energies across time and space. Here dedicated scholars, priestesses, colleagues and friends share their research and wonderings about this most passionate topic: the arts. The inquiries include as scholarship all creative works—visual arts, textiles, sculpture, dance, poetry, dream, altar making and storytelling.*

This book, *Vibrant Voices: Women, Myth and the Arts,* includes a diversity of voices from the wave crest of women and mythology. It is divided into five sections: From the Beginning: Research into Images of the Female Divine; Inquiry into the Art of Experiencing the Goddess; Honoring Our Artist–Scholar Foremothers; Artists, Their Words and Their Works; and Herstories and Solidarities.

From the Beginning:
Research into Images of the Female Divine

In "Art, Myth, and the Sacred Feminine," Arisika Razak sets the context for the volume by providing a deep-time view of the foundations of modern scholarship about women and the arts. She traces the origins of art as a necessary response to our sacred connections with spirit and land and to our earliest beginnings. She firmly places women's creativity at the center of human survival and advancement.

Miriam Robbins Dexter examines and documents sacred display figures that countered, with humanity and humor, the fierce extremes of patriarchy. In this article, she tracks the widespread, persistent use of figures that display female genitalia for both warding off attack and protecting women and the land.

Yuria Celidwen addresses the complexity of native populations' relationships with three archetypes of the divine female: the Lady of Guadalupe, Tonantzin and Coatlicue. She invites us to confront the shadow side of cultural icons that were imposed by colonizers but that persist as symbols of resistance and reconciliation.

Aprina Murwanti examines the *Mitoni*, the Javanese pregnancy ritual associated with Sri, the most important Javanese goddess, and the political and religious reasons for the decline of her presence in contemporary society. Murwanti uses practice-led research with visual and textile installation art—specifically, ritual woven sacred cloths—to study this goddess, whose culture is being resuscitated through this ritual.

Inquiry into the Art of Experiencing the Goddess

In Section 2 of this volume, scholars explore how nondominant modes of inquiry, including dreams, altars and rituals, are vital to scholarship about women and myth. A personalized approach to research is exemplified by Mei-Mei Sanford's examination of representations of the orishas—female and male deities who appear and interact with their devotees through trance, dreams and apparitions. Her exploration of non-iconic images of the divine and iconic exceptions in Yoruba religion focuses on nature, trance and art and the goddess Osun.

Toni Truesdale reflects on the fact that women's dwellings have traditionally been considered spiritual places of prayer, safety and sustenance. Through her vibrant, colorful illustrations, she gives voice and image to the idea that the hearth, fire, food and altars are metaphoric examples of the importance that women have placed on their daily life-sustaining routines.

Marna Hauk explores ancient dream temples, using dream recovery techniques to explore diverse modes of co-evolutionary contact that have the potential for healing and transformation. Hauk shares her arts-based findings and research, resuscitating ancient Hygeian dream healing ceremonies and practices to liberate the prophetic power of dreaming for social healing and for regenerating living earth systems and women's power.

Honoring Our Artist–Scholar Foremothers

Section 3 includes tributes to two artist–scholars, foremothers who not only shared their creative work with us but were instrumental in providing ASWM leaders with guidance through its early years as members of the advisory board. We celebrate the tapestry of culture making that lives in and through the legacies of these two amazing artists.

Lydia Ruyle (1935–2016) is best known for her series of Spirit Icon Banners, more than 300 larger-than-life banners of goddesses from many traditions, which have been featured in pilgrimages, festivals and conferences around the world. She also was a pioneer in restoring women to the field of art history. Her goals were to restore women's contributions to the public consciousness and to inspire her students to further study. Because much has been written about Lydia elsewhere, we have chosen to include a biography with a personal connection: one written by her longtime friend Joan M. Cichon. Joan's article includes a remembrance by Lydia's niece Katie Hoffner, which demonstrates Lydia's vigorous, determined approach to discovering and studying goddess artifacts wherever they were to be found.

Mary B. Kelly (1936–2016) was another remarkable artist-scholar whose research into women's textile arts greatly expanded our understandings of symbolism in folk art. In addition to painting and creating textiles, Mary wrote books about sacred weaving and ritual cloths. Those books are invaluable contributions to goddess scholarship, making visible the forgotten symbolic language of European textiles. Joan Marler's tribute to Mary makes clear that Mary's art and research both grew from her appreciation of the spiritual foundation of art. Because the online listing of much of Mary's work no longer exists, we have added to this article a complete list of her scholarly publications. We hope that this bibliography will facilitate further study of her remarkable work. We also have included images of Mary's series of goddess paintings, which she created in response to her research discoveries. We have included an appendix listing of her scholarly publications.

Artists, Their Works and Their Words

From the earliest planning stages, ASWM founders Patricia Monaghan and Sid Reger defined goddess scholarship as including representations and discussions of the arts. They recognized that many artists contribute to the advancement of knowledge through their creations and through innovative, independent scholarship. Section 4 of this volume presents the work of three contemporary artists whose visions from a diversity of cultures and folk traditions advance our understanding.

Cristina Biaggi extols Medusa's apotropaic gaze, using Medusa images from the National Archaeological Museum of Taranto as well as her own work inspired by Medusa. Her sculptures capture both the benevolent and the enraged aspects of this misunderstood goddess.

Laura Fragua-Cota shares her widely varied work—sculptures, two-dimensional work, mixed media and poetry—inspired by the Pueblo Indians and their past and present culture. Her article addresses the symbolic and narrative conveyance of Pueblo prayers and blessings and provides critical reflections on colonization and cultural appropriation.

Finally, Lydia Ruyle's lecture notes about mermaids represent a work in progress that she presented in the year before her passing. Ruyle explores the herstorical cultural iconography of the mermaid across cultures and shares her banner images of mermaid-related goddesses, including the Fish Goddess of Lepenski Vir, Melusine, Oshun, Sedna, Nu Gua and Mami Wata.

Section 4 also includes a gallery of twelve artists whose work has been featured in panels at past ASWM events. Our first event, in 2008, featured a panel of visual artists, which we titled The Holy Wind. This phrase was given to Sid by a young Navajo *hatalii* during a conversation about creativity. In his culture, he said, people did not concern themselves with "art" or "pieces of work that hang on a wall." Instead, they speak of "the holy wind," a spirit of creativity in which the maker, the material, the object and the community all are in harmony. All benefit from the making. In the lives and work of contemporary feminist artists, we have found a striving for creativity that will benefit all.

Each of the artists included in this section of the volume brings a clear, positive vision of the female divine. Rae Atira-Soncea illustrates a powerful birth-giving goddess. Helen Klebesadel's inspired Medusa resonates with domestic tactility; Carmen R. Sonnes's Mexican-American female divine throbs; and Lisa Noble's *Labyrinth Bee* is clear and profound. Sid Reger's mandala draws on ancient symbols of harvest and migration; Louie Laskowski's collage-like painting of a praying mantis praying to the Butterfly Goddess pulsates; Merry Grant Norris's mandala celebration of crones is inspiring; Barb Lutz's double goddess made of earth, in honor of Lydia Ruyle, is very moving; Lisa Levart's work *Goddess on Earth*, which she included in her books, is beautifully conceived and executed. Cristina Rose Smith dreams of homecoming in her evocative watercolor of the river swallow; Denise Kester vibrantly embraces planetary possibilities in vivid textures;

and Lauren Raine's compelling "Masks of the Goddess" put beautiful women's faces to awe-inspiring goddess archetypes from many world cultures.

Herstories and Solidarities

The final section of this book explores diverse perspectives on goddess archetypes in art and story, multi-ethnic solidarity and respectful engagement across cultures. These articles offer reflections on identity based on integration of myth and sacred story. The authors share inspiration about ancient archetypes and practices and reveal possibilities for cross-cultural redemption, connection and regeneration.

Simone Clunie's work explores the context and themes of goddess imagery in contemporary visual art. She traces the history of second-wave feminist art and describes the major factors that caused a resurgence of interest in goddess mythology. She then analyzes the creative mythic origins of the work of five major artists: Monica Sjöö, Mary Beth Edelson, Mayumi Oda, Yolanda Lopez and Ana Mendieta.

In her very readable article told like a story, Nancy Vedder-Shults examines the Hindu goddess Kali's contradictory aspects, her unbound nature beyond the constraints of human nature. She discusses her own emotional experience with Kali and with the Greek goddesses Demeter and Persephone. Vedder-Shults argues that storytelling can enrich scholarly engagement with myths in order to restore the myths' power as holistic modes of knowing.

Cristina Rose Smith explores how the female divine is manifested in mestiza cultures. Her interdisciplinary mestiza approach advances multicultural solidarity through sharing of personal and literary stories. She combines critical literary and auto-ethnographic approaches to study the renewal of integrative solidarity from her multiple ancestral traditions.

The final article in this volume is an invitation to move forward into a deeper conversation about cross-cultural research and scholarship. Kathryn Henderson offers speculations about how practitioners of goddess spirituality may engage with living traditions in a manner that avoids appropriation. She recounts her interviews with five spiritual leaders from various faith streams who responded from the wisdom of their experience and traditions.

Poetic Accompaniments

Opening the sections of this book are poems by other accomplished members of ASWM. Gina Belton's renga recognizes the arts as gifts and offerings to the ancestors. Ann Filemyr's "Calling You-who!" is a chant, a call to arms—to sing, to dance, to do, to experience joyously in the doing. Anne Finch's short invocation is haunting. Judy Grahn's "Geology Lesson" suggests a powerful, earth-shaping cultural continuity with women who have crafted this way before us. Marna Hauk situates the arts as a continuity, remembrance and honoring of matrilineal healers and elders. Patricia Monaghan's "Litha" is a lovely paean to striving, struggling and achieving that is rewarded with untold vistas of beauty and the need to keep moving.

The words and images of our contributors invite us—across time, context and art form—to engage with the sacred arts. We hope that this volume will be an invitation to you to connect with this generative research convergence across media, methods and cultures and to join us in celebrating the power of women, myth and art.

> *May our creative ventures be urged on by the delight and need of the lineage of foremothers and by generations of future beings, even if they are but distant echoes of the cacophonous, delightful hubbub, litany, elegy, invocation, dedication and earth making of the gathering of mythic women, goddesses, makers and matriarchs that they thank for continuing inspiration.*
>
> *May this volume be a kind gathering of insight, connection and transformation.*
>
> *May the words and images shared here open worlds and awaken depths of velvet memory and remembrance.*

SECTION 1

FROM THE BEGINNING: RESEARCH INTO IMAGES OF THE FEMALE DIVINE

A GEOLOGY LESSON

Here, the sea strains to climb up on the land
and the tree blows dust in a single direction.
The trees bend themselves all one way
and volcanoes explode often
Why is this? Many years back
a woman of strong purpose
passed through this section
and everything else tried to follow

~ *Judy Grahn*
From *Love Belongs to Those Who Do the Feeling*
(Red Hen Press, 2012, 2017)

ART, MYTH AND THE SACRED FEMININE

ARISIKA RAZAK

This is an essay about art—art made by women, art that celebrates women and art that respects women's accomplishments and characteristics. It is about the art that marks the dawn of consciousness: the art of our ancient ancestors of the Paleolithic and Neolithic eras, who became conscious of the world around them and responded with awe, ecstasy and the urge to create, imitate, represent and memorialize. It is about the early technologies, as they were expressed in art, and the role that women played in those technologies. It explores the changing cycles of women's bodies and how these cycles are celebrated in the early art of the Paleolithic and Neolithic eras as well as in the art of indigenous cultures today.

The essays that follow will, for the most part, discuss later elaborations of art: art created under patriarchy but that documents the heretical foundations of our goddess heritages; indigenous rituals that invoke our ancient connections to Spirit and Nature; and films that help us remember and re-create our lost or stolen womanist, feminist, matricentric herstories. Art has the power to bypass the oppressive structures generated by patriarchy, racism, homophobia and other elaborations of dominant culture hierarchies that deny us full representation as children of Spirit; it speaks directly to our hearts, generating epiphanies of individual and collective empowerment, self-love and unmediated, embodied spiritual awareness.

It is my hope that when you read these essays you will understand just how important, ubiquitous, common and uncommon our urge to create art is—not just for now but for uncounted millennia of human history. We are an art-making species, and whether we wear, carve, paint, dance, or sing art, we are as hard wired to create art as we are to love, nurture or elaborate religion. Art is the language of spirit for us. It's how we speak Spirit or, if we're lucky, how Spirit speaks us.

In the beginning, every human culture was connected to the earth. Our lives, our survival and our ability to be human were linked to the places we inhabited and the visible and invisible networks that supported the web of life in which we were embedded. We depended on the sustenance we drew from particular places on the earth and from the beings who fed on that earth and on whom we fed in turn. Over thousands of years and in various places, we learned to appreciate the cycles and seasons: the growth and maturation of plants, animals and human beings; the waxing and waning of the moon; the bleeding of women; the slow, repetitive movement of the stars; and the inevitable cycles of birth, transformation, death and rebirth. We learned to live by making relationships with the powerful life forms who shared the earth with us and the processes that shaped our lives, and we used those connections to make ritual covenants between those on whom we depended and that which in many cultures is termed the *Great Mysterious* or *Great Mystery*, that which is beyond human knowing but supports the whole of life.

Much of what the West considers art was, in modern indigenous cultures, a dialogue between powerful beings of the spirit world and the world of humans. Matter was not dead. It was inhabited, alive and volitional. The creation of jewelry, cloth, body designs and images was never the simple manifestation of individual artistic genius; it involved personal and ritual preparation, ceremonial prayers and knowledge passed through generations. It represented reciprocal exchanges between human beings and spirits of wood, fiber, flint and clay; invocations to the spirits of fire, water, wind and earth; and stories of the ancestors, the deities and natural and cosmological events.

Although the modern West often boasts of its technological prowess, it is the great human technologies of music, dance, ritual and storytelling that helped our ancestors to celebrate their joys and survive their tragedies. Long before we had formal theaters separating actor and audience, performer and witness, long before we had professional shamans to heal our physical and psychic wounds, long before we even had words or concepts to name our feelings, we engaged in solo and collective action that reflected an overabundance of emotion: We wailed and shouted together; leaped and danced in joy; rolled in cool mud; and painted our bodies with clay and ocher. We adorned our bodies with ornaments of shell and bone; trailed our hands in cool water and watched it ripple; and smeared our mouths with honey and fat, laughing together in joy and fulfillment.

These are the germs of artistic expression. When our bodies are so full of feelings that we can't contain them, we seek release. When awe and beauty overwhelm us, we naturally cry out. When grief and sorrow are so deep that we feel as if we are starting to drown, we moan, wail and whimper our pain. And when our earliest Paleolithic and Neolithic ancestors began to understand the recurring cycles of life, we sought—individually and collectively—the renewal of the elements on which our lives depended: the nurturing, life-giving rains, the animal herds that provided sustenance, the plants whose growth meant life and healing, and the fertility that grants us a perennial place despite the recurring cycles of loss and death.

Over time, we developed and enacted rituals of storytelling, ceremonial pleading and artistic representations that beseeched the life givers to return. We identified intermediaries who journeyed with and for us, who called the spirit back to the body, and sought the mysterious sources on which existence was founded. Long before we developed writing, we placed messages in rock shelters open to the sky, in caves deep within the body of the earth, and in high plateaus and cliffs to which we ceremonially returned. We wrote, in the language of artistic expression, not only for ourselves but also for the returning generations, about what was important, revered and necessary for our lives. This is the well from which human art was generated. Although modern technocapitalism and commodity culture have obscured this beginning, it is still the source drawn upon by many cultures, particularly the ones discussed in this book.

The feminine is at the center of our earliest artistic endeavors. It is seen in the use of red ocher millennia before our ancestors attempted to represent the human form. Some researchers believe that, although Neanderthals used red ocher to make conceptual links among the notions of living, dying and group affinity (belonging), Homo sapiens made conceptual links among red ocher, women, menstruation, and fertility.[1] Thousands of carvings of nude, seminude, full-bellied females, vulvas and therianthropes (human–animal hybrids) have been found in European caves. These carvings date to the Neolithic and Upper Paleolithic eras.[2] We have explored only a fraction of the thousands of rock paintings in North Africa and Southern Africa, but many of them speak to the importance of woman in either her primordial form as an ocher-stained vulva or her later form as a ceremonial leader, goddess, priestess or menstrual initiate.[3] The semi-abstract images found in textiles produced up through the 19th and 20th centuries reveal the importance of the female, whose body is the recurrent, perennial symbol of birth, death, rebirth and transformation, and the reverence with which our species once viewed the female body and the natural processes of the female body. Carol Christ wrote the following in her powerful essay "Why Women Need the Goddess":

> In the ancient world and among modern women, the Goddess symbol represents the birth, death, and rebirth processes of the natural and human worlds. The female body is viewed as the direct incarnation of waxing and waning, life and death cycles in the universe. . . . The life-giving powers of the Goddess in her creative aspect are not limited to physical birth, for the Goddess is also seen as the creator of all the arts of civilization, including healing, writing, and the giving of just law. Women in the middle of life who are not physical mothers may give birth to poems, songs, and books, or nurture other women, men, and children. They too are incarnations of the Goddess in her creative, life-giving aspect. At the end of life, women incarnate the crone aspect of the Goddess. The wise old woman, the woman who knows from experience what life is about, the woman whose closeness to her own death gives her a distance and perspective on the problems of life, is celebrated as the third aspect of the Goddess. Thus, women learn to value youth, creativity, and wisdom in themselves and other women.[4]

Although we do not know when the first human art was created, Gillian Morriss-Kay suggested that art production is a signal element of human culture, one with roots deep in our animal ancestry:

> Art, in its many forms, is practised by almost all human cultures and can be regarded as one of the defining characteristics of the human species. In all societies today, the visual arts are intimately intertwined with music, dance, ritual (marking life landmarks, death, religion and politics)

and language (poetry, song and story-telling). Vocalization, ritualized movement and visual display are part of animal courtship and dominance competition as well as human ritual and communication, so it is likely that the roots of music, dance and body decoration lie deep in the evolutionary history of the animal kingdom. Nevertheless, with the evolution of human cognition, they were deployed in current ways, with complex symbolic meaning becoming attached to them.[5]

Although the earliest date of art making by humans is contested, incised fragments of ocher accompanied by shell beads may well be the oldest signs of adornment in the world. These artifacts were found in a cave in South Africa and dated to between 70,000 and 100,000 years ago.[6] The use of ocher may go back even further than that; some researchers believe that ocher use began 164,000 years ago,[7] and others claim evidence that it occurred even earlier.[8] Although tool use was initially believed to be a defining characteristic of Homo sapiens, it has since been documented among many animal species,[9] leading to increased appreciation of aesthetic awareness and artistic creativity as hallmarks of modern humanity. Recent research has indicated that artistic creativity is not limited to Homo sapiens but rather included Neanderthals.[10] Pamela Willoughby summarized the interdisciplinary research found in Christopher Henshilwood and Francesco d'Errico's *Homo Symbolicus: The Dawn of Language, Imagination, and Spirituality* (2011):[11]

There are still traits that are characteristic of modern behavior—intentional burial, abstract designs, personal adornment, figurative representations and bone tools. For them [researchers Henshilwood and d'Errico], signs of modern behavior are present in Africa by at least 150,000 years ago, in the Middle East after 100,000 years ago, and probably by 60,000 to 50,000 years ago in Europe (presumably made by Neanderthals). . . . They make the intriguing suggestion that beads are present well before 70,000 years ago in South Africa, North Africa, and the Middle East.[12]

Trance, ritual, meaningful burial and literal and abstract representations of human beings, animals, shamans and therianthropes appear in art from as early as the Paleolithic and Neolithic eras and possibly to the dawn of human consciousness. This art is not an insignificant or accidental accompaniment to human culture but rather is at the center of human culture, representing the development of a self-aware being that can look both outward and inward in contemplating time, death, change and transformation. The development of consciousness may be the most important revolution of all time, and it is documented in art that was produced tens of thousands of years ago. The art discussed in this book represents a diversity of liberatory, spiritual, artistic and cultural expressions that have survived five thousand years of patriarchal marginalization, denigration and attempted genocidal erasure of those who seek to continue the practices of spiritual traditions and artistic endeavors in which women are at the center or at least deeply involved. The contemporary resurrection of the goddesses of ancient times, the rituals of trance of precolonial indigenous religions, the ceremonies supporting the blood mysteries[13] of women's bodies, the documentation of alternative-gender individuals and communities, the storytelling of contemporary films that present the ancient spiritual beliefs of subaltern cultures, and women's life-enhancing domestic arts all are efforts that seek not only to address the deep wrongs of patriarchy, racism and other oppressions but also to empower those who have been marginalized for so long.

The idea that our ancient ancestors in the Neolithic and Paleolithic eras were capable of imagination, creativity and spirituality is not new to women's spirituality scholars. Nor is the idea that art is a marker of early human spirituality, which centered on women. In *Dark Mother: African Origins and Godmothers*, Lucia Birnbaum asserted that the oldest signs of religious veneration are the pubic V shape and the pigment red ocher. She believes that ancient African immigrants took these signs with them when they migrated out of Africa 50,000 years ago.[14] Marija Gimbutas believed that her twenty years of excavations not only indicated that Old Europe—southeastern Europe during the Neolithic and Upper Paleolithic eras—was characterized by peaceful, matrifocal, egalitarian societies that worshipped a goddess or many goddesses but that the symbols, markings and human and therianthropic female images that she had found represented "an alphabet of the metaphysical"[15] that she was able to interpret.[16]

8

If this ancient art is an important marker of human cognition, who made it and why is it important to us? Why might it be of particular importance to women today? I suggest that, if art is one of humanity's oldest languages, it matters who made it that art. If women, elders, people of color and other oppressed genders are to move from the margins of discourse to the center and be rightfully acknowledged as the creators—or cocreators—of human culture and civilization, it most definitely matters who made the art and where and when the art was made. In cultures in which sexist, racist and ableist beliefs are the norm, the sex, gender, disability status and ethnicity of our early forebears makes a difference, especially if we are trying to elaborate a culture that holds all of our peoples, all of our talents and all of our cultures.

Early researchers, most of whom were European or Euroamerican men, initially assumed that the first signs of modern human artistic behavior were in Europe. Although that notion was in part due to the difference between the considerable number of stone images and artifacts found in Europe and the limited number of similar artifacts, which presumably had been made of wood, plant fibers and other easily degradable materials, found in tropical Africa, it also aligned with 19th and 20th century Eurocentric, white-supremacist beliefs. It reflected the lack of looking for signs of cognitive, artistic and intellectual development in Africa and the tendency to assign African achievements to other cultures.[17]

Male anthropologists and archeologists also asserted that all of the artists who had made the paintings and sculptures in Upper Paleolithic and Neolithic caves were men, a notion rooted in patriarchal beliefs about the secondary nature of women and "women's work." According to Adovasio, Soffer and Park, "until recently, the field called archaeology (along with geology, paleontology, and all the other specialties involved with our story) has een practiced almost exclusively by men, [and] it will be no surprise that the story they have told has been largely free of females, of women."[18]

However, the later work of feminist researchers and others who have excavated sites in Africa revealed that the artistic explosion that took place in Europe also occurred in Africa. Some researchers believe that hand stencils found in French and Spanish caves, estimated to have been created during the Upper Paleolithic era (approximately 40,000 years ago to 10,000 years ago), were made by women and children.[19] Others have suggested that, if early female figurines were depicted wearing knotted skirts, woven hats and other adornment, women, as the first weavers,[20] either carved some of these statues or advised male carvers in how to do so. (Alternatively, Afrocentric researchers see the heads of the Venus of Willendorf and the Venus of Brassempouy not as women wearing hats but as women whose hair reflects the hair and hairstyles—e.g., braids and cornrows—typical of African peoples, lending credence to the idea that the early settlers of Europe were black Africans.[21]) McCoid and McDermott suggested that the anatomically "incorrect" or "obese" female form—pendulous breasts, full or pregnant belly and large buttocks—of many Upper Paleolithic statues is the view of a pregnant woman looking down at her own body. They suggest that women may have carved these statues for themselves, as depictions of gynecologic or obstetric knowledge and to demonstrate appropriate growth during pregnancy.[22]

If early art found in sites dating back to the Paleolithic era represents the beginnings of symbolic cognition and culture as well as the primal language of ecstasy, awe, and spiritual and religious belief, the lack of women's participation in such art—if that lack were true—would be a deep cause for women's feelings of shame, self-loathing and insignificance. It would be a soul-deep validation of patriarchal beliefs that would have us believe that women are not only worthless but also innately deficient in what makes us human—a claim that is echoed in patriarchal elaborations of religious belief and Western science and biomedicine.

Luckily for us, this patriarchal view is simply not true. Those of us who—regardless of our ethnicities, our sexual orientations, our abilities and disabilities, our gender identities and our ages—have repudiated the patriarchal beliefs that surround us understand that it is not women (or the disabled, people of color, the LGBTQIQ communities, and so forth) who are deficient. It is the societies in which we live that have marginalized the accomplishments of women and other targeted groups, denying the value of the work that they do not simply for ourselves but for humanity as a whole.

It does not matter whether we are speaking of the modern techno-industrial, patriarchal West, the kyriarchical empires of the past or androcentric elaborations of cultures of color. In sexist and dominator societies, women's roles and significance—if acknowledged at all—are subordinated to male roles and values. Women's sexuality is denied or constrained, but men's sexuality is not; women's reproductive powers are denigrated; and women's creativity is marginalized or subjugated to male desire.

The patriarchal cult of war, which has led to valuing hunting over gathering, killing over birthing, and physical prowess as the determiner of righteousness, became the most important element of patriarchal culture.

The early veneration of menstrual blood—the symbol of women's creative and life-giving powers, which some researchers and theorists have linked to the development of human culture, cognition and art[23]—was replaced with menstrual scorn, the veneration of the blood of death, and the cult of the warrior. And although women in many indigenous cultures of Africa, Asia, Europe, North and South America and the Middle East have functioned as warriors, either out of necessity or out of their own desires, this role is not the most significant one for women.

The lives and experiences of women and members of other oppressed groups, genders and communities have played significant roles in the elaboration of culture. Although many feminists and researchers of women's spirituality have asserted that women served as leaders, shamans and healers in ancient times,[24] recent research has proposed that disabled women may have served in these roles and that burial sites suggest that these women were revered even in death.[25] The notion that our Paleolithic ancestors were able to elaborate culture based solely on able-bodied masculine prowess in the arts of war and the hunt, while women and children waited passively on the sidelines, is based on neither physical evidence from the past nor the experiences of the hunter-gatherer cultures of the present.[26]

Instead, the notion that women have always been confined to "lesser" domestic roles reflects the patriarchal bias of many societies, both Western and non-Western. Although it is true that Paleolithic stone tools were easier for archaeologists to recognize and analyze than were the remnants of Paleolithic string artifacts, it is also true that men's use of tools, in itself, was deemed more important than women's sewing or weaving. This bias of seeing women's work as less important than men's work is foundational to Western distinctions between art and crafts and the relegation of women's endeavors to the lesser category of crafts. Although the modern West esteems clothing designers but not the sewers, some researchers believe that during the Upper Paleolithic era the making of garments and the use of weaving conveyed great status for both the makers and the wearers. Soffer, Adovasio and Hyland made the following statement in their analysis of the garments worn by Paleolithic Venuses, which represent goddesses or Sacred Mothers:

> The exquisite and labor-intensive detailing employed in the depiction of the woven garments worn by one group of Venuses clearly shows that weaving and basket-making skills and their products were valued enough to be transformed into transcendent cultural facts carved into stone, ivory and bone. Simply put, we suggest that being depicted wearing such garments associated the wearer and, by extension, the maker of them, with a marked position of prestige.[27]

A corollary to this notion of the essential lesser nature of women is the idea that Stone Age tools, carvings and paintings were created only by and for men. No one can deny the fact that excavations in Europe and the so-called Middle East have revealed hundreds of images of nude or seminude females with full bellies, pendulous breasts, large buttocks and highly defined pubic areas. Some of the figures are colored with red ocher; some wear jewelry, belts or other adornment that accentuates their pubic areas. In spite of the care with which these images were carved or painted, many androcentric researchers still reject the idea that these images represent priestesses, goddesses, sacred ancestors, clan mothers or pregnant women. Instead, they equate the images with the static images found in modern, predigital pornography. This masculinist point of view reduces these carvings, which are so abundant in Europe, and the rock paintings found in Africa to simple representations of sex. But there is evidence that the carvings and paintings are multivalent representations of life, creativity, technology and the sacred.

Many researchers have testified to the presence of red ocher in burial sites, on beads and as adornments of female figurines and other artifacts, and several feminist researchers, women's spirituality scholars and others in the academic fields of anthropology and archeology have linked the use of red ocher to associations between menstruation and reproduction.[28] Although menstruation is visible in girl children at puberty, the menstrual flow ceases during pregnancy and while the child is nourished at the breast.[29] The visibility of menstrual flow and its cessation may have led to an association between the color red ocher, women's menstrual blood, fertility, and childbirth, a time when women's blood also visibly flows from the vagina.

Writing from a perspective of women's spirituality, visionary poet and writer Judy Grahn argued that women's menstruation led to the development of human consciousness and later to the development of writing, math, astronomy, cooking, clothing, cosmetics and language.[30] Grahn believes that menstrual seclusion enabled our early ancestors who simply experienced the dark to apprehend and name the dark. She has suggested that the many human creation stories that speak of a time of primal darkness and chaos refer to that moment:

> At one time, our ancestral apes could not see the landscape of the earth, not recognize the sun and moon, had no name for water. The ancient stories recall a time when our pre-human ancestors could not perceive shape, color, light, depth, distance . . . and had not names for them and no fixed sense of their qualities. This state of being, which we call "nature," rules from inside the animal body; emotions, physiological states, estrus, and mating simply happen, they are not up for question, examination, or rearrangement. . . . Although the inner animal life has its own order, its own integration with the whole, its own rationalism, we rely so much on our culture that the preconscious state before our ancestors learned to think outside themselves was a state we now call Chaos, and greatly fear.[31]

> Acquiring an externally based mind required early humans to connect to something outside of themselves as a frame of reference, to connect physically; and this was accomplished when the females evolved a menstrual cycle capable of synchronous rhythm or *entrainment*. Entrainment is the quality of two similarly timed beats to link up and become synchronized in each other's presence.[32]

Grahn believes that menstrual seclusion was a worldwide cultural phenomenon in which women were forbidden to see light. She suggests that, in the time before the existence of artificial light, menstrual synchrony existed and that the experience of being together in the dark with other women signaled a major change in human consciousness.

> When during the hundreds of thousands of times the ancestral prehumans secluded themselves during what was at least

> some of the time a collective menstruation at the dark of the moon, they noticed that the light was also hiding. They may . . . have come to notice that the light at times (dawn) was the same color as their blood. While they were menstruating, they noticed darkness was different from light.[33]

Wordlessly, a more conscious female pulled her sisters into seclusion with her. Wordlessly, they pushed their daughters into seclusion at the first sign of their blood. Wordlessly, they sat in the moonless night and "saw" darkness as a different state than light. They named it with the act of separation. They "saw" that when anyone menstruating was absent from the group, so was the night light. In this seeing, they perceived light and dark as different states. . . . With the act of sitting together in the dark, the early women entered a new world of consciousness. Their minds became "human" through an externalized vision that had as yet and perhaps for millennia to come no other expression than menstrual separation, the creation of consciousness by distinguishing menstruation from other activities. This separation endowed both menstruation and light with power, the power of memory and first cause, the power of rite to create human mind and culture.[34]

Grahn has discussed the use of red ocher as a cosmetic or material metaform, a process in which menstruation is visibly and ritually displayed on women's bodies as a sign of knowledge or used as a material to identify the cultural beliefs of a society. Another perspective on the importance of menstruation in the development of Homo sapiens—and on the use of red ocher to mimic menstruation—was presented by Camilla Power. Writing from what she describes as a Darwinian viewpoint, she suggested that our early female ancestors used red ocher to signal menstruation, as a sign of approaching fertility to males:[35]

> Once ovulation had been concealed in the human lineage, menstrual bleeding became the only good indicator of impending fertility. But while concealed ovulation withholds information from males about which females are fertile at any time, the salience of the menstrual signal undermines this effect, marking out imminently fertile females from pregnant or lactating ones. To resist male discrimination between cycling and noncycling females,

coalitions of late archaic/early modern Homo sapiens women began cosmetically manipulating menstrual signals—sham menstruation. Collective, deceptive and amplified use of red pigments as body paint confused information available to men about women's reproductive status, and effectively formed a pre-adaptation to ritual. This model predicts that the earliest art will be evidenced by a cosmetics industry, dominated by red pigments.[36]

Although I question the part of Power's thesis that places women in a dependent position in regard to men—who, in this model, reward attractive (i.e., potentially fertile) females with gifts of food and other sustenance— Power's focus on the significance of human ovulation and menstruation and her discussion of African rock paintings and contemporary South African hunter-gatherer societies offer important insights.

In Power's investigation of more recent southern African rock art in conjunction with contemporary hunter-gatherer traditions in south Africa, she asserted that flowing streams depicted as coming from women's vulvas represent the sacred menstrual flow, which is a sign of spiritual power equal to that of shamans.[37] She notes noted that red ocher— or, in its absence, red pigment derived from trees— is usually gathered by women, and that emerging menstrual initiates gave red ocher to women for adornment and to hunters for luck. She drew the following conclusion:

> It appears that menarcheal ritual provides a template for other rituals of transition, including first-kills, marriage and death. I argue that it . . . provides the metaphor for movement to the other world involved in trance death. The preoccupation of /Xam narratives with the dire consequences of violation of proper menarcheal observances confirms that no other ritual context is so vital to reproduction of the Khoisan cosmos, affecting the fertility of women, the land and the game, and success in the hunt.[38]

Although a number of scholars of women's spirituality have discussed the importance of menstruation as symbol and evidence of women's spiritual and earthly powers and ritual connection to the cycles of birth, death and transformation,[39] Power's analysis offers a highly secular and highly physical origin for the significance of menstruation and red ocher in the Upper Paleolithic era. She noted that some contemporary researchers still refuse to acknowledge the genital emphasis of some African rock art and instead choose to focus on facial characteristics and other artifacts.[40] She drew the following conclusion:

> Given the central importance of menstrual potency in Bushman [*sic*] ideology, ritual and narrative of initiation, resistance to seeing portrayal of the metaphor of power in rock art is surprising. This refers to our own culture's deep-seated taboos, but obstructs our understanding of Bushman [*sic*] cosmology and its representation.[41]

Power also discussed contemporary South African hunter-gatherer cultures' identification of (female) menstrual initiates with the (male) eland. Both are considered fat and are linked with rain and the well-being of the land. The association presents interesting ideas regarding gender fluidity, power and spirituality.[42]

Feminist scholars have revealed that women played active roles in the emergent material technologies of the Neolithic and Paleolithic eras. Although women's spirituality scholars have made this assertion for decades, it has often been based on religious or spiritual interpretations of the arts of the Neolithic and Paleolithic eras. Contemporary secular scholars have argued that women's participation in the String Revolution, the creation of agriculture, the formation of language and the use of ritual adornment demonstrate the centrality of women in the production of technology and art, which are central to our existence as humans. And more recent scholarship has spoken to the growing interest in the notion that women—and the natural changes in women's bodies—may have been foundational to the evolution of human culture. Adovasio, Soffer and Park (2007) asserted the following:

> Thanks to the work of numerous scholars in several fields, it has come to light that female humans have been the chief engine in the unprecedentedly high level of human sociability, were the inventors of the most useful of tools (called the String Revolution), have shared equally in the provision of food for human societies, almost certainly

16

drove the human invention of language, and were the ones who created agriculture.[43]

Why are these accomplishments of women not common knowledge? And what do we have to do to disseminate them? These are certainly questions that feminist researchers and scholars of women's spirituality have struggled with for years. In spite of decades of research and publication, in many modern-day societies the pivotal role of women in the evolution and sustenance of human culture has been denied. Moreover, the physical characteristics for which women were esteemed in ancient times—the life-giving nature of reproductive cycles, the production of milk by women's bodies, the mysterious fact that women bled in synchronicity with the moon but did not die, and the emergence of male and female children from women's bodies—have become touchstones for the degradation of women.

As Power's work has demonstrated, the significance of women's bodies as icons of the sacred and as carriers of the inherent wisdom of women has been carried into the modern era by selected indigenous cultures. Jean Bolen discussed this in "Forward" in *The Heart of the Goddess: Art Myth and Meditations of the World's Sacred Feminine*, a book that contains many female images drawn from precolonial cultures of color:

> Most of us have been brought up to be ashamed of our bodies and our genitals, and the dominant culture values only youthful, slender, (and usually Caucasian) figures as beautiful. But as I lived with the images of this book, what was strange became familiar, those that were initially off-putting to me became beautiful in their own way or awesome, worthy of respect and acceptance.[44]

Because Bolen is a physician and psychiatrist who has primary knowledge of the many ills and diseases experienced by modern women, her comments are especially important. Although she acknowledges that a woman's experiences of pregnancy and birth are affected by personal desire, history of emotional or physical abuse, grief, war, and so forth, she wrote of the "embodied and unmediated" spirituality that can occur during the reproductive cycle,[45] noting that the stages of pregnancy and childbirth are potentially linked to profound, transformative spiritual experiences:

> I know intuitively that if the Goddess had not been oblit-
> erated from consciousness and culture, quickening would
> be valued as a profound religious experience. A pregnant
> woman would know that she shares in the essence of the
> Goddess as creator, who brought forth life from her own
> body. Sensing her own divinity would occur simultane-
> ously with feeling life stir within her own womb. At that
> moment, she could know and say, "The Mother Goddess
> and I are one."[46]

In a culture that so values thinness that healthy women literally starve themselves to death, I think that a supported review of goddess images from the Paleolithic era should be required reading for women who live under the tyranny of the unattainable norms of Western beauty. And although (wanted) pregnancy and childbirth are not necessary acts, reflection on what Vicki Noble has designated as the quintessentially shamanic act of child-birth would do much to diminish the feminist denigration of motherhood and the patriarchal elevation of socially powerless mothers.

For some women, reclaiming the goddess and rejecting patriarchal religions are key to reclaiming fully embodied, creative, artistic, sexual selves. However, we need to acknowledge that some cultures never lost the goddess. Despite centuries of colonization, forced Christianity, slavery and attempted genocide, many indigenous societies have held on to the memory of woman as Creatrix, culture bearer, healer, law giver, mother and extinguisher of life at its end. Writing of her Laguna Pueblo culture, Paula Gunn Allen explained:

> Where I come from, God is a Woman; her name is Thinking.
> She is accompanied by her sister-goddesses Memory and
> what I will translate as Intuition, and she is the elder of
> the female gender. She is called Grandmother, in recogni-
> tion of the spiritual significance of proper relationship and
> of her revered place among us, and also Spider—maybe
> because she both spins and lives in the fragile, inordi-
> nately strong, potentially deadly, and ever wondrous web
> of All-That-Is. Where I come from society is (tradition-
> ally, though colonization and white law dictate otherwise

18

now) matrilineal, matrilocal, and matrifocal. . . . Where I
come from all spirituality is gender based, and as near as
historical, geographical paleontological, environmentalist,
horticultural, or other measures show, the planet and the
people are/were all the better for gender-based, elder-fe-
male focused spiritual systems. . . . Warfare is actually
prohibited and pacifism, nurturing, healing, inclusiveness,
egalitarianism among all members of the community of
being, and profound spiritual and ritual awareness continue to characterize that system.[47]

Many indigenous societies are struggling to retain their original matricentric traditions. The patriarchal societies of West Africa—including those
of the Yoruba and the Igbo—still exhibit some of the women-reverencing
traditions that informed earlier iterations of their societies, and their art
still celebrates the central roles of women in society. According to Diop,
matriarchy and reverence for the role of the mother formed the cultural
foundation of most early African societies.[48] It is not, as Allen observed,
that woman was revered simply for her birth-giving abilities. It is and
was that woman embodied the Creatrix, carrying with her the gifts of culture making, thriving and survival, and in selected West African societies
woman represents the spiritual powers that punish those who violate the
social rules that ensure balance and harmony among the natural, spiritual
and human realms.

The book you are now reading is an attempt to redress the exclusion
of women from the false tapestry of history that has been produced by
patriarchal deception and misinformation. The idea that women's biology
somehow renders women as less than men—that it essentially and eternally
condemns women to lesser roles that deny the significance of women's
participation in the great revolutions that supported human evolution—is
false. The idea that women's contributions to civilization were insignificant erases the fact of Paleolithic women's participation in hunting as well
as gathering and marginalizes the importance of the foodstuffs gathered
by women and children.[49] It diminishes the importance of making slings,
carrying bags, and setting snares to trap game, all of which certainly were
done by women as well as men. Most importantly, it denies the intelligence
and creativity required for these activities.

In the prepatriarchal periods of the Upper Paleolithic era, women were beings of intellect, emotion, spirituality and physicality. Women were and are innately curious and creative. As bearers of children, mates to men, creators of technology, witness to perennial cycles of life, death and rebirth, women have pondered the cycles of change that moved through their bodies and linked them to the cosmos, the natural world, and the human world that they created. Women developed mythic, religious and spiritual beliefs that consoled them in the face of their mortality and the mortality of those they loved.

If you are reading this book, you will find that this history and these activities—the material and the spiritual—have been documented in women's art. The production of art in new, 21st century forms is alive and well, and it rests on a foundation of earlier artwork that extends back to the Paleolithic era. These new art forms have arisen from a diversity of historic and contemporary cultures, just as the old art forms did. It is important that this work be seen in the context of the long past of women's artistic and material endeavors and that women artists be seen not as muses or inspirers of men but as complex inventors, thinkers and cultural creatives who are part of a tradition that extends back to the dawn of human consciousness.

References

Adovasio, J. M., Olga Soffer, and Jake Page. *The Invisible Sex: Uncovering the True Roles of Women in Prehistory*. Walnut Creek, CA: Left Coast Press, 2007.

Allen, Paula Gunn. "The Anima of the Sacred: Empowering Women's Spirituality." In *Off the Reservation: Reflections on Boundary-Busting, Border-Crossing Loose Canons*, 84–92. Boston: Beacon, 1998.

Barber, Elizabeth J. W. *Prehistoric Textiles: The Development of Cloth in the Neolithic and Bronze Ages with Special Reference to the Aegean*. Princeton, NJ: Princeton University Press, 1992.

———. *Women's Work: The First 20,000 Years: Women, Cloth, and Society in Early Times*. New York: W. W. Norton, 1994.

Birnbaum, Lucia Chiavola. *Dark Mother: African Origins and Godmothers*. Lincoln, NE: iUniverse Inc., 2002.

Bolen, Jean Shinoda. Foreword to *The Heart of the Goddess: Art, Myth, and Meditations of the World's Sacred Feminine*, by Hallie Iglehart Austen. Berkeley: Wingbow, 1990.

————. *Crossing to Avalon: A Woman's Midlife Pilgrimage*. New York: HarperCollins, 1994.

Christ, Carol. "Why Women Need the Goddess." In *The Politics of Women's Spirituality: Essays on the Rise of Spiritual Power Within the Feminist Movement*, edited by Charlene Spretnak, 71–86. New York: Anchor Press, 1982.

Clegg, Legrand, II. "The First Invaders." In *African Presence in Early Europe*, edited by Ivan Van Sertima. 3rd ed. New Brunswick, NJ: Transaction Press, 1987, 23–35.

Diop, Cheikh Anta. *The Cultural Unity of Black Africa: The Domains of Patriarchy and of Matriarchy in Classical Antiquity*. Chicago: Third World, 1978.

Formicola, Vincenzo, Antonella Pontrandolfi, and Jiří Svoboda. "The Upper Paleolithic Triple Burial of Dolní Vestonice: Pathology and Funerary Behavior." *American Journal of Physical Anthropology* 115, no. 4 (2001): 372–79.

Gadon, Elinor. *The Once and Future Goddess: A Symbol for Our Time*. San Francisco: Harper & Row, 1989.

Gimbutas, Marija. *The Language of the Goddess*. San Francisco: Harper & Row, 1989.

Henshilwood Christopher S., and Francesco d'Errico. *Homo Symbolicus: The Dawn of Language, Imagination, and Spirituality*. Philadelphia, John Benjamins Publishing Co., 2011.

Jeffries, Rosalind. "The Image of Woman in African Cave Art." In *Black Women in Antiquity*, edited by Ivan Van Sertima, 98–122. New Brunswick, NJ: Transaction, 1989.

Knight, Chris. *Blood Relations: Menstruation and the Origins of Culture*. Princeton, NJ: Yale University Press, 1995.

Lhote, Henri. *The Search for the Tassili Frescoes: The Story of the Prehistoric Rock Paintings of the Sahara*. Translated by Alan Houghton Brodrick. London: Hutchinson, 1959.

McCoid, Catherine Hodge, and Leroy D. McDermott. "Toward Decolonizing Gender: Female Vision in the Upper Paleolithic." *American Anthropologist* 98, no. 2 (1996): 319–26.

Morriss-Kay, Gillian M. "The Evolution of Human Artistic Creativity." *Journal of Anatomy* 216, no. 2 (2010): 158–76.

Owens, Linda. *Distorting the Past: Gender and the Division of Labor in the European Upper Paleolithic*. Tübingen, Germany: Kerns Verlag, 2005.

Power, Camilla. "Women in Prehistoric Rock Art." In *New Perspectives on Prehistoric Art*, edited by Gunter Berghaus, 75–103. Westport, CT and London: Praeger, 2004.

Roebroeks, Wil, Mark J. Sier, Trine Kellberg Nielson, Dimitri De Loecker, Josep Maria Parés, Charles E. S. Arps, and Herman J. Mücher. "Use of Red Ochre by Early Neandertals." *Proceedings of the National Academy of Sciences of the United States of America* 109, no. 6 (2012): 1889–94. doi: 10.1073/pnas.1112261109.

Shumaker, Robert W., Kristina R. Walkup, and Benjamin B. Beck. *Animal Tool Behavior: The Use and Manufacture of Tools by Animals*. Revised and updated. Baltimore: John Hopkins University Press, 2011. First published 1980.

Snow, Dean. "Sexual Dimorphism in European Upper Paleolithic Cave Art." *American Antiquity* 78, no. 4 (2013): 746–61.

Soffer, Olga, J. M. Adovasio, and D. C. Hyland. "The 'Venus' Figurines: Textiles, Basketry, Gender, and Status in the Upper Paleolithic." *Current Anthropology* 41, no. 4 (2000): 511–37.

Tedlock, Barbara. *The Woman in the Shaman's Body: Reclaiming the Feminine in Religion and Medicine*. New York: Bantam, 2009. First published 2005.

Willoughby, Pamela R. Review of *Homo Symbolicus: The Dawn of Language, Imagination and Spirituality*, by Christopher S. Henshilwood and, Francesco d'Errico, eds. *PaleoAnthropology* 2012: 231–32. doi:10.4207/PA.2012.REV126.

Wreschner, Ernst E., Ralph Bolton, Karl W. Butzer, Henri Delporte, Alexander Häusler, Albert Heinrich, Anita Jacobson-Widding, et al. "Red Ochre and Human Evolution: A Case for Discussion [and Comments and Reply]." *Current Anthropology* 21, no. 5 (1980): 631–44.

Endnotes

1 Ernst E. Wreschner et al., "Red Ochre and Human Evolution: A Case for Discussion [and Comments and Reply]," *Current Anthropology* 21, no. 5 (1980): 631–44; Camilla Power, "Women in Prehistoric Rock Art," in *New Perspectives on Prehistoric Art*, ed. Gunter Berghaus (Westport, CT and London: Praeger, 2004), 75–103; Chris Knight, *Blood Relations: Menstruation and the Origins of Culture* (Princeton, NJ: Yale University Press, 1995).

2 Elinor Gadon, *The Once and Future Goddess: A Symbol for Our Time* (San Francisco: Harper & Row, 1989), 3–20; Marija Gimbutas, *The Language of the Goddess* (San Francisco: Harper & Row, 1989).

3 Power, "Women in Prehistoric Rock Art"; Rosalind Jeffries, "The Image of Woman in African Cave Art," in *Black Women in Antiquity*, ed. Ivan Van Sertima, 98–122 (New Brunswick, NJ: Transaction, 1989).

4 Carol Christ, "Why Women Need the Goddess," in *The Politics of Women's Spirituality: Essays on the Rise of Spiritual Power Within the Feminist Movement*, ed. Charlene Spretnak (New York: Anchor Press, 1982), 79–80.

5 Gillian M. Morriss-Kay, "The Evolution of Human Artistic Creativity," *Journal of Anatomy* 216, no. 2 (2010): 158.

6 Christopher S. Henshilwood and Francesco d'Errico, *Homo Symbolicus: The Dawn of Language, Imagination, and Spirituality* (Philadelphia, John Benjamins Publishing Co., 2011).

7 Morriss-Kay, "The Evolution of Human Artistic Creativity," 160.

8 Wreschner et al., "Red Ochre and Human Evolution."

9 Robert W. Shumaker, Kristina R. Walkup, and Benjamin B. Beck, *Animal Tool Behavior: The Use and Manufacture of Tools by Animals*, rev. ed. (1980; rev. and updated, Baltimore: John Hopkins University Press, 2011).

10 Wil Roebroeks, Mark J. Sier, Trine Kellberg Nielson, Dimitri De Loecker, Josep Maria Parés, Charles E. S. Arps, and Herman J. Mücher, "Use of Red Ochre by Early Neandertals," *Proceedings of the National Academy of Sciences of the United States of America* 109, no. 6 (2012): 1889–94, doi: 10.1073/pnas.1112261109.

11 Henshilwood and d'Errico, *Homo Symbolicus*.

12 Pamela R. Willoughby, review of *Homo Symbolicus: The Dawn of Language, Imagination and Spirituality*, by Christopher S. Henshilwood and, Francesco d'Errico, eds., *PaleoAnthropology* 2012: 231–32, doi:10.4207/PA.2012. REV126.

13 The blood mysteries typically include menarche, sexuality, pregnancy and menopause. Although transgender men can become pregnant and bear children and people of any gender may become parents via adoption, this term originated within the cisgender female pagan or Neopagan community.

14 Lucia Chiavola Birnbaum, *Dark Mother: African Origins and Godmothers* (Lincoln, NE: iUniverse Inc., 2002).

15 Gimbutas, *The Language of the Goddess.*

16 Gimbutas, *The Language of the Goddess.*

17 Henri Lhote, the original discoverer of the Tassili Frescoes in Algeria, labeled the distinctively African Horned Goddess the White Lady. He claimed that, in spite of her African scarification patterns, fringed skirt, armbands and ankle bracelets, there was another cultural influence in her creation. See Henri Lhote, *The Search for the Tassili Frescoes: The Story of the Prehistoric Rock Paintings of the Sahara*, trans. Alan Houghton Brodrick (London: Hutchinson, 1959).

18 J. M. Adovasio, Olga Soffer, and Jake Page, *The Invisible Sex: Uncovering the True Roles of Women in Prehistory* (Walnut Creek, CA: Left Coast Press, 2007), 1–2.

19 Dean Snow, "Sexual Dimorphism in European Upper Paleolithic Cave Art," *American Antiquity* 78, no. 4 (2013): 746–61.

20 Olga Soffer, J. M. Adovasio, and D.C. Hyland, "The 'Venus' Figurines: Textiles, Basketry, Gender, and Status in the Upper Paleolithic," *Current Anthropology* 41, no. 4 (2000): 523–24.

21 Legrand Clegg, II, "The First Invaders," in *African Presence in Early Europe*, ed. Ivan Van Sertima, 3rd ed. (New Brunswick, NJ: Transaction Press, 1987), 23–35; Jeffries, "The Image of Woman in African Cave Art."

22 Catherine Hodge McCoid and Leroy D. McDermott, "Toward Decolonizing Gender: Female Vision in the Upper Paleolithic," *American Anthropologist* 98, no. 2 (1996): 319–26.

23 Grahn, Judy. *Blood, Bread, and Roses: How Menstruation Created the World.* (Boston: Beacon, 1993); Knight, *Blood Relations*; Vicki Noble, *Shakti Woman: Feeling Our Fire, Healing Our World: The New Female Shamanism* (New York: HarperSanFrancisco, 1991); Power, "Women in Prehistoric Rock Art."

24 Grahn, *Blood, Bread, and Roses*; Noble, *Shakti Woman*; Barbara Tedlock, *The Woman in the Shaman's Body: Reclaiming the Feminine in Religion and Medicine* (2005; repr., New York: Bantam, 2009).

25 Some researchers believe that disabled individuals may have held special roles as tribal shamans, based on a European burial site that displays a woman who had a facial deformity and was covered in red ochre and buried beneath two mammoth bones, holding a fox—all of which were indications of high status. See Vincenzo Formicola, Antonella Pontrandolfi, and Jiří Svoboda, "The Upper Paleolithic Triple Burial of Dolní Vestonice: Pathology and Funerary Behavior," *American Journal of Physical Anthropology* 115, no. 4 (2001): 372–74.

26 Linda Owens, *Distorting the Past: Gender and the Division of Labor in the European Upper Paleolithic* (Tübingen, Germany: Kerns Verlag, 2005); Elizabeth J. W. Barber, *Prehistoric Textiles: The Development of Cloth in the Neolithic and Bronze Ages with Special Reference to the Aegean* (Princeton, NJ: Princeton

University Press, 1992); Elizabeth J. W. Barber, *Women's Work: The First 20,000 Years: Women, Cloth, and Society in Early Times* (New York: W. W. Norton, 1994). Owens examined the roles—including gatherers, hunters of small game, fishers and flintknappers—played by men and women in contemporary Arctic cultures. She hypothesized that these roles may be similar to the roles played by women in Europe in the Upper Paleolithic era and then reviewed the archeological evidence in terms of plant and animal remains. She argued that plant gathering may have comprised a larger part of the diet during the Upper Paleolithic era than had been assumed. She also suggested that bone tools identified as spear points may instead be needles used in the making of clothes. Barber argued that the development of string technology—twining fibers together to make nets, cloth, carrying bags, and so forth—was begun in the Paleolithic era by women and was one of the most significant technological developments of early humans.

27 Soffer, Adovasio, and Hyland, "The 'Venus' Figurines," 524.

28 Wreschner et al., "Red Ochre and Human Evolution"; Grahn, *Blood, Bread, and Roses*; Knight, *Blood Relations*; Power, "Women in Prehistoric Rock Art."

29 Although menses can occur during lactation, it is less likely to do so when children are breast-fed exclusively (i.e., not supplemented with bottles) for the first few years.

30 Grahn, *Blood, Bread, and Roses*.

31 Grahn, *Blood, Bread, and Roses*, 10.

32 Grahn, *Blood, Bread, and Roses*, 13.

33 Grahn, *Blood, Bread, and Roses*, 14.

34 Grahn, *Blood, Bread, and Roses*, 15.

35 Power, "Women in Prehistoric Rock Art," 75.

36 Power, "Women in Prehistoric Rock Art," 75.

37 Power, "Women in Prehistoric Rock Art," 87–93.

38 Power, "Women in Prehistoric Rock Art," 83.

39 della Madre, 2005; Gadon, *The Once and Future Goddess*; Grahn, *Blood, Bread, and Roses*; Noble, *Shakti Woman*; Sjoo and Mor, 1987.

40 Power, "Women in Prehistoric Rock Art," 87.

41 Power, "Women in Prehistoric Rock Art," 88.

42 Power, "Women in Prehistoric Rock Art," 83–99.

43 Adovasio, Soffer, and Page. *The Invisible Sex*, 3.

44 Jean Shinoda Bolen, foreword to *The Heart of the Goddess: Art, Myth, and Meditations of the World's Sacred Feminine*, by Hallie Iglehart Austen (Berkeley: Wingbow, 1990), xiv.

45 Jean Shinoda Bolen, *Crossing to Avalon: A Woman's Midlife Pilgrimage* (New York: HarperCollins, 1994), 57.

46 Bolen, *Crossing to Avalon*, 56–57.

47 Paula Gunn Allen, "The Anima of the Sacred: Empowering Women's Spirituality," in *Off the Reservation: Reflections on Boundary-Busting, Border-Crossing Loose Canons* (Boston: Beacon, 1998), 92.

48 Cheikh Anta Diop, *The Cultural Unity of Black Africa: The Domains of Patriarchy and of Matriarchy in Classical Antiquity* (Chicago: Third World, 1978).

49 In some contemporary hunter-gatherer groups, women and children gather sixty to eighty percent of the food consumed by the group.

SACRED DISPLAY: DIVINE AND MAGICAL FEMALE FIGURES OF ANCIENT EURASIA

MIRIAM ROBBINS DEXTER *

Introduction

This article focuses on magical female dancing and display figures, especially those that appear in prehistoric and early historic Eurasian cultures. Very similar female figures were depicted throughout Eurasia in a broad chronological sweep, beginning with figures depicted in the aceramic (pre-pottery), pre-agricultural Neolithic—dating at least from 8000 BCE in Southeast Anatolia—and the early and middle Neolithic in southeastern Europe—Bulgaria, Romania and Serbia—continuing through the late Neolithic and the Bronze Age in Western China and the Indus Valley and working its way into early historic Greece, East Asia, India, Ireland and elsewhere.

Sacred Display: A Definition

Female figures making a *sacred display* of their genitals are found in two iconographic forms: 1) a bent-knee dance in which the legs often form an M position and 2) a crouch that strongly displays the genitals. Some figures, such as the Irish Sheela-na-gig from Kiltinan, do both—doing a magical dance while opening and displaying her vulva. In prehistory as well as the modern era, piscine imagery is frequently connected with these figures.

Sacred display figures represent both the beneficent and the ferocious aspects of the divine feminine: They are apotropaic, warding off the enemy, and—a natural concomitant—they are protective of their people. They bring

---

* My co-author on the work of *Sacred Display* (rather than this article) is Victor H. Mair.

both fertility and good fortune. The apotropaic function of female genitals has been found as early as the Aurignacian era of the Upper Paleolithic, ca. 35,000-32,000 BCE.

The V in Upper Paleolithic Cave Art

The phenomenon of sacred display goes back many thousands of years. Cave art dating to the Upper Paleolithic—ca. 35,000 BCE through ca. 10,000 BCE—depicts a powerful symbol: the V, the female pubic triangle. A female figure composed of only a huge pubic triangle and legs was recently highlighted in a documentary film about Chauvet Cave, a vast underground cavern in the Ardèche Gorges in the south of France, which was discovered in 1994 by spelunkers.[1] At the time the cave was discovered, it had not been disturbed for 20,000 years, because a massive rockslide had sealed the original entrance. Because the cave had been undisturbed for so long, the paintings inside are exceptionally vivid—so much so that at first there were doubts as to their authenticity. But the paintings are covered in layers of calcite and concretions, which take thousands of years to grow, so the paintings cannot be forgeries.

The documentary film, *The Cave of Forgotten Dreams*, directed by Werner Herzog, shows a female figure with large pubic triangle, carved on a limestone outcropping; she dates to the Aurignacian period (ca. 35,000-32,000 BCE).[2] She is located in the last and deepest chamber of the 1,300-foot long cave, the Salle du Fond, and she may well have had an apotropaic function,[3] guarding the entrance to the farthest gallery, the holy of holies. She is in an area where lion paintings are found. The association of apotropaic female figures and felines has continued for many thousands of years. The cave includes four other female representations, each limited to the pubic triangle and indicating an entrance to an adjacent cavity.

Sometime after the female figure guarding the "Salle du Fond" was carved, a bison that some call the Sorcerer[4] was superimposed on her.[5] Although some have written that the bison and the female figure were engaging in a "hieros gamos,"[6] that has held true only since the bison was carved. The female figure was carved earlier than the bison, so the original intent was to depict not sex between male and female but the sacrality of the pubic triangle. The Chauvet Cave was a place of ritual rather than habitation.[7] Bones, including skulls, of cave bears have been found within.[8]

One bear skull, unfortunately lacking collagen for use in DNA analysis, was placed on a rock—likely by a human who was using the cave.[9]

In the Upper Paleolithic, female figures with large pubic triangles, often called Venus figures, also were often sculpted. The oldest yet discovered is the tiny female figure, carved from a mammoth tusk, that was found in 2008 in Hohle Fels cave in southwestern Germany (*Figure 1*). She dates to between 40,000 and 30,000 BCE, the Aurignacian period—the same dating as for the female figure from Chauvet Cave.[10] A flute made from a vulture bone was found just 70 cm from the female figure.[11] The combination of music and a sacred female figure probably indicates a ritual space.

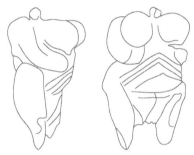

Fig. 1. 35,000-year-old female figure in the Hohle Fels
cave in southwestern Germany. Photograph n.d.

There was an earlier find in Städel cave in the Swabian Alb, a plateau in Germany: a sculpture of an anthropomorphic lion, dating to the same Aurignacian era as the Chauvet Cave's pubic triangle. The combination of animal and human characteristics has led researchers to interpret this sculpture as a shaman taking the form of a lion. The lion seems to be standing on tiptoe, perhaps an indicator of a shamanic dance. Although many pieces were missing from the original find, about 1,000 more pieces were found in a more recent investigation of Städel cave.

The statue has six stripes on its upper left arm. The small plate on its abdomen originally was interpreted as a penis in a hanging position. Recently, paleontologist Elisabeth Schmid has classified it as a pubic triangle. The navel is especially pronounced, and a horizontal crease runs across the lower abdomen; these are features typically belonging to female figures.[12] If this is a female figure, it is further indication of the association of female and feline, which has been found in the earliest Upper Paleolithic artifacts and has continued through time.[13]

The Neolithic

Spiritual phenomena related to caves and rock art continued into the Neolithic. A cave painting at Peri Nos Cape at Lake Onega in the Republic of Karelia[14] depicts a dancing figure, likely doing a religious, perhaps shamanic, dance. Neolithic rock art also depicts a female figure holding a bow and doing a magical dance.[15] The bow and sometimes arrows, according to Elisabeth During Caspers, are the paraphernalia of what she calls the shaman, male or female, as hunting magician. The religious adept employs the bow and arrow as objects of divination.[16]

In the earliest Neolithic period, this magical dance was combined with display of the female genitals; in such a display, the female figure often was depicted nude with a large, magical vulva.

Göbekli Tepe

In the earliest Neolithic, the image of the sacred pubic triangle and the function of apotropaia evolved into female display figures. One dancing figure found in level II of the Southeast Anatolian site of Göbekli Tepe dates to the aceramic, pre-agricultural Neolithic of no later than 8000 BCE; she is crouching in a magical dance or stance, with her arms and legs bent in an M position. She was carved on a stone slab that was found on the floor at the entrance to a room in the lion pillar building.

One had to step on the Göbekli Tepe female figure to enter the room; she was therefore the ground upon which one walked.[17] Because she protected the entrance to the room—just as the pubic triangles in Chauvet Cave protected the entrances to galleries—the female figure of Göbekli Tepe too was apotropaic, similarly to most Upper Paleolithic, Neolithic and later female figures that did sacred display. She was the goddess who protected the worshippers in the temple. This apotropaic function has been assigned to female display figures for millennia; the early historic Greco-Roman Medusa and the medieval Irish and British Sheela-na-gigs are examples of historic female figures whose functions included the apotropaic.

The female figure was found between pillars containing depictions of felines, continuing the association of the apotropaic female figure and the feline throughout Anatolia, the Indus Valley and historic India. Those associations likely continued an association that had begun in the Upper Paleolithic.

The T-shaped limestone pillars excavated in numerous small buildings at Göbekli Tepe have attracted media attention, and there is much speculation about the function of this site. In a *National Geographic* article published in June 2011,[18] Charles Mann began, "We used to think agriculture gave rise to cities and later to writing, art and religion. Now the world's oldest temple suggests the urge to worship sparked civilization." This is a quite revolutionary thought, since it directly disagrees with V. Gordon Childe's theory of the Neolithic Revolution, in which scarcity of food led to the need for plant domestication and sedentarism, which then would have given rise to both hierarchical societies and religion. However, as Mann reported, there is, as yet, no good evidence for social hierarchy. Klaus Schmidt, the excavator, speculated that peoples living within a hundred-mile radius of Göbekli Tepe created the site as a holy gathering place, yet nearby are several other sites, including Nevali Cori and Çayonu, which also show evidence of T-shaped pillars. There are multiple sophisticated religious sites in Southeast Anatolia, which may have been a larger area of gatherings. That this area—near the Karaca Dağ Mountains—gives us the first evidence of domesticated einkorn wheat may be significant as well.[19]

Lepenski Vir, Serbia

Lepenski Vir, in the Iron Gates section of the Danube River in Serbia, contains several female fish sculptures, copies of which are now in the Lepenski Vir Museum. One in particular is crouching; her arms reach down to indicate a deeply incised vulva (Figure 2). One can see two tiny breasts by the hands, perhaps representing those of an adolescent girl.

Fig. 2. Crouching stone "fish" figure from the Mesolithic site of Lepenski Vir. Lepenski Vir Museum. Photograph by Gregory L. Dexter, n.d.

The other sculpture is a fish figure with elaborate vesica piscis design—piscine imagery that we also see elsewhere.

Elsewhere in Southeastern Europe—Romania and Bulgaria

Neolithic dancing figures have been found throughout southeastern Europe. In Stara Zagora, Bulgaria, there are several such figures depicted on pots and potsherds and dating to the early Neolithic; the figures appear to be doing a magical dance. In two potsherds, the figure has one arm raised and the other lowered—a typical and magical position.[20] Similar figures have been found in Romania. Two figures excavated and published by Cornelia-Magda and Gheorghe Lazarovici also demonstrate this magical dance. The first, excavated by Cornelia-Magda Lazarovici, dates to Cucuteni A-3 (4300–4050 BCE); it is from Scânteia, Romania.[21] Its arms are raised and its legs form a crouching position in mirror image to its arms. The second, excavated by Gheorghe Lazarovici, dates to Vinca B (4300–4200 BCE); it is from Zorlentu Mare, Romania.[22] Further, there are Romanian pots that suggest the *hora*, or round dance; these pots are related to the ritual life of the communities that make them.[23]

Sacred Display and Chinese Pots

A pot from the Machang phase of the Majiayao culture of Liuwan in Western China (ca. 2300–2000 BCE) depicts a female figure in a display position. The pot was found in the Hexi corridor, part of the Northern Silk Road, a route from North China to the Tarim Basin and East Central Asia. The figure has tiny breasts much like those of the Lepenski Vir figure and a distended navel similar to that of the Upper Paleolithic lion sculpture. The woman's hands are positioned in such a way that they clearly are meant to expose her genitalia.

There are several pots from Western China that show the body of a human with arms and legs spread out in an M position; there are finlike appendages on the knees and shoulders. The fins link these images to the piscine imagery of the Lepenski Vir fish figures.

Yangshao Pots

Gheorghe and Cornelia-Magda Lazarovici and Senica Țurcanu, in their book on the Romanian Cucuteni culture, discussed pots that had been excavated from the Chinese Yangshao culture and dated to 5000–3000 BCE. The Yangshao civilization flourished along the Yellow River, through numerous provinces. One Yangshao pot illustrated by the authors is remarkably similar to the pots that depict figures with finlike protuberances at their elbows and knees.[24]

Artifacts from the Yangshao culture include pots with representations of fish, birds, animals, celestial bodies and the "primordial egg"—all symbols exceptionally similar to those found on artifacts from the southeastern European Cucuteni culture. Although the distance between southeastern Europe and China (more than 4,000 km) is huge, the authors point out that, in the same way, the Cardial Ware complex spread from east of the Mediterranean Sea, from Mersin to the Bay of Biscay to the south of Brittany—also a distance of 4,000 km. Given enough time and roadways between the cultures, such symbols and mythological themes can spread incredible distances. We will see shortly that we may assume a similar trajectory between southeastern Europe and the Indus Valley.

Additional East–West Connections

Petroglyphs incised into a high cliff face at Kangjiashimenzi, near Qutubi, north central Xinjiang, in Western China (*Figure 3*), dating to ca. 1000 BCE, depict dancing figures with triangular bodies,[25] strongly resembling those incised and painted on pots from the Cucuteni-Tripolye culture of Romania and other cultures from Ukraine and Poland, which date to ca. 4000–3500 BCE.[26]

Fig. 3. Female silhouettes, painted and incised, Cornelia-Magda (Mantu) Lazarovici, excavator. C-M Lazarovici, 2009: 93, fig. 9. Cucuteni A-B, B = Tripolie BII and CI; ca. 4100–3500 CAL BCE. Sites from Romania, Poland, Ukraine. Courtesy of Cornelia-Magda Lazarovici.

The V

The V, which takes the shape of a triangle open at the top, is found inscribed on many artifacts of Neolithic southeastern Europe, which is often called Old Europe. This V was also used as the base for many symbols of the Danube script.[27] It is an important symbol in the art and language of many cultures,[28] because it can be expanded by means of multiple diacritics.[29] The V may well have as its base the magical and enlarged vulva of the female figures that were excavated by the thousands from Neolithic and Chalcolithic sites throughout prehistoric Anatolia and Europe[30] and that continued to be depicted in iconography and text into the early historic period.[31] Even though the V must have been an abstract symbol, given the multiplicity of diacritical markers, we believe that the core spiritual meaning would have remained within each symbol.

By the time the Danube script was being formulated, female figures with large pubic triangles were being crafted throughout southeastern Europe and elsewhere.

The M

In Old European cultures, the legs of a figure often were depicted in an M position;[32] this M is a character of the Danube script as well, and it represents the position taken by the legs in a ritual dance.[33] In representations of that dance, the legs are usually bent in an M position, and often the arms mirror the legs, raised and forming an M. One or both of the arms may hang from the elbows, and the legs can be spread wide or with one leg up but one leg down.

The Indus Valley culture also incorporated the iconography of the M.[34]

The M of the Danube script is the underpinning of a particular type of female figure, the display figure that Marija Gimbutas associated with birthing and "the frog goddess as life regenerator,"[35] and we find that the frog, a symbol of both fertility and the fertilizing rain, is depicted with its legs in this position.[36] K. de B. Codrington illustrated a figure from Mathura, the front of which is a crouching Lajja Gauri and the back of which is a frog.[37] Codrington dated the figure to the early 2nd century CE. Thus, one display figure brings together the principles of female human fertility and the fertility thought to be brought by frogs.

The Indus Valley

The cultures of the Indus Valley, also known as the Indus/Saraswati Valley[38] had many features that echoed those of the earlier Danube cultures, including sacred display figures. These civilizations produced few weapons and did not leave evidence of hierarchy. Each produced a script—still undeciphered—as well as beautiful pottery and other evidence of high culture.[39] There are several characters in the Danube script that have correlates in the Indus script.[40] Further, there is evidence that the cultures used comparable ornamentation.

Very well made armlets or bangles were used by the Indus/Saraswati Valley peoples,[41] as well as India's early historic and recent cultures. Bangles appear not only as indications of jewelry on artifacts but also as grave goods themselves. An elderly woman was buried with seven shell bangles, worn smooth, seemingly from having been worn for many years.[42]

Bangles have also been found in excavations of Danube cultures. The ritual pit of the Lady—or priestess—of Tartaria shows signs of great honor paid to this elderly woman. A *Spondylus gaederopus* armlet was found in her ritual pit; it showed signs of having been deeply worn—that is, worn throughout a lifetime.[43] This bangle may have been one sign of her office rather than customary ware of other women of the culture. Indeed, we postulate that this may have been the first use of bangles/armlets. A like phenomenon is the transition of tall "witches'" or priestesses' hats to bridal hats in Central Asia.[44] That is, the hats became generalized to ceremonial garb for young women, where before they had been used by priestesses in special female burials—for example, in the Tarim Basin[45] and the Altai Mountains.[46] Perhaps the bangle was originally a marker of a priestess or shaman, exemplified by the Spondylus shell bracelet found in the burial pit of the Lady of Tartaria. Later, the bangle would have become a more general marker for women in the Indus Valley and then in historic India.

Display figures with armlets have been found in several excavations of Neolithic southeastern European sites: An armlet encircles the left arm of a figure from Durankulak, Bulgaria, dating to 4550–4450 BCE; one encircles the right arm of a pregnant figure from the Pavlovac site (FYROM); and three encircle the right arm of a Vinca terra-cotta figure from the Stublive site in Serbia.[47]

There are other correlates between Indus Valley cultures and those of Old Europe. Early historic Indic female figures have correlates in the earlier, Bronze Age Indus Valley culture and the Bactria–Margiana Archaeological Complex; these cultures produced seals that depict both Durga-like (that is, in the image of the Great Goddess Devi/Kali/Durga) and Lajja-Gauri-like (female display) figures. A large wooden sculpture (28 inches tall) of a nude female from the Harappan culture, dated to ca. 2400 BCE, is squatting and displaying her genitals.[48]

This figure and Indus Valley seals[49] of female figures in display position relate Indus Valley iconography to later Hindu and Buddhist Lajja Gauri figures, nude figures that hold their legs in positions that boldly display their genitals. In fact, the Indus script itself includes a crouching figure that seems to be in a sacred stance or dance.

Pre-Durga

In Indus Valley stamp seals, a yogi (more likely, a yogini) has a tiger beard.[50] This is enough to make most archaeologists deem it a male figure with breasts. However, a 3rd century BCE to 3rd century CE display figure from the Nilgiris District is a ferocious-looking female figure with breasts and the beard of a tiger[51]—a historic age depiction that echoes the earlier, Indus depiction of a goddess turning into a tiger.

The historic-age Great Goddess Durga has been depicted with felines. Her mount is the lion in the *Devi Mahatmyam*, but she is associated with the tiger elsewhere. The tiger may have been replaced by the lion later.[52]

There is a carved steatite[53] seal from the Mohenjo-daro culture of the Indus Valley, dating to ca. 2600-1900 BCE. It depicts a woman standing between a Shami tree and a tiger. The tiger has the leaves of a tree as head-dress. The woman is undergoing metamorphosis: Her feet have become hooves or claws, and she has developed a tail and horns.[54]

Two other seals from Mohenjo-daro depict tree goddesses that appear to be summoning tigers, which are looking back at them.[55]

In a seal from Mohenjo-daro, the tiger and the woman are united.[56] The woman has the distinctive horns of a markhor goat. A square stamp seal from Kalibangan also depicts the unification of woman and tiger, with a tiger-bodied goddess that has the horns of a markhor goat.[57]

The human–tiger motif is repeated on another seal from Kalibangan. A woman with long, flowing hair is standing between two males; she is wearing a long skirt, and she has bangles on her arms.[58] Nearby is the tiger goddess, also with long, streaming hair,[59] and her arms too are covered from wrists to shoulders with bangles. The tiger-woman is wearing a headdress with animal horns and a tree branch.

The female deity of the tree is depicted on a seal from the site of Nausharo. A seal from Mohenjo-daro illustrates the tree deity along with seven female figures, with long braids, that border the bottom of the seal. The seven female figures may represent the Pleiades[60] and may have evolved into the Saptamatrika, the powerful seven mother goddesses.

The pre-Indic iconography may underlie the possibility of a later Buddhist goddess-feline, such as the Tantric lionheaded goddess Simhamukha.[61]

East Indian Female Figures—Southern Asia—Kali

With the Indus Valley material in mind, we consider again the Hindu Great Goddess Devi/Kali/Durga.

The Indic goddess Kali brings death but also protects the worshiper from death—that is, she is apotropaic, like the Paleolithic carved pubic triangles guarding the entrances to chambers in Chauvet Cave, the Neolithic Göbekli Tepe woman, and the Irish and British Sheela-na-gigs. Kali has been represented in the same bent-knee or dancing pose taken by several of the prehistoric figures we have discussed.[62] Many other Indic female figures are portrayed in the dancing position as well.[63] Kali, as well as other Indic goddesses, can appear in the cremation grounds, the place of death, dancing on the corpse just as she dances upon her consort, Shiva, to awaken him.[64]

Kali is one of the forms of the Indic Great Goddess Devi; in one of Devi's ferocious forms, Durga, she appears as a rather bloodthirsty savior of the Indic gods in her battles against the asuras, the demons. Kali becomes a major figure in the *Devi Mahatmyam* (from the *Markandeya Purana*), one of the earliest and most significant Tantric hymns to the Great Goddess Devi in her many manifestations, which was written in the 4th or 5th century CE. In chapter seven of the *Devi Mahatmyam*, the asuras Chaṇḍa and Muṇḍa, are threatening Devi and trying to capture her. Devi becomes furious, and her countenance becomes dark.

> Then, [as Durga] contracted her brows, out of the flat sur-
> face of her forehead came Kali, the gaping-mouthed one,
> having a sword and noose.[65]

Thus, in this version of the myth, Kali is born from Durga's forehead. She wears a tiger's skin and a necklace of skulls. She is emaciated, and her eyes are sunken and reddish. She kills Chaṇḍa and Muṇḍa and then receives the epithet Chamunda.

Indic Lajja Gauri Figures

The large wooden sculpture that we discussed earlier, as well as the Indus Valley seals of female figures in a display position, relate Indus Valley iconography to later, Hindu and Buddhist Lajja Gauri figures—nude figures that hold their legs in positions that display their genitals. These figures date from the 1st century BCE through approximately the 16th century CE and have been found in temples throughout India. Some Lajja Gauris have human heads, but by the first few centuries of this era most of the heads had been replaced by lotuses[66] and snakes.[67] There is also a froglike Lajja Gauri with a lotus head.[68] The Buddhist Lajja Gauris retained human heads but with the addition of the long ears emblematic of Buddhist iconography.[69] The snakes and lotuses symbolize fertility: Snakes can shed and then regenerate their skin, and so they give a visual demonstration of the possibility of regeneration, while the lotus is a symbol of regenerative vegetation. Many images of Lajja Gauris were abstracted as flowers.[70] Some of the early Lajja Gauris were depicted with vegetation growing out of their mouths or navels.[71]

It is the concept of fertility that is important. The female gives birth to all things out of her body:

> Thereupon, O Gods, I shall maintain the whole world by
> means of life-sustaining vegetables, produced from my
> own body, until it rains.[72]

This is a promise made by the Goddess Devi/Durga. Thus, both Durga and the Lajja Gauris are sources of vegetation. According to Laura Amazzone,[73] on the ninth day of the great festival of Durga in contemporary India, the goddess manifests as nine forms of sacred plants;[74] Durga is the power inherent in all vegetation.[75]

Another symbol of the Lajja Gauris, who bring good fortune to the temples in which they reside, is the "brimming vase [of fortune]," the *pūrṇa kumbha; kumbha* means both pot and womb.[76] In village societies of India, the pot is the symbol of the divine feminine, the mother.[77] The Mangala Gaur celebration is important for new brides in Maharashtra. In the month of Shravan, within a year after a new bride's marriage, she performs the Shiva lingam puja for the well-being of her husband and her new family.[78] Sanskrit *maṅgala* means "happiness, welfare, auspiciousness,"[79] so the festival is the Gauri Auspiciousness or the Auspiciousness of Gauri. Further, at one point during the Durga festival a pot is identified with the goddess; edible fruit and plants are placed in the pot, which also contains water from the Ganges, and the priest says a prayer to identify the pot with the source of the nectar of immortality, the *amṛta*,[80] which is produced by the churning of the Sea of Milk. Thus, the brimming pot of auspiciousness or good fortune is associated with the genital display of the propitious Lajja Gauris.

In one silver seal from Kashmir Smast (*Figure 4*), the legs of the Lajja Gauri are in an M position and the mirrored arms are in a W position.[81] A seal with a comparably positioned Lajja Gauri, from the Allahabad District, dates to the Kushana period.[82]

One of the names given to Devi, the great goddess, is Gauri, the shining one. Sanskrit *gaura* means yellowish and also white, brilliant, and shining; it is a description given to several goddesses, including Parvati Gauri, the wife of Shiva.[83] Devi is given the epithet Gauri in *Devi Mahatmyam* 4.11, 41; since she is paired there with Shiva, she is Parvati Gauri. A gauraki is "a girl 8 years old

Fig. 4. Silver seal of Lajja Gauri from Kashmir Smast, silver, 1.9 cm × 1.9 cm, 2nd century CE. Private collection of Max Le Martin, purchased from an auction gallery in British Columbia, Canada. Photograph n.d.

prior to menstruation," that is, a virgin.[84] Forms of Gauri are worshipped throughout rural India.[85] Lajja means shame in Bengali and other Indic languages, so the Lajja Gauri could be a shameful young woman, because she makes a bold display. This is a rather negative naming, in contrast to the fact that Lajja Gauris are believed to bring good fortune.[86] Indeed, an alternate etymology was given by Dr Ramchandra C. Dhere in his book, *Lajja Gauri*. He believed that Lajja is a form of Lanja/Lanjika, which means naked.[87] Certainly, that definition would better fit the nude female figures.

Medusa

In the earliest Greek texts that contain myth, Homer's *Iliad* and *Odyssey*, Medusa was a monstrous head associated with the underworld.[88] She was the only mortal of three Gorgon sisters. The adjective γοργός means terrible, fierce, and frightful. Medusa's staring eyes play a role in her myth from her textual inception: her eyes literally petrify.

Medusa was apotropaic, and for that reason shields bearing Gorgon heads abound in Greek iconography.

In *The Theogony*, written by the Greek poet Hesiod, Perseus decapitates the Gorgon (*Figure 5*). We may note that in this illustration the wings are Medusa's, not those of the horse Pegasus; Medusa, with her wings and snaky hair, is the descendent of the Neolithic bird and snake goddess.[89] Interestingly, despite being thought of as monstrous, Medusa was attractive enough for the god Poseidon to want to sleep with her; the two lay in a soft meadow, in the midst of spring flowers.[90]

Medusa's apotropaic function was manifested iconographically by the numerous Gorgon antefixes that have been found in Greece and Italy. Over time, Medusa also accrued a lolling tongue,

Fig. 5. Perseus slaying winged Medusa, Melos, terra-cotta relief, circa 450 BCE. British Museum, 1842.7.28.1134. Courtesy of the British Museum. Photograph by Gregory L. Dexter, n.d.

comparable to that of the Indic Kali. The Medusa head was placed on soldiers' shields, over doorways, as antefixes on roofs, on doors of ovens and kilns, and on Athena's aegis. Again, we may compare her to the prehistoric figures: the goddess as vulva on the limestone outcropping in Chauvet Cave, who protected the entrance to the Salle du Fond, and the dancing female figure from Göbekli Tepe, who protected the temple at whose entrance she lay.

In addition to Medusa's head being a protectress, her blood had a function: In Euripides's *Ion*, we are told that one drop of Medusa's blood is deadly but that the other drop brings healing.[91] Further, we are told by Apollodorus that the blood from Medusa's left side is poisonous but that from the right is healing.[92] Thus, Medusa represents regeneration as well as death.

Fig. 6. Gorgon pediment from Artemis Temple in Corfu. 590–580 BCE. The Medusa on this pediment is nine feet tall. Her waist is cinched with serpents, and there are snakes in her hair. She appears with a lion and her children, Pegasus and Chrysaor. Courtesy of the Kekyra Archaeological Museum. Photograph by Gregory L. Dexter, n.d.

Just like the prehistoric figures, Medusa has a bent-knee pose. The Medusa portrayed on the pediment of the Artemis temple in Kerkyra is in this posture (*Figure 6*). In an Etruscan artifact, she is in full display pose with her legs in an M position.

Irish and British Sheela-na-gigs

Sheela-na-gigs also served an apotropaic function; in the medieval era, many Sheela-na-gigs were sculpted and placed above the doors to churches and castles. These Sheela-na-gigs protect these powerful and sacred places. Sheela-na-gigs were sometimes presented as old and emaciated and sometimes as young and even pregnant. They may represent all of a woman's life phases. The magical stance or dance and the erotic display that we have found in other female figures are shared by the Irish Sheela-na-gig from Kiltinan, which stands on one foot with her left hand lifted to her face and her right hand displaying her vulva (*Figure 7*). Her knees are bent as if in a dance.

The Sheela-na-gigs take magical postures –the crouching Moate Sheela-na-gig (*Figure 8*) takes a position comparable to that of the Lepenski Vir fish figure. Further, both the Moate and the Cavan Sheela have huge mouths, similar to the fishy mouth of the Lepenski Vir fish figure. The Cavan Sheela has a magically large vulva that hangs down below her knees. She is emaciated as well, with well-defined ribs, just like the Indic goddess Kali.

Fig. 8. Moate Sheela-na-gig. This Sheela is above a door behind the Moate castle in County Westmeath, Ireland. Photograph courtesy of Starr Goode, n.d.

Fig. 7. Kiltinan Sheela-na-gig from Fethard, County Tipperary, Ireland. Photograph courtesy of Joe Kenny (www.fethard.com), n.d.

We can see the vesica piscis, the double-pointed oval, in the huge vulva of the Cavan Sheela-na-gig. Vesica piscis literally means fish bladder, and this takes us back to the Lepenski Vir fish figure and the figures on Neolithic Chinese pots that have finny protuberances.

One would touch the vulva of a Sheela in order to obtain fertility—the ability to have a child. Birth is magical, miraculous and sacred, and this was especially true in antiquity, when the rates of infant and mother mortality were very high. The Sheela-na-gigs represent more than a human woman giving birth. There is the addition of magical postures and the juxtaposition of the aged woman and the young, fertile woman. Two Neolithic figures may illustrate this concept. The first, a figure from the Neolithic site of Achilleion, Thessaly, in Central Greece, is depicted in a normal birth-giving position. The second, from the island of Malta in Southern Europe (south of Sicily), is also depicted in a birthing position, but to that is added magical gestures (*Figure 9*).

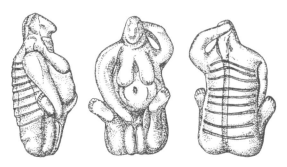

Fig. 9. Birth-giving woman from Malta, in a magical stance. End of 4th millennium BCE. Figure 7.2 of Marija Gimbutas, *The Civilization of the Goddess: The World of Old Europe*, ed. Joan Marler (San Francisco: Harper, 1991), with permission from the literary estate of Marija Gimbutas.

Female Display Figures of the Pacific

Female display figures also have been found in the Pacific. Douglas Fraser found that Pacific display figures (in Sepik art in New Guinea, Borneo, Sumatra, Hawaii, New Zealand and some other cultures) were brought from Changsha in the Chu culture area of South China to this region during the late Zhou period. These cultures had the Gorgon in their repertoire by the 3rd-4th centuries BCE, employing them as tomb guardian figures.[93] The Gorgon was not depicted in the art of the original Malayo-Polynesian peoples when they first migrated into the Pacific, ca. 2000–700 BCE.[94]

Fraser found the same motif on the northwest coast of America, among the Nootka, the Kwakiutl, the Haida, the Tsimshian and the Tlingit. In this area, when the display figure is not a human female, it is a bear, otherwise depicted in northwest coast art with a long, protruding tongue.[95] This strikingly reminds one of the bear display figure from the early Neolithic Anatolian site of Çatalhöyük.[96]

Display figures also have been found in the pre-Columbian art of central Peru, the Peruvian coast and Ecuador.[97] In Ecuador the figures sit with their legs in an M position and their arms mirroring their legs, upraised in a W position.[98] This position strongly recalls figures found throughout Neolithic southeastern Europe and the Indus Valley, which we have already discussed.

Robert von Heine-Geldern believed that the images were transmitted from the West to China via a route in Central Asia. This diffusion of the idea of female display figures explains why so many parts of the world, hitherto thought unconnected, have Gorgon-like figures. In its origins and development, sacred display is a distinctly Eurasian phenomenon.

Conclusion

Evidence demonstrates that female display figures have had apotropaic and protective functions, from the earliest Upper Paleolithic era—for example, in Chauvet Cave—through the modern era. Sheela-na-gigs were placed on the walls of churches and castles, presumably to ward off the enemy and protect those inside. Gorgon antefixes were placed on the walls of houses, on roofs, on ovens, on shields and even in the aegis of the goddess Athena, for the same purposes. Further, gorgon figures were placed on tombstones[99] and sarcophagi,[100] most likely as a symbol of, and hope for, regeneration. Even today, Indic Lajja Gauri figures are thought to bring good fortune to the temples in which they reside.

Fig. 10. Sign in front of Starbucks in Del Mar,
California. Photograph by Gregory L. Dexter, n.d.

There is also a contemporary and pervasive image of the display figure that many of us may take for granted (*Figure 10*). The early form of the Starbucks logo depicted a woman in a double-tailed mermaid display position, with her two fish legs uplifted.

There is a continuum between erotic magical figures and erotic religious figures. There is no sharp line of demarcation between magic, including folk magic, and religion, since what may be cult magic, folk magic or even myth to one person may be religion to another. These fierce and often voluptuous female figures, nude and dancing a magical dance or nude and crouching to display their vulvas, are magical figures and, likely, religious figures. They date to the earliest Neolithic in Anatolia and Europe, the mature Neolithic in southeastern Europe and the late Neolithic/Bronze Age in eastern and central Asia and the Indus Valley, and they appeared in early historic Europe, East Asia and South Asia and later cultures throughout the world. The sacred display of these female figures reflects the huge numinosity of the prehistoric divine feminine.

These figures represent apotropaia, protection, birth, death and regeneration. In displaying their genitals, they are potent images of the gateway to the womb—the womb of the Great Mother, the literal matrix of birth, the place to which one returns at death and the source of regeneration.[101]

References

Amazzone, Laura. *Goddess Durgā and Sacred Female Power.* Lanham, MD: Hamilton, 2010.

Apollodorus, *Atheniensis Bibliothecae.*

Bocherens, Hervé, Dorothée G. Drucker, Daniel Billiou, Jean-Michel Geneste, and Johannes van der Plicht. "Bears and Humans in Chauvet Cave (Vallon-Pont-d'Arc, Ardèche, France): Insights from Stable Isotopes and Radiocarbon Dating of Bone Collagen." *Journal of Human Evolution* 50 (2006): 370–6.

Bolon, Carol R. *Forms of the Goddess Lajja Gauri in Indian Art.* Vol. 49 of *Monographs on the Fine Arts.* University Park, PA: Pennsylvania State University Press, 1992.

Bradshaw Foundation. "The Salle du Fond Chamber—The Venus and the Sorcerer." Accessed August 3, 2017. www.bradshawfoundation.com/chauvet/venus_sorcerer.php.

Brown, Robert L. "A Lajjā Gaurī in a Buddhist Context at Aurangabad." *The Journal of the International Association of Buddhist Studies* 13, no. 2 (1990): 1–18.

Clottes, Jean. "France's Magical Ice Age Art: Chauvet Cave." *National Geographic*, August 2001, 104–121.

Codrington, K. de B. "India. Iconography: Classical and Indian." *Man: A Monthly Record of Anthropological Science* 35 (May 1935): 65–6.

Conard, Nicholas J. "A Female Figurine from the Basal Aurignacian of Hohle Fels Cave in Southwestern Germany." *Nature* 459 (May 14, 2009): 248–52.

Davis-Kimball, Jeannine. *Warrior Women: An Archaeologist's Search for History's Hidden Heroines*. New York: Warner, 2002.

Dexter, Miriam Robbins. *Whence the Goddesses: A Source Book*. Athene Series. New York: Pergamon, 1990.

———. "Ancient Felines and the Great-Goddess in Anatolia: Kubaba and Cybele." In *Proceedings of the 20th Annual UCLA Indo-European Conference*, edited by Stephanie W. Jamison, H. Craig Melchert, and Brent Vine, 53–67. Bremen, Germany: Hempen, 2009.

———. "The Ferocious and the Erotic: 'Beautiful' Medusa and the Neolithic Bird and Snake." Journal of Feminist Studies in Religion 26, no. 1 (2010): 25–41.

———. "Substrate Continuity in Indo-European Religion and Iconography: Seals and Figurines of the Indus Valley Culture and Historic Indic Female Figures." *In Archaeology and Language: Indo-European Studies Presented to James P. Mallory*, Journal of Indo-European Studies Monograph Series no. 60, edited by Martin E. Huld, Karlene Jones-Bley, and Dean Miller. Washington, D.C.: Institute for the Study of Man, 2012, 197–219.

———. "Further Thoughts on the V and the M in the Danube Script: The Danube Script and the Old European Goddess." In *On the Trail of Vlassa, Fifty Years of Tărtăria Excavations*. Proceedings from a conference sponsored by Eftimie Murgu University, Reşiţa, Romania and the Institute of Archaeomythology, Sebastopol, September 1–5, 2011. Forthcoming.

Dexter, Miriam Robbins, and Starr Goode. "The Sheela na gigs, Sexuality, and the Goddess in Ancient Ireland." *Irish Journal of Feminist Studies* 4, no. 2 (2002): 50–75.

Dexter, Miriam Robbins, and Victor H. Mair. *Sacred Display: Divine and Magical Female Figures of Eurasia*. Amherst, NY: Cambria, 2010.

Murray, Gilbert, ed. 1902. *Euripides, Fabulae* I (includes the Ion) Reprint 1951. Oxford: Clarendon Press.

Jagadiswarananda, Swami, trans. *Devi Mahatmyam*. Madras, India: Sri Ramakrishna Math, 1953.

Donaldson, Thomas. "Propitious–Apotropaic Eroticism in the Art of Orissa." *Artibus Asiae* 37 (1975): 75–100.

During Caspers, Elisabeth. "Another Face of the Indus Valley Magico-Religious System." In *South Asian Archaeology 1991: Proceedings of the Eleventh International Conference of the Association of South Asian Archaeologists in Western Europe. Berlin, 1–5 July 1991*, edited by Adalbert J. Gail. Stuttgart, Germany: F. Steiner, 1993, 65–86.

Fraser, Douglas. "The Heraldic Woman: A Study in Diffusion." In *The Many Faces of Primitive Art: A Critical Anthology*. Englewood Cliffs, NJ: Prentice Hall, 1966, 36–99.

Garfinkel, Yosef, 2003, "The Earliest Dancing Scenes in the Near East." *Near Eastern Archaeology.* 66.3: 84-95

Gimbutas, Marija. *The Language of the Goddess*. San Francisco: Harper, 1989.

———. *The Civilization of the Goddess: The World of Old Europe*. Edited by Joan Marler. San Francisco: Harper, 1991.

———. *The Living Goddesses*. Edited and supplemented by Miriam Robbins Dexter. Berkeley/Los Angeles: University of California Press, 1999.

Gimbutas, Marija, Shan Winn, and Daniel Shimabuku. *Achilleion: A Neolithic Settlement in Thessaly, Greece, 6400–5600 B.C.* Vol. 14 of *Monumenta Archaeologica*. Los Angeles: Institute of Archaeology, University of California Los Angeles, 1989).

Goode, Starr, and Miriam Robbins Dexter. "Sexuality, the Sheela na gigs, and the Goddess in Ancient Ireland." *ReVision* 23, no. 1 (2000): 38–48.

Haarmann, Harald, and Joan Marler. *Introducing the Mythological Crescent: Ancient Beliefs and Imagery Connecting Eurasia with Anatolia*. Wiesbaden, Germany: Harrassowitz Verlag, 2008.

Hesiod, *Theogony.*

Heun, Manfred, Ralk Schäfer-Prefl, Dieter Klawan, Renato Castagna, Monica Accerbi, Basilio Borghi, and Francesco Salamini. "Site of Einkorn Wheat Domestication Identified by DNA Fingerprinting." *Science* 278 (1997): 1312–4.

Hiltebeitel, Alf. "The Indus Valley 'Proto-Śiva,' Reexamined through Reflections on the Goddess, the Buffalo, and the Symbolism of Vāhanas." *Anthropos* 73, no. 5/6 (1978): 767–97.

Jayakar, Pupul. *The Earth Mother: Legends, Goddesses, and Ritual Arts of India*. San Francisco/New York: Harper and Row, 1990.

Kenoyer, Jonathan Mark. *Ancient Cities of the Indus Valley Civilization.* Oxford: Oxford University Press and the American Institute of Pakistan Studies, 1998.

Kinsley, David. *Hindu Goddesses: Visions of the Divine Feminine in the Hindu Religious Tradition.* Vol. 12 of *Hermeneutics: Studies in the History of Religions.* Berkeley/Los Angeles: University of California Press, 1988.

(Lazarovici) Mantu, Cornelia-Magda.

1992 "Representări antropomorfe pe ceramica aşezării Cucuteni A3 de la Scînteia (jud. Iaşi)." *Studii şi Cercetări de istorie veche şi arheologie* 43 (3): 307-315.

1995 "Câteva consideraţii privind cronologia absolută a neo-eneoliticului din România." *Studii şi Cercetări de istorie veche şi arheologie* 46 (3-4): 213-235.

2008 "Symbols and Signs in Cucuteni-Tripolye Culture" In *Journal of Archaeomythology* 4, 1: 65-93. From the Proceedings of the conference, "International Symposium on Neolithic Signs and Symbols: the Earliest Literacy?", Novi Sad, May, 2004. Joan Marler and Miriam Robbins Dexter, eds. Sebastopol: Institute of Archaeomythology.

Lazarovici, Cornelia-Magda, Gheorghe-Corneliu Lazarovici, and Senica Ţurcanu. *Cucuteni: A Great Civilization of the Prehistoric World.* Iaşi, Romania: Palatul Culturii, 2009.

Lazarovici, Gheorghe, Cornelia-Magda Lazarovici, and Marco Merlini. *Tărtăria and the Sacred Tablets.* Cluj-Napoca, Romania: Editura Mega, 2011.

Los Angeles County Museum of Art. Dancing Vajravārāhī/Vajrayoginī, Himalayas, central Tibet. LACMAM74_106_1.

Lubell, Winifred Melius. *The Metamorphosis of Baubo: Myths of Women's Sexual Energy.* Nashville and London: Vanderbilt University Press, 1994.

Mair, Victor H. "Prehistoric and East Asian Flutes." In *Studies in Chinese Language and Culture-Festschrift in Honour of Christoph Harbsmeier on the Occasion of His 60th Birthday*, edited by Christoph Anderl and Halvor Eifring. Oslo: Hermes Academic Publishing, 2006.

Mallory, James P., and Victor H. Mair. *The Tarim Mummies.* London: Thames and Hudson, 2000.

Mann, Charles C. "The Birth of Religion." *National Geographic,* June 2011.

Jamie McCartney. "The Great Wall of Vagina" (art exhibit). www.greatwallofvagina.co.uk.

McIntosh, Jane R. *The Ancient Indus Valley: New Perspectives.* Santa Barbara, CA: ABC Clio, 2008.

Monier-Williams, Sir M. 1899. *Sanskrit-English Dictionary.* Oxford: Clarendon Press.

Mookerjee, Ajit. Kali: *The Feminine Force.* New York: Destiny, 1988.

Mukherjee, Samir Kumar. "Terracotta Art in the Gangetic Valley under the Kushanas." In *Indian Terracotta Sculpture: The Early Period.* Mumbai: Marg, 2002, 74–85.

Newberry, John. Indus Script Monographs. Victoria, BC, Canada: J. Newberry, 1988–1990.

Parpola, Asko. *Deciphering the Indus Script.* Cambridge: Cambridge University Press, 1994.

Polosmak, Natalya. "A Mummy Unearthed from the Pastures of Heaven." *National Geographic*, October 1994, 79–103.

Schulz, Matthias. "Is the Lion Man a Woman?" *Spiegel Online*, December 9, 2011, www.spiegel.de/international/zeitgeist/is-the-lion-man-a-woman-solving-the-mystery-of-a-35-000-year-old-statue-a-802415.html.

Shaw, Miranda. *Buddhist Goddesses of India.* Princeton, NJ/Oxford: Princeton University Press, 2006.

Sonawane, V. H. "Some Remarkable Sculptures of Lajjā Gaurī from Gujarat." *Lalit Kalā* 23 (1988): 27–34.

TantraWorks. "Tantra in Ancient Times." Accessed August 3, 2017. www.tantra-works.com/Ancient_Tantra.html#indus.

Thackeray, J. Francis. "A 'Venus' and 'Man-Bison' in Upper Palaeolithic Art at Chauvet Cave." *The Digging Stick* 25, no. 1 (2008): 21.

Wang Binghua. *Xinjiang Tianshan shengzhi chongbai yanhua* [Tianshan Petroglyphs: A Testimony of Fertility Worship]. Edited by The Historical Relics and Archaeology Institute of the Xinxiang Uygur Autonomous Region. Beijing: Cultural Relics Publishing House, 1990.

Wessels-Mevissen, Corinna. "Creative Legacy of the Nilgiri Hills: Terracotta Offerings from South Indian Megalithic Burials." In *Indian Terracotta Sculpture: The Early Period*, edited by Pratapaditya Pal. Mumbai: Marg, 2002, 24–35.

Wikipedia. "Lajja Gauri." Accessed July 2, 2011. en.wikipedia.org/wiki/Lajja_Gauri.

Wikipedia. "Marathi People." Accessed July 2, 2011. en.wikipedia.org/wiki/
Marathi_people#Mangala_Gaur.

Wikipedia. "Soapstone." Accessed July 2, 2011. en.wikipedia.org/wiki/
Soapstone.

Endnotes

1 Jean Clottes, "France's Magical Ice Age Art: Chauvet Cave," National
Geographic, August 2001, 104–21.

2 Hervé Bocherens, Dorothée G. Drucker, Daniel Billiou, Jean-Michel Geneste,
and Johannes van der Plicht. "Bears and Humans in Chauvet Cave (Vallon-Pont-
d'Arc, Ardèche, France): Insights from Stable Isotopes and Radiocarbon Dating
of Bone Collagen," *Journal of Human Evolution* 50 (2006): 370, 374. Chauvet
Cave has yielded the oldest parietal art yet.

3 Bradshaw Foundation, "The Salle du Fond Chamber—The Venus and the
Sorcerer," accessed August 3, 2017, www.bradshawfoundation.com/chauvet/
venus_sorcerer.php. That article states, "Perhaps the female representation
relates directly to the corridor to the chamber, which opens just behind her. A
cluster of convergent data suggests that the Venus is Aurignacian and that she
was created in the first period of the decoration of the Chauvet Cave."

4 Clottes, "France's Magical Ice Age Art," 2001; J. Francis Thackeray, "A
'Venus' and 'Man-Bison' in Upper Palaeolithic Art at Chauvet Cave," *The
Digging Stick* 25, no. 1 (2008): 21.

5 According to the Bradshaw Foundation, "the Venus is the earliest of the
designs. The feline on the left, the Sorcerer, and the multiple lines on the right,
are all painted or engraved later" (Bradshaw Foundation, "The Salle du Fond
Chamber—The Venus and the Sorcerer").

6 Thackeray, "A 'Venus' and 'Man-Bison,'" 21; Clottes, "France's Magical Ice
Age Art," 2001.

7 Clottes, "France's Magical Ice Age Art," 2001, 111.

8 Bocherens et al, "Bears and Humans in Chauvet Cave," 2006, 372 and
375. The authors analyzed the DNA of cave-bear bones found at the site. The
radiocarbon age of eight samples of cave-bear bone collagen clustered between
30,690 before present (BP) plus or minus 180 BP and 28,850 BP plus or minus
170 BP. One sample, a jawbone buried in red clay and then exposed by water
erosion, measured 37,410 BP plus or minus 290 BP. Unfortunately, a bear skull
that seemed to have been consciously placed on a rock in the Salle du Crâne

contained insufficient collagen and therefore could not be dated. The bear bones that were able to be dated originated from areas close to paintings and hearths. According to the authors, the dates for the bear bones cannot be converted into historical ages, because the Carbon-14 calibration curve goes back only 26,000 years. The authors suggest that calendar ages are older than Carbon-14 ages in this time range. Although both humans and bears used the cave between ca. 32,000 and 28,000 BP, it is possible that the two species alternated in habitation over the course of years or centuries.

9 Clottes, "France's Magical Ice Age Art," 2001, 212.

10 Nicholas J. Conard, "A Female Figurine from the Basal Aurignacian of Hohle Fels Cave in Southwestern Germany," *Nature* 459 (May 14, 2009): 248–52. The image of the 35,000-year-old female figure from the Hohle Fels Cave in southwestern Germany is from Miriam Robbins Dexter and Victor H. Mair, *Sacred Display: Divine and Magical Female Figures of Eurasia*, Amherst, NY: Cambria, 2010, figure 47.

11 Victor Mair, "Prehistoric and East Asian Flutes," in *Studies in Chinese Language and Culture-Festschrift in Honour of Christoph Harbsmeier on the Occasion of His 60th Birthday,* ed. Christoph Anderl and Halvor Eifring (Oslo: Hermes Academic Publishing, 2006).

12 Matthias Schulz, "Is the Lion Man a Woman?" *Spiegel Online,* December 9, 2011, www.spiegel.de/international/zeitgeist/is-the-lion-man-a-woman-solving-the-mystery-of-a-35-000-year-old-statue-a-802415.html.

13 Miriam Dexter, "Ancient Felines and the Great-Goddess in Anatolia: Kubaba and Cybele," in *Proceedings of the 20th Annual UCLA Indo-European Conference*, ed. Stephanie W. Jamison, H. Craig Melchert, and Brent Vine (Bremen, Germany: Hempen, 2009), 53–67.

14 Harald Haarmann and Joan Marler, *Introducing the Mythological Crescent: Ancient Beliefs and Imagery Connecting Eurasia with Anatolia.* Wiesbaden, Germany: Harrassowitz Verlag, 2008, figure 4. A figure from the roof stone at Peri Nos, Lake Onega, Republic of Karelia in the Russian Federation.

15 Haarmann and Marler, *Introducing the Mythological Crescent*, 2008, figure 16. A rock painting from Astuvansalmi (Ristiina, Finland).

16 Elisabeth During Caspers, "Another Face of the Indus Valley Magico-Religious System," in *South Asian Archaeology 1991: Proceedings of the Eleventh International Conference of the Association of South Asian Archaeologists in Western Europe. Berlin, 1–5 July 1991,* ed. Adalbert J. Gail (Stuttgart, Germany: F. Steiner, 1993), 70.

17 We thank Joan Marler for the following insight: "She is the earth beneath our feet, and her body is the temple" (personal communication with the authors, September 2, 2011).

18 Charles C. Mann, "The Birth of Religion," *National Geographic*, June 2011.

19 Manfred Heun, Ralk Schäfer-Prefl, Dieter Klawan, Renato Castagna, Monica Accerbi, Basilio Borghi, and Francesco Salamini, "Site of Einkorn Wheat Domestication Identified by DNA Fingerprinting," *Science* 278 (1997): 1312–4.

20 An early Neolithic potsherd showing a dancing pose. Nova Zagora Historical Museum, Bulgaria.

21 A dancing figure excavated in Scânteia, Romania, by Cornelia-Magda Lazarovici. It dates to Cucuteni A-3 (4300–4050 BCE). From Lazarovici 1992.

22 This female silhouette from Zorlenţu Mare, Romania, which dates to Vinca B, 4300–4200 BCE, was excavated by Gheorghe Lazarovici. From G. Lazarovici 2008 fig. 4c.

23 Cornelia-Magda Lazarovici, Gheorghe-Corneliu Lazarovici, and Senica Ţurcanu, *Cucuteni: A Great Civilization of the Prehistoric World* (Iaşi, Romania: Palatul Culturii, 2009), 75 and for figures that may represent the magic dance, 76 and cat. nos. 135, 242 and 263.

24 Lazarovici, Lazarovici, and Ţurcanu, *Cucuteni*, 11, figure 2C and, for discussion of the notable resemblances between pottery from southeastern European cultures and that of the Yangshao culture, as well as samples of highly congruent symbols from writing systems of the two cultures, 11–3.

25 Wang Binghua, 1990, figure 7.

26 Cornelia Magda Lazarovici 2008, figures 9–13. Similar Middle Neolithic figures have been found throughout Southeastern Europe and elsewhere. See also Marija Gimbutas, *The Language of the Goddess* (San Francisco: Harper, 1989), 239–43; Marija Gimbutas, *The Civilization of the Goddess: The World of Old Europe,* ed. Joan Marler (San Francisco: Harper, 1991), 170 and the following.

27 See Gheorghe Lazarovici, Cornelia-Magda Lazarovici, and Marco Merlini, *Tărtăria and the Sacred Tablets* (Cluj-Napoca, Romania: Editura Mega, 2011), 114 for further information regarding the V as a sacred sign of the Danube script, incisions in a V shape on the forehead of an anthropomorphic protome from Tărtăria, and comparable incisions on the base of the head of a monumental idol from the Zau culture. Linear motifs such as Vs decorate a vessel found in the Middle Neolithic Starčevo settlement of Porodin as well as a mask of a ram from Balatonszárszó-*Kis-erdei-dűlő.* According to the authors, "the linear sequential organization of the frieze and the selected geometric elements

indicate that the decoration did not function as a pure aesthetic ornament, but carries a symbolic meaning and message" (153). The V is discussed throughout their book, with relation to many artifacts dating to the Upper Paleolithic through the Neolithic (183–208, 222 and the following).

28 Pupul Jayakar, *The Earth Mother: Legends, Goddesses, and Ritual Arts of India* (San Francisco/New York: Harper and Row, 1990), wrote about rural art in India, comparing it to the art and symbols of the Indus Valley and saying that "the goddess was the seed of the universe in the form of a triangle."

29 Lazarovici, Lazarovici, and Merlini, *Tărtăria and the Sacred Tablets,* 285.

30 Gimbutas *The Language of the Goddess*; Gimbutas, *The Civilization of the Goddess*; Marija Gimbutas, *The Living Goddesses*, ed. and supp. Miriam Robbins Dexter (Berkeley/Los Angeles: University of California Press, 1999).

31 Dexter and Mair, *Sacred Display: Divine and Magical Female Figures of Eurasia.*

32 See, for example, the clay tablet dating to ca. 7000–3500 BCE in the Museum of Alexandria, Romania.

33 Dexter, "Further Thoughts on the V and the M in the Danube Script: The Danube Script and the Old European Goddess," in *On the Trail of Vlassa, Fifty Years of Tărtăria Excavations*, proceedings from a conference sponsored by Eftimie Murgu University, Reşiţa, Romania and the Institute of Archaeomythology, Sebastopol, September 1–5, 2014.

34 A figure from Harappa, dated to the Kot Diji phase, 2800–2600 BCE. It illustrates the V and the M.

35 Gimbutas, *The Living Goddesses*, 46.

36 See, for example, the black greenstone pendant of a frog figure from Sesklo, shown in Marija Gimbutas, Shan Winn, and Daniel Shimabuku, *Achilleion: A Neolithic Settlement in Thessaly, Greece, 6400–5600 B.C.* Vol. 14 of *Monumenta* Archaeologica (Los Angeles: Institute of Archaeology, University of California Los Angeles, 1989), plate 7.11.

37 K. de B. Codrington, "India. Iconography: Classical and Indian," *Man: A Monthly Record of Anthropological Science* 35 (May 1935): 65, plate E. See also Carol R. Bolon, *Forms of the Goddess Lajja Gauri in Indian Art,* vol. 49 of *Monographs on the Fine Arts* (University Park, PA: Pennsylvania State University Press, 1992), figures 66–68.

38 The Indus Valley culture flourished in the river valley between the ancient Indus river and the now dried-up Saraswati/Ghaggar Hakra River (Jane R.

McIntosh, *The Ancient Indus Valley: New Perspectives* Santa Barbara, CA: ABC Clio, 2008, 3, 19ff, and 116). There were many more settlements along the Saraswati (approximately one thousand) than along the Indus (approximately fifty) (20). Therefore, a better designation for the culture would be the Saraswati Valley (or, at least, the Indus/Saraswati Valley) culture.

39 Miriam Robbins Dexter, "Substrate Continuity in Indo-European Religion and Iconography: Seals and Figurines of the Indus Valley Culture and Historic Indic Female Figures," in *Archaeology and Language: Indo-European Studies Presented to James P. Mallory,* Journal of Indo-European Studies Monograph Series no. 60, ed. Martin E. Huld, Karlene Jones-Bley, and Dean Miller (Washington, D.C.: Institute for the Study of Man, 2012), 197–219.

40 Lazarovici, Lazarovici, and Merlini, *Tărtăria and the Sacred Tablets,* 315, 317–9, 326 (table) and 329.

41 Jonathan Mark Kenoyer, *Ancient Cities of the Indus Valley Civilization* (Oxford: Oxford University Press and the American Institute of Pakistan Studies, 1998), 122). Bangles were traditionally worn on the left arm of adult women of the Indus Valley.

42 Kenoyer, *Ancient Cities of the Indus Valley Civilization,* 144, cat. no. 90 and text figure 7.43.

43 Lazarovici, Lazarovici, and Merlini, *Tărtăria and the Sacred Tablets,* 109, 125 and 146–7 and figures VIIB. 23–24.

44 Jeannine, Davis-Kimball, *Warrior Women: An Archaeologist's Search for History's Hidden Heroines* (New York: Warner, 2002), 38.

45 James P. Mallory and Victor H. Mair, *The Tarim Mummies* (London: Thames and Hudson, 2000), 220, figure 132.

46 Natalya Polosmak, "A Mummy Unearthed from the Pastures of Heaven," *National Geographic*, October 1994, 79–103.

47 Lazarovici, Lazarovici, and Merlini, *Tărtăria and the Sacred Tablets,* 221–2.

48 TantraWorks, "Tantra in Ancient Times," accessed August 3, 2017, www. tantraworks.com/Ancient_Tantra.html#indus. We thank Vicki Noble for this reference.

49 A is an Indus Valley cylinder seal from the Mature Harappan Period, 2700–2300 BCE. In black marble, it is from the private collection of Max Le Martin. B is a Bactria–Margiana Archaeological Complex Lajja Gauri as flower and lion, dated to the 3rd century or early 2nd century BCE. It is from the Metropolitan Museum of Art in New York.

50 Kenoyer, *Ancient Cities of the Indus Valley Civilization*, figure 6.19, cat. no. 23 and the book's cover.

51 Corinna Wessels-Mevissen, "Creative Legacy of the Nilgiri Hills: Terracotta Offerings from South Indian Megalithic Burials," in *Indian Terracotta Sculpture: The Early Period*, ed. Pratapaditya Pal (Mumbai: Marg, 2002), 24, figure 3. Ferocious goddess, part of a lid, burial offering at Nilgiris, red terracotta, dated between the 3rd century BCE and the 3rd century CE. Staatliche Museen zu Berlin–Preussischer Kulturbesitz, Museum fuer Indische Kunst.

52 Alf Hiltebeitel, "The Indus Valley 'Proto-Śiva,' Reexamined through Reflections on the Goddess, the Buffalo, and the Symbolism of Vāhanas," *Anthropos* 73, no. 5/6 (1978): 777.

53 Soapstone (also known as steatite or soaprock) is a metamorphic rock, a talc-schist. It is largely composed of the mineral talc and is thus rich in magnesium. Wikipedia, "Soapstone," accessed July 2, 2011, en.wikipedia.org/wiki/Soapstone.

54 Miranda Shaw, *Buddhist Goddesses of India* (Princeton, NJ/Oxford: Princeton University Press, 2006), 429, figure 21.3; Jayakar, The Earth Mother, figure 6.

55 A is from Jayakar, *The Earth Mother*, figure 5. B is from Kenoyer, *Ancient Cities of the Indus Valley Civilization*, text figure 6.22, cat. no. 26.

56 Seal from Mohenjo-daro. National Museum, New Delhi, India. Jayakar, *The Earth Mother*, figure 7.

57 Square stamp seal from Kalibangan (K-50). Asko Parpola, *Deciphering the Indus Script* (Cambridge: Cambridge University Press, 1994), 254, figure 14.26; Kenoyer, *Ancient Cities of the Indus Valley Civilization*, 117, figure 6.32.

58 Cylinder seal impression from the Harappan culture at Kalibangan: tiger figure and female figure wearing bangles and skirt, with two anthropomorphic figures. Next to that scene, the body of the female figure merges with that of the tiger figure. The tiger-woman wears a headdress with animal horns and a tree branch. Parpola, *Deciphering the Indus Script*, figure 14.25.

59 Painted pottery from Samarra, depicting female figures, probably dancers, with streaming hair. See Garfinkel 2003: 86.

60 Nude female figure in pipal tree, Mohenjo-daro. Steatite seal depicting a deity standing in a pipal tree and looking down on seven female figures that have long braids and are wearing skirts. Both the deity and the seven female figures are wearing multiple bangles. Kenoyer, *Ancient Cities of the Indus Valley Civilization*, figure 6.1, cat. no. 24.

61 Shaw, *Buddhist Goddesses of India*, 428–9; Amdo region, Tibet, 19th century. The Newark Museum, 1936, 36.518, plate 15.

62 Cosmic Form of the Goddess Kali (recto). Folio from a book of iconography. Nepal, Himalayas. Los Angeles County Museum of Art.

63 Red figure of a dancing Vajravārāhī/Dorje Pagmo, Nepal, Himalayas, central Tibet. Himalayas 1, Los Angeles County Museum of Art, LACMAM74_106_1. Dancing Vajravārāhī/Vajrayoginī, Himalayas, central Tibet. Los Angeles County Museum of Art.

64 Kali dancing on Siva to awaken him. Los Angeles County Museum of Art.

65 *Devi Mahatmyam* 7.6., ca. 500 CE. Translations from the Sanskrit are by Miriam Robbins Dexter. The following Sanskrit text is in Jagadiswarananda, *Devi Mahatmyam, 7.6:*

*Bhrukuṭīkuṭilāttasyā lalāṭaphalakāddatam
Kālī karālavadanā viniṣkrāntāsipāśinī.*

66 Lajja Gauri, stone, from Naganatha Temple, Karnataka, India, dated to the late 7th century CE. See, for example, Bolon, *Forms of the Goddess Lajja Gauri in Indian Art*, figure 48.

67 Lajja Gauri with snake head, stone, from Madhya Pradesh, India, dated to the 6th or 7th century CE. Bolon, *Forms of the Goddess Lajja Gauri in Indian Art*, figure 98.

68 A frog-like Lajja Gauri with lotus head, terracotta, from the Allahabad District, Uttar Pradesh, India, dated to the 4th century CE. Bolon, *Forms of the Goddess Lajja Gauri in Indian Art*, figure 38.

69 Lajja Gauri with human face, stone, from the Rajkot District, Gujarat, dated to the 7th century CE. Bolon, *Forms of the Goddess Lajja Gauri in Indian Art*, figure 82.

70 Lajja Gauri as flower, in a stūpa II railing medallion from Sanchi, Raisen District, Madhya Pradesh, dated to the 1st century CE. Bolon, *Forms of the Goddess Lajja Gauri in Indian Art*, figure 111.

71 Two flower Lajja Gauri figures, stone, in stūpa railing medallions from Bharhut, Sama District, Madhya Pradesh, dated to the 1st century CE. Bolon, *Forms of the Goddess Lajja Gauri in Indian Art*, figures 119, 120.

72 The following Sanskrit text is in Jagadiswarananda, *Devi Mahatmyam, 11.48:*

*Tato'hamakhilaṁ lokamātmadehasamudbhavaiḥ
bhariṣyāmi surāḥ śākairāvṛṣṭeḥ prāṇadhārakaiḥ.*

73 Laura Amazzone, *Goddess Durgā and Sacred Female Power* (Lanham, MD: Hamilton, 2010), 99, 183. See also David Kinsley, *Hindu Goddesses: Visions of the Divine Feminine in the Hindu Religious Tradition*, vol. 12 of *Hermeneutics:*

Studies in the History of Religions (Berkeley/Los Angeles: University of California Press, 1988), 95, 111.

74 Amazzone, *Goddess Durgā and Sacred Female Power*, 99, 183.

75 Kinsley, *Hindu Goddesses*, 111.

76 Bolon, *Forms of the Goddess Lajja Gauri in Indian Art*, 13–4, figure 10: Lajja Gauri as pot, terracotta, from Ter, Osmanabad District, Maharashtra, Ter Museum 785, dated to the 3rd or 4th century CE.

77 Jayakar, *The Earth Mother*, 31.

78 Wikipedia, "Marathi People," accessed July 2, 2011, en.wikipedia.org/wiki/Marathi_people#Mangala_Gaur.

79 Monier-Williams 1899: 772.

80 Kinsley, *Hindu Goddesses*, 111–2.

81 From the private collection of Max Le Martin, purchased at an auction gallery in British Columbia. Dated to the 2nd century CE. 1.9 cm × 1.9 cm.

82 Samir Kumar Mukherjee, "Terracotta Art in the Gangetic Valley under the Kushanas," in *Indian Terracotta Sculpture: The Early Period* (Mumbai: Marg, 2002), 84, figure 12. Kaushambi, Allahabad District, Kushana Period, Patna Museum, dated to the 1st–3rd cCenturies CE.

83 Monier Williams 1899: 369.

84 Monier-Williams 1899: 370.

85 Jayakar, *The Earth Mother*, 130 ff.

86 For additional information about the Lajja Gauris, see Bolon, *Forms of the Goddess Lajja Gauri in Indian Art*; Robert L. Brown, "A Lajjā Gaurī in a Buddhist Context at Aurangabad," *The Journal of the International Association of Buddhist Studies* 13, no. 2 (1990): 1–18; Thomas Donaldson, "Propitious–Apotropaic Eroticism in the Art of Orissa," *Artibus Asiae* 27 (1975): 75–100; V. H. Sonawane, "Some Remarkable Sculptures of Lajjā Gaurī from Gujarat," *Lalit Kalā* 23 (1988): 27–34. Donaldson demonstrated that the erotic art decoration of the temples of Orissa served two functions that display figures worldwide seem to serve: blessing the temple and warding off natural disasters.

87 Wikipedia, "Lajja Gauri," accessed July 2, 2011, en.wikipedia.org/wiki/Lajja_Gauri.

88 For additional information about Medusa, see Miriam Robbins Dexter, "The Ferocious and the Erotic: 'Beautiful' Medusa and the Neolithic Bird and Snake," *Journal of Feminist Studies in Religion* 26, no. 1 (2010): 25–41.

89 Miriam Robbins Dexter, *Whence the Goddesses: A Source Book, Athene Series* (New York: Pergamon, 1990).

90 Hesiod, *Theogony*, ca. 700 BCE, 270–83.

91 Euripides, *Ion,* lines 1003–5.

92 Apollodorus, *Atheniensis Bibliothecae* 3.10.3. Apollodorus was born ca. 180 BCE.

93 Douglas Fraser, "The Heraldic Woman: A Study in Diffusion," in *The Many Faces of Primitive Art: A Critical Anthology* (Englewood Cliffs, NJ: Prentice Hall, 1966), 51.

94 Fraser, "The Heraldic Woman," 51.

95 Fraser, "The Heraldic Woman," 57–60. Fraser regarded this as a particular index of Late Zhou influence. See also Dexter and Mair, *Sacred Display*, figure 34, for a Mother Bear doorway of a Tlingit culture tribal house on Chief Shakes Island, Wrangell, Alaska, dated to the 19th century CE.

96 See the bear display figure at the Anatolian Civilizations Museum, Ankara, Turkey. Tableau of display figure and bovine heads. See also Dexter and Mair, *Sacred Display*, figure 35, a bear stamp seal from Çatalhöyük.

97 Fraser, "The Heraldic Woman," 71–4.

98 Fraser, "The Heraldic Woman," 74–5.

99 See Fraser, "The Heraldic Woman," 42.

100 Numerous examples of gorgons on sarcophagi are extant—for example, in the Antalya Museum in southern Turkey. Here are a number of sarcophagi that include garlands and images of Medusa.

101 Today more and more artists are honoring sacred display. "The Great Wall of Vagina," (www.greatwallofvagina.co.uk) by British artist Jamie McCartney, was exhibited in London in May and June 2012. The exhibit consisted of monumental wall sculptures of castings of the vulvas and labia of 400 women. Its purpose was to enable women to see that there is beauty, not shame, in the female genitalia. We thank the poet Annie Finch for referring us to this exhibit.

THE GODDESS SRI SPIRIT IN JAVANESE *MITONI* PREGNANCY RITUAL: TRADITIONAL *LURIK* WOVEN CLOTHS IN INSTALLATION ART

APRINA MURWANTI

Introduction

Feminist artists have been taking inspiration from goddesses and featuring goddesses in their works since at least the 1970s. The goddess plays an important role as a symbol of women's power in visual art practice. The feminist art movement of the 1970s is a significant inspiration for female artists, today, to use goddesses to represent women's power in their visual art practice. By using goddesses in their works, second-wave feminist artists also portrayed women and their important positions, both social and spiritual. Female artists explored "historical female ancestors" to empower their artworks.[1] G. F. Orenstein found that the use of the pre-patriarchal goddess by second-wave feminist artists was based not on an interest in "mythical expression" or their personal experiences with the goddess but rather on artistic, historical and archeological studies.[2]

In exploring the Javanese goddess Sri, I use a slightly different perspective than did second-wave feminist artists. My creative practices not only are based on artistic and historical study of the goddess but also include study of Sri's mythical expression that I have found, firsthand, in Java. In my practice, I use as the main visual reference the personal engagement with Sri that I experienced in a *Mitoni* ritual during my first pregnancy, in 2006. I tell stories of Sri through installation art using woven textiles named *lurik* cloths, the most sacred cloths in *Mitoni*. I tell these stories from my perspective as a Javanese Muslim female artist. For me, telling those stories is important, because the disappearance of Sri from Java has been entangled with many issues, including the politicization of religion. The disappearance of Sri has reduced the number of ritual practices in Java which, in turn, has reduced the demand for *lurik* cloths, affecting the livelihood of craftspeople in the *lurik* home industry.

In this project, I used a practice-led research methodology interwoven with the material culture of actual objects tied together by a bricolage aesthetic. Practice-led research acknowledges art practice as a form of research.[3] I utilized material culture in my research to observe, discuss and highlight *lurik* cloth, *Mitoni* ritual and their relationship with Sri in the traditional Javanese context. Material culture engages the past through its emphatic approach in identifying cultural objects.[4] Bricolage is useful in connecting the fragmented narratives of the cultural histories and mythology that underpin the *Mitoni* ritual, the *lurik* cloths and Sri with visual art theories and studio practice. Bricolage in installation arts becomes a conduit of memory and history in narrative threads that activate the mythopoetic approach.[5]

The Importance of the Goddess Sri in Javanese Culture

Sri is known as the goddess of agriculture and fertility.[6] Moreover, she is believed to represent the death, reincarnation and rice growth.[7] Dewi Sri (Goddess Sri) is a Javanese goddess who reflects Hindu influence in Javanese ritual and ceremony.[8] Javanese ritual is believed to have come from the Majapahit Empire, which ruled Java from 1331 to 1389.[9] The Hindu god Shiva and goddess Sri were closely identified with elements of Javanese local deities, because the Majapahit emperors claimed to be descendants of Siva and Sri.[10] Sri is believed to have become the Javanese Earth Mother during the Majapahit period,[11] but the ritual of worshipping Sri as the goddess of fertility was an indigenous local tradition in Java prior to that outside incursion.[12]

Two characters of Sri exist in Java. The first character, Sri Widawati, is the wife of Vishnu (also spelled Wisnu) and mother of Kamajaya, the god of love.[13] She was widely known as Lakshmi in India, and she was associated with the Javanese-Hindu fertility rite.[14] Lakshmi is the goddess of fortune, wealth, beauty and fertility in India.[15] Irvine explained that there were many incarnations of Sri Widawati: Dewi Citrawati; Sinta (also spelled *Sita*), the wife of *Rama*, an incarnation of Vishnu; *Rukmini*; and Sumbadra.[16]

The second character of Sri was associated with rice fields and harvesting; she is the granddaughter of Vishnu. Because of the similarity of the name Sri, people perceived this second character of Sri as one of the reincarnations of Sri Widawati.[17] This second version of Sri is also associated with her brother Sadana, the god of harvests, who was believed to be the reincarnation of Vishnu.[18] There is a famous folktale in Java, titled *Sri Sadana*, in which Sri was searching for her brother Sadana, who had run away from the palace.[19] During Sri's journey, an evil giant, who disguised himself with many forms of animals, chased Sri across the land. During her escape, Sri suggested to an elder named Kyai Wrigu that he encircle his house with *lawe* (cotton yarn) to protect his baby from the demon.[20] Similarly, the *Mitoni* pregnancy ritual includes a segment in which a *lawe* (coconut leaf) is placed around the mother's belly and cut with a keris (Javanese sword), symbolizing the disappearance of obstacles. The use of *lurik* cloths, made from lawe and worn with a motion of encircling to symbolize prayers of protection, in the *Mitoni* recalls the story of Sri in the *Sri Sadana* folktale. The activity of encircling the human body or a sacred object with textiles or yarns—symbols of protection—has been adopted in the performance of sacred rituals in many cultures worldwide.[21]

Sri and representations of her various incarnations also were depicted in *wayang purwa*, the tradition from Central Java of shadow puppet play. The shadow puppets are not realistic, because *wayang purwa*'s recent visual style was developed by *wali songo* (the nine proselytes) to infuse Islamic sharia (basic rules and law of Islam) into the art form of Java. In Islam, the depiction of real-life creatures, especially animals and humans, is *haram* (highly forbidden), except for use in educational materials for children.[22]

Places Sacred to Sri

Traditionally, Javanese people arranged special spaces in the palace and in the rice fields to recall Sri's spirit. The *keraton* (Javanese palace) and the traditional Javanese house each contained a special room named a *krobongan*, which was devoted to Sri. The *krobongan* was usually decorated to be the most beautiful room in the palace or the house.[23] The special sacred places in the paddies looked like small houses, the size of birdhouse, built of natural materials and surrounded by offerings. Such houses are believed to have the power to call Sri to fertilize the paddies and spread prosperity.

Mitoni, Lurik Cloths and Sri

Sri is an important female figure. She underpinned the Javanese *Mitoni* ritual and Javanese society.[24] My direct participation in the *Mitoni* ritual during my first pregnancy, in 2006, connected me with the story of Sri. I felt protected, safe and secure.

Mitoni is a Javanese traditional ritual for a woman in the seventh month of pregnancy. It wishes her a safe labor. The *Mitoni* ritual is divided into five main segments. It begins with an act of *sungkeman* (asking for blessing from the woman and her husband), followed by *siraman* (holy bathing). Next are the ceremonial acts of breaking a water pitcher, splitting coconuts and cutting yarn or coconut leaves, all of which symbolize the breaking of obstacles. The next phase, *Nyamping*, is the distinctive act of wrapping the woman in seven pairs of traditional Javanese cloths, including *lurik* cloths *(Figure 11)*. Finally are the *dhawetan* or *dodol dhawet* and the *rujakan*, in which the

Fig. 11. My Mitoni ritual, Nyamping segment. Photograph by Santi Sidhartani, n.d.

woman and her husband pretend to sell sour and sweet dishes.[25] All segments symbolize the prayers of the family for a healthy, safe delivery. *Lurik* cloths are the most sacred cloths in the *Mitoni* ritual.[26]

Lurik cloths are Javanese traditional woven cloths with horizontal and vertical lines in check or plaid patterns.[27] The word *lurik* comes from the Javanese word *rik*, "a symbol for fence and protection lines."[28] *Rik* also can be interpreted as "a shallow moat or line that cannot be erased or removed, surrounding the wearer."[29]

Lurik cloths *(Figures 12 and 13)* have existed in Java for more than two centuries. Many pattern variations of *lurik* cloths were available in Central Java and East Java, but particular patterns of *lurik* cloths were used in the *Mitoni* ritual.[30] One set of *lurik* cloths for the *Mitoni* ceremony contained patterns of *dringin* (drizzle), *tumbar pecah* (crushed coriander) and *liwatan* (leap). The pattern *lurik toh watu* or *tuluh watu* (sacred stone) was also worn as a *jarit* (Javanese wrap skirt) in the *Mitoni* ceremony in the past.[31] The wearing of *lurik tuluh watu* was believed to give the wearer strength and tenacity.[32] Wearing a *lurik* cloth with *tuluh watu* pattern also had a strong philosophical meaning that symbolized "the lasting relationship between the mother and the child throughout life and their life-long inseparability."[33] There is strong motherhood wisdom in the philosophy of wearing *lurik* cloths.

Fig. 12. Lurik cloth with dringin pattern.
Photograph by Aprina Murwanti, 2012.

Fig. 13. Lurik cloth with tumbar pecah pattern. Photograph by Aprina Murwanti, 2012.

Many of the goddesses in world cultures associated with weaving were associated with magic and fertility.[34] The immortal characters that created life in these folk stories, usually depicted as goddesses, were portrayed as "spinners and weavers."[35] The common associations of goddess figures with weaving, life giving, magic and sacredness[36] are similar to those that existed in the Javanese pre-Islamic era, when Sri was worshipped and played a pivotal role in Javanese society. In West Java, Nyi Pohaci (Sri) was a weaver worshipped for granting human prosperity. In Bali, the Balinese traditional woven textile was used for worshipping the Dewi Sri in the temple.

Furthermore, the connection between textiles and fertility also relates to the myth that traditional, handmade textiles generate magical protective powers for pregnancy and birth. This myth is found in traditions from Bethlehem, the Himalayas, Mayan culture and Germany, which connect textiles to fertility, birth, pregnancy and the cycle of life.[37] In the *Mitoni* ritual, *lurik* cloth was believed to protect and save both the mother and the baby in her womb. The repetitive action of encircling *lurik* cloths around the woman's body during the *Mitoni* is a metaphor of protection; meanwhile, the patterns in the *lurik* cloths contain symbols of prayer and positive expectations from the family.

The rule of the Majapahit Empire in Java ended in the early 1500s, and the previous role of Brahman priests as spiritual advisers to local rulers was overtaken by the *wali* (great Islamic proselytizers).[38] This decline in Hindu influence explains, in part, why finding statues of Sri in Java is difficult. The Islamic influence in Java also explains how the story of a once-powerful goddess, Sri, vanished from Javanese culture.

The concept of Sri as the divine of the *Mitoni* ritual and the *lurik* cloth, as well as the central figure in most traditional Javanese rituals, is not compatible with Islamic doctrine. Islamic beliefs center on the single power of Allah as the almighty god; representing any other figure as associated with divine power is strongly forbidden. This is one of the reasons that figures of Sri were gradually removed from Javanese culture. Sadly, this religious prohibition also contributed to the decline of *Mitoni* ritual practice, so important to women and their families, and, in turn, affected the economic condition and social position of *lurik* craftspeople in Central Java.

Goddess in Feminist Installation Art Practice

By the 1970s, feminist artists had reclaimed and reglorified the goddess as the symbol of women's empowerment and as a way of redressing the patriarchal history of "removing the goddess in history."[39] During the 1970s, female Western artists regarded the ancient goddess as representing women's "talent, powers, creativity and important cultural contributions."[40] Insights into how goddesses were depicted in the West's second wave of feminist art are useful in studying how the use of ritual, the goddess and mythology was politically motivated to venerate women's power, both in art and in society.[41] Depictions of the goddess were regarded as engagement with ritual. In my study, Sri represents women's empowerment as mothers and birth givers, because she was an important female figure underlying the Javanese *Mitoni* ritual and she represented the importance of women in the society. Sri linked rituals, textile tradition and sociocultural issues in one political context in Java, and she does so again in my art installations.

Ana Mendieta's works during the 1970s are excellent examples of the use of goddess figures in installation art practice. In her work *Incantation to Olokun-Yemaya*, Mendieta merged and associated herself with Olokun, the Cuban goddess who came from the bottom of the ocean.[42] Olokun is the grandmother of the goddess Yemaya.[43] Both Olokun and Yemaya are invoked when one is in need of a "place to call home."[44] Mendieta demonstrated that the silhouette she had made from her body trace enabled her to channel herself to her "home"—her origin culture—and to symbolically connect with the goddess.

Judy Chicago's *The Dinner Party* installation also used goddess imagery that spanned Western and Eastern cultures.[45] By borrowing these goddesses, Chicago inspired women to claim their power in society. Regarding the craft strategies in Chicago's installation, Orenstein noted that *The Dinner Party* linked "feminist iconography and feminist reinterpretation of the creation myth" through monumental artworks involving traditional female craft.[46] Chicago's feminist narrative in *The Dinner Party* was enriched by her use of mythical women figures and handmade objects.

Misrepresentation of Goddess Sri and Other Javanese Female Divines

Representations of female divines from a male perspective are often misleading. Such representations include images in paintings by Basuki Abdullah and Agus Djaya and in Jim Supangkat's sculpture (1975) of Ken Dedes. In Abdullah's paintings *Djoko Tarub* (1940–1960) and *Janoko Bertapa* (1940–1960), he depicted nymphs and princesses from Javanese folklore as seductive, sexually inviting women. In *The Battle between Rahwana and Djataju in the Abduction of Sita* (1940s), Abdullah visualized the goddess Sita as a pale, powerless, helpless woman. In his painting *Nyai Roro Kidul*, he highlighted the beautiful physical appearance and sexuality of the Javanese mystical queen of the Javanese South Sea rather than her divine power. Similarly, Agus Djaya's version of *Nyai Roro Kidul* (1950s) is sexually inviting, with a seductive glance in Nyai Roro Kidul's eyes, ignoring her fundamental quality as a powerful divine who ruled the Javanese South Sea. Jim Supangkat depicted Ken Dedes, the first queen of Singhasari in Java, in a controversial way: Her head and shoulder are shown in a classical Javanese sculpture, but her body—from breast to toe—is given a comic style, suggesting that she is "a prostitute."[47] Supangkat's visualization of Ken Dedes is far from the "feminine beauty, purity and magical power" that she symbolized in Javanese culture.[48]

These misleading depictions of Javanese female divines motivated me to evoke the narratives of Sri from a female perspective—my own perspective. Concerns about the representation of Sri and the relationship of such imagery to changes in sociocultural conditions drew my attention to a similar phenomenon of glorification of the goddess figure in Western art practice during the 1970s. I found that not only were narratives about the Dewi Sri connected with the history of the *Mitoni* ritual and *lurik* cloth but the demise of those narratives was linked with the role of patriarchy in Indonesia's art and society.

In crafting my ethnographic narrative of the practices that engage Sri, I used my personal experience and creative practice and positioned my artistic endeavor as political statement. I employ two philosophical frameworks in my installation art practice: first, Joseph Beuys's concept of "social sculpture" and, second, Carol Hanisch's well-known feminist concept "The personal is political," which was reinterpreted by feminist artists in the 1970s and by Asian female artists contemporaneously.

I utilize Beuys's concept of social sculpture, which extends the concept of sculpting from visual art to a sociocultural and sociopolitical context. In asking "how [do] we mould and shape the world in which we live?"[49] Beuys provided artists with the opportunity to respond, through creative practice, to the particular society and culture in which they live. With this perspective, the practice of art as a form of sociopolitical activism can be seen as an invitation to the art's viewers to engage in social and political discussions. Shaping the world in social sculpture provides an opportunity to draw society's attention to something. My installation art is my political sign, an invitation to the audience to explore the entangled stories underneath the disappearance of Sri.

The phrase "The personal is political," which was popularized by liberation activist Carol Hanisch,[50] was widely borrowed and transformed as a political rationale for 1970s-era feminist activism and art.[51] "The personal is political" was used to interpret women artists' work in western Europe and the United States as well as in the critical reading of Asian women's art. "The personal is political" idea was implemented in art when "'personal stories' began to be interpreted as the logical consequence of much larger political structures."[52] Thus, "personal experiences" were also seen, anew, "as symptoms of a larger political factor which inspires the artwork."[53] In my art installation, I used my personal experience of the *Mitoni* ritual and my perspective as a Javanese Muslim female artist as the political foundation.

Installation Art Practice and Exhibition

I created two major art exhibitions for this project: *Recalling the Goddess Sri* (2012) and *Mitoni. Lurik and the Stitches of Lament* (2013). Both exhibitions were shown in Wollongong, Australia. *Lurik* was the main material used in those installations. In a form of bricolage to connect all of the stories, I used a hand-stitching technique to construct soft sculpture objects. Hand stitching has three functions in these two installations: first, a metaphoric act of mending the wounds imparted by society and lamenting the disappearance of Sri; second, a response to the Islamization of Java; and, third, a technique for constructing the objects in the installations.

The costumes for covering the body—made by use of the stitching and sewing process of traditional Javanese costume making—were results "of the twin historical processes of Islamization and creation of states ruled by the Dutch."[54] Prior to the arrival of Islam, the traditional Javanese costume for a man or a woman was unsewn cotton cloth that draped around the body. The transformation of Javanese costume was political and economic, with the Dutch promoting covering of the body, which benefited the Vereenigde Oost-Indische Compagnie (VOC) or Dutch East India Company. Textile importation was the VOC's main business in Indonesia.[55] In addition, Islamic missionaries promoted costumes that were more modest to their eyes, in order to spread their religious culture and doctrine in Java. Gradually, stitched garments became integrated into traditional Javanese costume design. These historical and political dimensions of stitched garments and stitching in Java gave me an opportunity to highlight the histories that related specifically to my personal interests. I made use of old Javanese traditions and traditions of Islamization in Java, by employing stitching as the main technique in constructing the objects for my installations.

By transforming *lurik* cloths into soft sculptural objects and using stitching to construct the objects in my installations, I highlighted the stories of the *Mitoni* ritual, *lurik* cloths and Sri—stories that had been buried and hidden as a consequence of the spread of Islam. In this way, the action of stitching became a political statement about my being both a Javanese woman and a Muslim. By stitching, I questioned freedom in society from a perspective of dual self-identity. In addition, my stitching was intended to metaphorically stitch together the wounds in Javanese society. The use of *lurik* cloth and stitching in the making of the objects in my installations was intended to engage both artistic and political qualities of this practice-led research and to engage the viewers of the work.

Recalling the Goddess Sri

In this art installation *(Figures 14-17)* is a central object: the figure of a woman, a representation of Sri. The figure is surrounded by soft sculptured offerings to her. The installation is centered on the floor and inspired by the way the Javanese give offerings in traditional ritual. By arranging objects that were inspired by a part of the *Mitoni* ceremony, I brought the sacred ambiance of Javanese ritual into the art installation. Light and shadows were utilized as features to dramatize

Fig. 14. Aprina Murwanti, *Recalling the Goddess Sri,* art installation of lurik cloths and soft sculptures, FCA Gallery, University of Wollongong, 2012. Photograph by Aprina Murwanti.

the atmosphere of the site. The figure of Sri emerges from the floor and represents the spirit of waking up and expressed reciprocity. One of my

Fig. 15. Detail of the goddess Sri and the rice cones offering in Aprina Murwanti, *Recalling the Goddess Sri,* art installation of lurik cloths and soft sculptures, FCA Gallery, University of Wollongong, 2012. Photograph by Aprina Murwanti.

intentions in this work was to connect my art practice with the heart of social conscience and position my art as a statement of refusal to be part of political oppression.

In making the Sri figure, I used myself as a model. Sri was believed to be a form of spirit, and therefore she was too vague to imagine. Instead, I started with the logic that Sri was the greatest ancestor of Javanese women and that I may be one of her descendants. I traced myself to capture her presence and thus encapsulate her spirit in the work. I traced my face and used that tracing to reconstruct her face. In fact, the thought of myself as one of her descendants strengthened the bond that I already felt with her. Through this authoritative act of self-tracing, I connected her with my personal story. A similar creative method of self-tracing was used by Ana Mendieta in her *Silueta* series.

Recalling the Goddess Sri includes soft sculptures in the shapes of flowers and fruits, inspired by offerings in the *Mitoni* ritual. *Liwatan lurik*, hung on the walls, encircles the space. There is a chandelier made by soft sculptures, inspired by chandeliers in *krobongan*–Sri's sacred room in Javanese palaces. A couple of coconut-shaped soft sculptures with embroidery of the Javanese symbols of long-lasting love, Kamaratih and Kamajaya, also inspired by *Mitoni* ritual, are included in the offerings to the goddess. The hand-stitched soft sculptures are imperfect, highlighting humanness in the installation.

Fig. 16. Viewers of Aprina Murwanti's *Recalling the Goddess Sri* exhibition, FCA Gallery, University of Wollongong, 2012. Photograph by Bharoto Yekti, 2012.

Fig. 17. Detail of Kamaratih and Kamajaya in Aprina Murwanti, *Recalling the Goddess Sri*, art installation of lurik cloths and soft sculptures, FCA Gallery, University of Wollongong, 2012. Photograph by Aprina Murwanti.

Mitoni, Lurik and the Stitches of Lament

This art installation *(Figures 18-21)* was made through a bricolage process in which I interconnected ethnographic narratives from myths and folklore with my art and ideas. I used playfulness to express my lament for Javanese cultural loss and my personal fears, melancholies and disappointments. The animal figures are inspired by folktales about Sri, fabric patterns used in *Mitoni* ritual, Javanese palaces and offerings for Sri. The empty chair, a fragile throne made from *lurik* cloths, indicates Sri's absence.

My position in this installation is that of a bricoleur and storyteller who has woven together the threads of these fragmented stories. I used stitching to link the fragmented narratives about Sri that are contained in the *Mitoni* ritual and *lurik* cloths with the social and political stories. The metaphor of stitching

Figure 18. Aprina Murwanti, *Mitoni, Lurik and the Stitches of Lament*, art installation, FCA Gallery, University of Wollongong, 2013. Courtesy of Photography by Appleart.

Figure 19. Aprina Murwanti, *Mitoni, Lurik and the Stitches of Lament*, art installation, FCA Gallery, University of Wollongong, 2013. Courtesy of Photography by Appleart.

Fig. 20. Aprina Murwanti, *Mitoni, Lurik and the Stitches of Lament*, art installation, FCA Gallery, University of Wollongong, 2013. Photograph by Aprina Murwanti.

enabled the pieces and bits of fragmented narratives to connect and retell these stories.

I installed amulets in the chandelier; these amulets combine my identities as a Muslim and as a Javanese. I used soft, sculptured scissors, a razor blade, flowers and goddess images in the amulets to represent Javanese myth. Scissors, razor blades and other sharp utensils are believed to protect a pregnancy from evil. I also installed on the chandelier hand embroideries of Javanese goddess amulets. One of the amulets is embroidered with the Arabic calligraphy for Allah. I united Javanese mythical beliefs and Islamic symbols in the chandelier object. My intention in *Mitoni, Lurik and the Stitches of Lament* is to highlight that the story of Sri in Java is surrounded by complex influences and interventions.

Conclusion

In this project, I extended the process of evoking Sri, through traditional Javanese *Mitoni* pregnancy ritual, to an installation art practice. By evoking and revisualizing the spirit of Sri in installation art, I connected and retold multiple stories associated with Sri, with a focus on the effect of politicization of religion. Using *lurik* cloths as the main material in the installations, I lamented the disappearance of Sri from Javanese society and expressed my disagreement with and critique of misleading representations of Javanese female divines. To make a statement, I stitched together the wounds and the ethnographic narratives; I brought the story into the present; I applied realities and myths to a discussion with political context. I utilized "The personal is political" phrase and social sculpture to evoke and revisualize Sri's spirit from my own perspective. I offered an alternative perspective for seeing and exploring the goddess through the lens of an Asian Javanese Muslim female artist.

Fig. 21. Aprina Murwanti, *Mitoni, Lurik and the Stitches of Lament*, art installation, FCA Gallery, University of Wollongong, 2013. Photograph by Aprina Murwanti.

References

Bailly, C. R. "Sri-Lakshmi Majesty of The Hindu King." *In Goddesses Who Rule*, edited by Elisabeth Benard and Beverly Moon. New York: Oxford University Press, 2000.

Bishop, Claire. *Installation Art: A Critical History*. New York: Routledge, 2005.

Broude, Norma, and Mary D. Garrard, eds. *The Power of Feminist Art: The American Movement of the 1970s, History and Impact*. New York: Harry N. Abrams Inc., 1994.

Budiwiyanto, J. "Penerapan unsur-unsur arsitektur tradisional Jawa pada interior public space di Surakarta" [Implementation of Traditional Javanese Architectural

Elements in Public Space Interiors in Surakarta]. *Gelar: Jurnal Seni Budaya* [Degree: Journal of Cultural Art] 7, no. 1 (2009): 1–21.

Djoemena, Nian S. Lurik: Garis-garis Bertuah: *The Magic Stripes.* Jakarta: Djambatan, 2000.

Geertz, Clifford. *The Religion of Java.* Chicago and London: The University of Chicago Press, 1960.

Gera, Judit. "The Search for Identity in the Art of Ana Mendieta and Arnaldo Roche-Rabell." *Americana E-Journal of American Studies in Hungary* 6, no. 1 (2010). Accessed May 5, 2013. americanaejournal.hu/vol6no1/gera.

Gordon, Beverly. Textiles: The Whole Story: Uses, Meanings, Significance. New York: Thames & Hudson, 2011.

Hanisch, Carol. "The Personal is Political: The Women's Liberation Movement Classic with a New Explanatory Introduction." First published in *Notes from the Second Year: Women's Liberation* (New York: Shulamith Firestone and Anne Koedt, 1970). Now available online with a new introduction, Carol Hanisch, 2009. www.carolhanisch.org/CHwritings/PIP.html.

Heringa, Rens. "Dewi Sri in Village Garb: Fertility, Myth and Ritual in Northeast Java." *Asian Folklore* Studies 56, no. 2 (1997): 335–77.

Hulsbosch, Marianne, Elizabeth Bedford, and Martha Chaiklin. "Asian Material Culture in Context." In *Asian Material Culture*, edited by Marianne Hulsbosch, Elizabeth Bedford, and Martha Chaiklin. Amsterdam: Amsterdam University Press, 2009, 9–16.

Irvine, David. *Leather Gods and Wooden Heroes: Java's Classical Wayang.* Singapore: Marshall Cavendish International, 2005.

Kneebone, Susan. "Naturally Disturbed: A Critical Inquiry into Pastoralist Memory and Environmental History as Realised Through Visual Art." PhD major studio project, South Australian School of Art, University of South Australia (Adelaide, Australia), 2010.

Koentjaraningrat, R. M. *Introduction to the Peoples and Cultures of Indonesia and Malaysia.* Menlo Park, CA: Cummings, 1975.

Koestriastuti. "Java: Central Java." In *Tenun: Handwoven Textiles of Indonesia*, edited by Jay E. Sian. Jakarta: Cita Tenun Indonesia, 2010.

Lestari, S. Interview in Cawas village, Central Java, Indonesia, April 28, 2011.

Lippard, Lucy R. *Overlay: Contemporary Art and the Art of Prehistory.* New York: Pantheon, 1983.

Mendieta, Ana. *Incantation to Olokun-Yemaya.* 1977.

Miklouho-Maklai, Brita L. *Exposing Society's Wounds: Some Aspects of Contemporary Indonesian Art Since 1966.* Adelaide, Australia: The Flinders University of South Australia, 1991.

Murwanti, Aprina. "Mitoni, Lurik and the Stitches of Lament." PhD diss., University of Wollongong (Wollongong, Australia), 2014.

Patrijunianti, Endang. "Lurik." In *Ensiklopedia Nasional Indonesia* [National Encyclopedia of Indonesia]. Jakarta: PT Delta Pamungkas, 2004, 450–51.

Pringgawidagda, Suwarna. *Upacara tingkeban* [Tingkeban Ceremony]. Yogyakarta, Indonesia: Adicita Karya Nusa, 2003.

Prown, Jules David. "Mind in Matter: An introduction to Material Culture Theory and Method." *Winthertur Portofolio* 17, no. 1 (1982): 1–19.

Purwadi. *Sejarah asal-usul nenek moyang orang Jawa* [History of the Origin of Javanese Ancestors]. Yogyakarta, Indonesia: Panji Pustaka, 2010.

Raffles, Thomas Stanford. *The History of Java.* Yogyakarta, Indonesia: Narasi, 2008.

Rahardjo, Supratikno. *Peradaban Jawa: Dari Mataram Kuno sampai Majapahit Akhir* [Javanese Civilization: From Ancient Mataram to Late Majapahit]. Depok, Indonesia: Komunitas Bambu, 2011.

Reckitt, Helen, and Peggy Phelan. *Art and Feminism.* Themes and Movements. New York: Phaidon, 2001.

Setyasih, S. Interview in Semarang, Central Java, Indonesia, April 25, 2011.

Sullivan, Graeme. *Art Practice as Research: Inquiry in the Visual Arts.* Thousand Oaks, CA: SAGE Publications, 2005.

———. "Research Acts in Art Practice." *Studies in Art Education* 48, no. 1 (2006): 19–35.

———. *Art Practice as Research: Inquiry in the Visual Arts.* 2nd ed. Thousand Oaks, CA: SAGE Publications, 2010.

Sumintarsih. "Dewi Sri dalam tradisi Jawa" [Dewi Sri in Javanese Tradition]. *Jantra* 2, no. 3, (2007): 136–44.

Taylor, Jean G. "Costume and Gender in Colonial Java: 1800–1940." In *Outward Appearances: Dressing State and Society in Indonesia,* edited by Henk Schulte Nordholt. Leiden, The Netherlands: KITLV, 1997, 86–116.

Endnotes

1 Norma Broude and Mary D. Garrard, eds., *The Power of Feminist Art: The American Movement of the 1970s, History and Impact*. (New York: Harry N. Abrams Inc., 1994), 25.

2 Orenstein, G. F., "Recovering Her Story: Feminist Artists Reclaim the Great Goddess," in *The Power of Feminist Art: The American Movement of the 1970s, History and Impact*, ed. Norma Broude and Mary D. Garrard (New York: Harry N. Abrams, Inc., 1994), 174.

3 Graeme Sullivan, *Art Practice as Research: Inquiry in the Visual Arts* (Thousand Oaks, CA: SAGE Publications, 2005); Graeme Sullivan, "Research Acts in Art Practice," *Studies in Art Education* 48, no. 1 (2006): 19–35; Graeme Sullivan, *Art Practice as Research: Inquiry in the Visual Arts*, 2nd ed. (Thousand Oaks, CA: SAGE Publications, 2010).

4 Marianne Hulsbosch, Elizabeth Bedford, and Martha Chaiklin, "Asian Material Culture in Context," in *Asian Material Culture*, ed. Marianne Hulsbosch, Elizabeth Bedford, and Martha Chaiklin (Amsterdam: Amsterdam University Press, 2009), 9–16; Jules David Prown, "Mind in Matter: An introduction to Material Culture Theory and Method," *Winthertur Portofolio* 17, no. 1 (1982): 1–19.

5 The term *mythopoetic* is take from Susan Kneebone, "Naturally Disturbed: A Critical Inquiry into Pastoralist Memory and Environmental History as Realised Through Visual Art" (PhD major studio project, South Australian School of Art, University of South Australia, Adelaide, Australia, 2010).

6 Rens Heringa, "Dewi Sri in Village Garb: Fertility, Myth and Ritual in Northeast Java," *Asian Folklore Studies* 56, no. 2 (1997): 335–77; Sumintarsih, "Dewi Sri dalam tradisi Jawa" [Dewi Sri in Javanese Tradition], *Jantra* 2, no. 3, (2007): 136–44.

7 Supratikno Rahardjo, *Peradaban Jawa: Dari Mataram Kuno sampai Majapahit Akhir* [Javanese Civilization: From Ancient Mataram to Late Majapahit] (Depok, Indonesia: Komunitas Bambu, 2011), 199.

8 Rahardjo, *Peradaban Jawa*; Sumintarsih, "Dewi Sri dalam tradisi Jawa."

9 R. M. Koentjaraningrat, *Introduction to the Peoples and Cultures of Indonesia and Malaysia* (Menlo Park, CA: Cummings, 1975).

10 David Irvine, *Leather Gods and Wooden Heroes: Java's Classical Wayang* (Singapore: Marshall Cavendish International, 2005); Sumintarsih, "Dewi Sri dalam tradisi Jawa."

11 Irvine, *Leather Gods and Wooden Heroes*; Sumintarsih, "Dewi Sri dalam tradisi Jawa."

12 Rahardjo, *Peradaban Jawa*.

13 Irvine, *Leather Gods and Wooden Heroes*.

14 Irvine, *Leather Gods and Wooden Heroes*; Sumintarsih, "Dewi Sri dalam tradisi Jawa."

15 C. R. Bailly, "Sri-Lakshmi Majesty of The Hindu King," in *Goddesses Who Rule*, ed. Elisabeth Benard and Beverly Moon (New York: Oxford University Press, 2000).

16 Irvine, *Leather Gods and Wooden Heroes*, 277.

17 Irvine, *Leather Gods and Wooden Heroes*.

18 Irvine, *Leather Gods and Wooden Heroes*; Sumintarsih, "Dewi Sri dalam tradisi Jawa."

19 Irvine, *Leather Gods and Wooden Heroes*; Sumintarsih, "Dewi Sri dalam tradisi Jawa."

20 Purwadi, *Sejarah asal-usul nenek moyang orang Jawa* [History of the Origin of Javanese Ancestors] (Yogyakarta, Indonesia: Panji Pustaka, 2010).

21 Beverly Gordon, *Textiles: The Whole Story: Uses, Meanings, Significance* (New York: Thames & Hudson, 2011).

22 This regulation is written in Hadith, the narrative record of the sayings or customs of Prophet Muhammad and his companions. Mentions include HR.Bukhori 5494, Muslim 3944 and HR.Bukhori 5495; HR.Bukhori 416 and Muslim 822; HR.Bukhori 5644; HR.Bukhori 5493 and Muslim 3929; HR.Muslim 3945; and HR.Muslim 2073.

23 J. Budiwiyanto, "Penerapan unsur-unsur arsitektur tradisional Jawa pada interior public space di Surakarta" [Implementation of Traditional Javanese Architectural Elements in Public Space Interiors in Surakarta], *Gelar: Jurnal Seni Budaya* [Degree: Journal of Cultural Art] 7, no. 1 (2009): 1–21.

24 Sumintarsih, "Dewi Sri dalam tradisi Jawa"; Aprina Murwanti, "Mitoni, Lurik and the Stitches of Lament" (PhD dissertation, University of Wollongong, Wollongong, Australia, 2014).

25 Suwarna Pringgawidagda, *Upacara tingkeban* [Tingkeban Ceremony] (Yogyakarta, Indonesia: Adicita Karya Nusa, 2003).

26 Nian S. Djoemena, *Lurik: Garis-garis Bertuah: The Magic Stripes* (Jakarta: Djambatan, 2000).

27 Djoemena, *Lurik*; Endang Patrijunianti, "Lurik," in *Ensiklopedia Nasional Indonesia* [National Encyclopedia of Indonesia] (Jakarta: PT Delta Pamungkas, 2004), 450–51; Koestriastuti, "Java: Central Java," in *Tenun: Handwoven Textiles of Indonesia*, ed. Jay E. Sian (Jakarta: Cita Tenun Indonesia, 2010).

28 Patrijunianti, "Lurik," 450.

29 Koestriastuti, "Java: Central Java," 77.

30 Djoemena, *Lurik*.

31 Clifford Geertz, *The Religion of Java* (Chicago and London: The University of Chicago Press, 1960); Thomas Stanford Raffles, *The History of Java* (Yogyakarta, Indonesia: Narasi, 2008).

32 Djoemena, *Lurik*.

33 Geertz, *The Religion of Java*, 44.

34 Gordon, *Textiles: The Whole Story*, 38.

35 Gordon, *Textiles: The Whole Story*, 38.

36 Gordon, *Textiles: The Whole Story*.

37 Gordon, *Textiles: The Whole Story*, 41–42.

38 Irvine, *Leather Gods and Wooden Heroes*, 7.

39 Lucy R. Lippard, *Overlay: Contemporary Art and the Art of Prehistory* (New York: Pantheon, 1983); Orenstein, "Recovering Her Story."

40 Orenstein, "Recovering Her Story," 181.

41 Broude and Garrard, eds., *The Power of Feminist Art*.

42 Ana Mendieta, *Incantation to Olokun-Yemaya*, 1977.

43 Judit Gera, "The Search for Identity in the Art of Ana Mendieta and Arnaldo Roche-Rabell," *Americana E-Journal of American Studies in Hungary* 6, no. 1 (2010), accessed May 5, 2013, americanaejournal.hu/vol6no1/gera.

44 Gera, "The Search for Identity in the Art of Ana Mendieta and Arnaldo Roche-Rabell."

45 Lippard, *Overlay*.

46 Orenstein, "Recovering Her Story."

47 Brita L. Miklouho-Maklai, *Exposing Society's Wounds: Some Aspects of Contemporary Indonesian Art Since 1966* (Adelaide, Australia: The Flinders University of South Australia, 1991), 30.

48 Miklouho-Maklai, *Exposing Society's Wounds*, 30.

49 Claire Bishop, *Installation Art: A Critical History* (New York: Routledge, 2005), 104.

50 Carol Hanisch, "The Personal is Political: The Women's Liberation Movement Classic with a New Explanatory Introduction," first published in *Notes from the Second Year: Women's Liberation* (New York: Shulamith Firestone and Anne Koedt, 1970), now available online with a new introduction (Carol Hanisch, 2009), www.carolhanisch.org/CHwritings/PIP.html.

51 Broude and Garrard, eds., *The Power of Feminist Art*; Helen Reckitt and Peggy Phelan, *Art and Feminism*, Themes and Movements (New York: Phaidon, 2001).

52 Reckitt and Phelan, *Art and Feminism*, 20.

53 Reckitt and Phelan, *Art and Feminism*, 30.

54 Jean G. Taylor, "Costume and Gender in Colonial Java: 1800–1940," in *Outward Appearances: Dressing State and Society in Indonesia*, ed. Henk Schulte Nordholt (Leiden, The Netherlands: KITLV, 1997), 94.

55 Taylor, "Costume and Gender in Colonial Java."

TONANTZIN-COATLICUE-GUADALUPE: CHRISTIAN SYMBOLISM, COLONIZATION AND SOCIAL JUSTICE

Yuria Celidwen

Introduction

Feelings of atonement and empowerment arise in personal and cultural narratives from the reconciliation of seemingly opposite views of life. Abusive situations compel us to stand up and call for dignity and respect. Through understanding the causes of suffering, we can gain compassion. By acknowledging our unconscious bias as individuals and as societies living in cultural constructs, we can grow in collective awareness. Based on this premise, in this article I aim to contribute to the dialogue about psychological atonement between the peoples of indigenous descent in Latin America, on one side, and the Christian faith—specifically, the Catholic Church—on the other side. To some, placing these two groups in confrontation may seem surprising, especially when 97.3% of the population of Mexico admits to practicing some form of Christianity, with the largest group being Catholic (89.3%), followed by Protestant and Evangelical (8%).[1] The standpoint I use here is that of the indigenous peoples as a subjugated group, originally oppressed by religious mandates of the Spanish Catholic crown, when pre-Hispanic cultures were violently deprived of their cultural values, symbols and social status, and then further persecuted precisely by those representing the Christian faith during the colonization period that started in the 16th century.

The dialogue that I propose entails an exploration of the aspects of the shadow side of the Catholic faith. In depth psychology, the shadow is akin to the unconscious, the side of the psyche or mind that is unacknowledged by the individual This side includes the personal characteristics, good and bad aspects of instincts, abilities and moral qualities, all of which the ego has repressed, never recognized or never even been conscious of. Generally, these character traits are experienced in others through the mechanism of projection.[2] In this article, I make the point that the shadow of the Catholic Church was projected as conflictive fear and aversion to the otherness of the indigenous populations in Latin America, and it was acted out through manipulation, subjugation and oppression by means of religious imposition and conversion.

The driving forces of the shadow manifest not only in individuals but also culturally in social groups and the dynamics of any community attempting to act as a whole. The innovative field of interpersonal neuro-biology—brought forward by Daniel Siegel, one of its pioneers in the past decade—proposes that integration is central to the developing mind as it aims to interlace separate modes of information processing into a coherent whole, giving rise to flexible, adaptive, harmonious functioning.[3] That is, seeking integration is inherent in the capacity of the psyche, and such integration can be achieved by acknowledging aspects that are unconscious or dissociated. From that perspective, I find it imperative to recognize and unveil the cultural narratives that underlie destructive behavior, since these are part of the identity function of the brain that is unacknowledged, separated and dissociated from a state of awareness and wholeness.

Based on these concepts, the process that I call shadow-facing involves a dialogue between the complex cultural aspects of identity conditioning as seen in its holistic nature, in both its nurturing and destructive tendencies. Once both aspects have been acknowledged, it is possible to understand their causes and conditions and therefore achieve a psychological integration. I argue that it is imperative to understand the unconscious bias we have been conditioned to by self-serving systems of power and to focus rather on the community at large. The objective is to transform self-centered dispositions into ways of relating that are conducive to communal, collaborative living.

I propose that, by realizing the connotations of the narratives that create our identity, we necessarily comprehend the ideologies by which we live. By understanding the origins of these ideologies, we can better respond and re-create new perspectives that can benefit us all. As we understand the complexity of our beliefs and behavior, we open ourselves to compassion. I claim that transformation begins with the realization that sensible beings matter and that to stand for justice means to call for social engagement in the form of a radical revolution of collaboration that burns away the impurities of a self-image that is concerned only with its own well-being. This alchemical process transforms the psyche through relentless scrutiny. The result is a mind compelled to live compassionately and ethically, replacing the establishment of power and subjugation with trust, unity, dignity and freedom.

In this article, I concentrate on developing a dialogue by acknowledging the aspects of the shadow side of the cultural constructions defined by the Catholic faith in Mexico. This process is essential for changing the conditions of misery and dehumanization brought upon the collective psyche of those living in unprivileged situations. The shadow aspects that I examine are expressly the symbolic and depth-psychological aspects of the development of the icon of the Lady of Guadalupe. I address how that image initially was used as a semiotic medium for the manipulation of the native population, as Patricia Harrington suggested, through which the traditional polytheistic beliefs were forced into conversion to Catholicism in the 16th century.[4] I deduce that the tones of the devouring aspect of this archetype are correlated with the sense of defeat that still subdues many indigenous populations in Mexico and the rest of Latin America. This self-defeating mechanism is particularly evident in regards to obstacles that indigenous peoples face in their efforts to protect sacred landscapes from exploitation and destruction. Hence, my perspective necessarily assumes an anti-neoliberal stance.

I approach this inquiry as a way of a metaphorical, convivial meal. I intend to provide food for thought and for emotion, bringing together mind and heart for reconciliation. This offering comes in four main courses. First, the table is set by describing the dynamism of the Lady of Guadalupe as the mother archetype of compassion, strength and unity for the indigenous, dispossessed and immigrant populations of Hispanic descent. Her image has been used as an icon of insurgency (in the movement for Mexican Independence and the Mexican Revolution), but also of conquest and subjugation (during the Spanish colonization of Mexico) and revolution (in liberation theology movements). Second, the spice comes with the exploration of the devouring aspect of the Lady of Guadalupe as an image of indoctrination and oppression of indigenous peoples. This elucidation is supported with historical accounts of the use of the icon by Spanish colonizers and a mythological analysis of the symbols in its iconography. Third, at the table sit the Nahuatl mother goddesses Tonantzin and Coatlicue and the Lady of Guadalupe, all sharing an inquiry on the symbolic archetypal elements they have in common. Finally, dessert comes with the sharing of the bread: The bodies of the three goddesses join as a compassionate mother/goddess archetype. In modern days, this archetype manifests in the very figure of Pope Francis, who has taken unprecedented steps as the head of the Catholic Church, offering an apology to the indigenous peoples of Latin America and acknowledging the practices of violation and abuse that were carried out by Spanish colonizers in the name of the Catholic faith. Moreover, he has encouraged Catholic devotees to come together in an act of forgiveness, unity and reconciliation. This process of shadow-facing is, in my opinion, a heartening start to a sense of restitution and a restoration of trust.

Setting the Table: Our Lady in Time

Every 12th of December, the Basilica of Our Lady of Guadalupe in Mexico City is flooded with pilgrim devotees who come from near and far to honor the figure of the Mesoamerican Mary (*Figure 22*). The Basilica is the most visited Catholic shrine in the world, with approximately 20 million visitors per year.[5] The communal celebrations each December are largely joyful events for the numerous pilgrims, who stand during an all-night vigil and take part in nine days of jubilation and prayer. In the past century, the Lady of Guadalupe has been adopted as a symbol of Hispanic cultural identity for destitute, indigenous and immigrant populations around the world.[6] These populations regard the image as an exemplary icon of spiritual refuge, for its archetypal qualities of motherhood and compassion.[7] She has become such an influential representation of the indigenous divine feminine[8] that just having made the pilgrimage is cause for admiration.

Fig. 22. Man walking on his knees to the Lady of Guadalupe shrine, on pilgrimage for the Lady of Guadalupe, December 2015. Basilica de la Virgen de Guadalupe, Mexico. Photograph by Yuria Celidwen, 2015.

As a foundational symbol in the history of Mexico, the image of Guadalupe was used as the insignia of empowerment and unity in the nation's two most important fights for social justice. In 1810, the Catholic priest Miguel Hidalgo carried a flag with the image of Guadalupe encouraging the natives to fight for independence from the Spanish authorities.[9] A hundred years later, during the Mexican Revolution, General Emiliano Zapata carried a banner with the image of Guadalupe to protest for the rights to land.[10] From that time to today, carrying a banner with the image of the Lady of Guadalupe has come to signify the unified call for equality and freedom.

Regardless of the Lady's historical presence in Mexico, the Lady's association with battles for justice and civil rights goes even further back in time and outside Latin America. By 1340, the image of the Virgin Mary as the Lady of Guadalupe in Extremadura, Spain, already was associated with Spanish royalty, as an icon of the Christian struggle for freedom against the Moors.[11] Therefore, it is not surprising that Mary was adopted as an emblem of Spain as it advanced in its Christian conquest campaigns in the New World.[12] Spanish colonizers carried statues and banners of Mary with them as they conquered indigenous territories. They replaced native idols with images of the Virgin.[13] In the advancing conquest of Mexico, within the first hundred years of contact—by 1620—the native population had been eradicated almost in its entirety. Natives found their deaths in battle, suicide or disease. As the worship of the traditional Nahuatl pantheon was banned, with the conversion of the indigenous population to Catholicism, natives were dehumanized, tortured and abused to bring about completely subjugation. People were slaughtered if they refused religious conversion.[14] The native population suffered from such traumatic psycho-cultural disso-lution that they found ways to stop bearing children in order to protect them from oppression. There were mass suicides and epidemics from viruses to which the native population had no immunity.[15] All of these factors brought the population close to extinction.[16] From this, Harrington affirmed that the natives must have associated the images of Mary with the destruction of their culture during the period of conquest.[17]

The Spice: Our Devouring Lady

As the destruction of the indigenous pantheon advanced, and its substi-tution with the new Christian faith was established, the population developed ingenious practices to continue their worship in secret. Figurines of the Nahuatl mother goddess Coatlicue, "Snakes-Her-Skirt" (*Figure 23*), were placed inside the statues of the Lady of Guadalupe, so that the traditional worship of the chthonic goddess could continue. The hill of Tepeyac, where

the Basilica of Our Lady of Guadalupe was later built, was a well-known place for Nahuatl ritual festivals to honor several chthonic mother goddesses, of whom the most revered was Tonantzin.[18] Friar Bernardino de Sahagún mentioned that the ritual site of Tonantzin—a Nahua appellative meaning "Our mother"— was merged with that of the Lady of Guadalupe and that the Lady later adopted the goddess's name, becoming Tonantzin Guadalupe.[19] It was through this strategy of merging mythic pagan elements with those of the newly established

Fig. 23. Mother goddess Coatlicue. Aztec. Basalt, 2.57 m, circa 1500 CE. National Museum of Anthropology, Mexico. Photograph by Yuria Celidwen, 2015.

faith, used by both the native population and the Catholic Church, that religious conversion was established.[20]

Tonantzin is also identified with Nahuatl chthonic mother goddess Coatlicue, the mother of the moon, the stars and the sun, according to the Nahuatl creation myth (*Figure 24*).[21] These elements would have been familiar and recognizable in the picture of Guadalupe. Going back to the *Leyenda de los Soles*, Coatlicue is one of the five creator goddesses who gave their lives to give birth to and energize the fifth and present sun, Huitzilopochtli,

Fig. 24. Mother goddess Tonantzin. Nahuatl. Ceramic, circa 16th century CE. National Museum of Anthropology, Mexico. Photograph by Yuria Celidwen, 2015.

which personifies the new era and the most important Nahuatl god.[22] This is another motif that appears in the mythology of Mary as Guadalupe, mother of Jesus Christ, the son of God, the solar god image of the new faith. Other significant similarities between the two faiths are that Coatlicue and Guadalupe are both represented as a conciliation of opposites: day and night, light and darkness, life and death. They are the Great Mother in the archetypes of compassion, fierceness, nurturance, death, strength, transformation and protection.

The stories related to the apparition of the Lady of Guadalupe in Mexico were first told in Spanish in the 1648 booklet *Imagen de la Virgen María, Madre de Dios de Guadalupe* [Image of the Virgin Mary, Mother of God of Guadalupe] by theologian Miguel Sánchez. In the following year, 1649, a religious tract called *Huei tlamahuiçoltica* [The Great Happening], written by the vicar of the Catholic sanctuary at the hill of Tepeyac, Luis Laso de la Vega, appeared in Nahuatl. That narrative is divided into seven parts, one of which is the *Nican Mopohua*. This section seems to have come from an original manuscript by Antonio Valeriano, a Nahua scholar who worked alongside friar Bernardino de Sahagún on the *Florentine Codex: General History of the Things of New Spain*.[23] The *Nican Mopohua* is the story of the apparition of the Virgin Mary as seen by a Nahua young man named Cuauhtlatoatzin (Talking Eagle). The narrative says that in the young man's grief the Virgin appeared to him as an indigenous young woman, the Lady of Guadalupe. She embraced him and said out loud, "Do not be troubled or weighed down with grief, my son. Am I not here, who am your Mother?" After this, she asked him to gather the roses that were blooming around him and to bring them to the bishop of New Spain, Juan de Zumárraga. The bishop initially dismissed the man's account and demanded proof of his veracity. The young man showed him his *tilma* (a traditional Nahua robe of rough cloth) that held the roses. Imprinted on the cloth was the image of the Lady of Guadalupe. Cuauhtlatoatzin, the narrative continues, then converted to Catholicism and was baptized as Juan Diego. Later a shrine in honor of the Lady of Guadalupe was built on the site of these apparitions. In 2002, Juan Diego Cuauhtlatoatzin was canonized by the Catholic Church.[24]

It must be assumed that the aforementioned narrative is part of the Catholic mythology for the Lady of Guadalupe, as there is no historical record of these apparitions. What is indeed known, however, is that the image was painted in the sixteenth century on a six-by-three-foot cloth made of linen and hemp. It follows a Byzantine painting style that uses tempera made with organic materials such as pine soot, calcium sulfate, copper and iron oxides, sulfur, and mercury compounds and cochineal dyes.[25] The style of imagery is evidently Spanish and the methods in use reflect European Christian iconography of the period.

The reasons developed below support the argument that the image was created to promote the religious conversion of the indigenous people, as the symbols depicted on it were identified and reinterpreted as part of Catholic mythology. The stellar symbols and the colors have meaningful religious connotations for both the Nahuatl and Catholic traditions. Indeed, it has been suggested that the image was created as a means of establishing the new faith.[26]

The theory of depth psychology states that the unconscious is "the source of the instinctual forces of the psyche and of the forms or categories that regulate them, namely the archetypes."[27] I suggest that, because the mind creates a sense of self from archetypes and images perceived, the story of the apparition was intended to be a model for an attitude to be adopted by the indigenous population toward the institution of the Catholic Church and the Spanish colonizers. Therefore, I argue that the elements on the image of the Lady of Guadalupe present established Christian symbols intended to institutionalize religious and political power and domination. An examination of these symbols enables us to come to terms with their sources and possible significance.

Sharing the Table: An Inquiry into Symbols

The central figure in the image of the Lady of Guadalupe (*Figure 25*) is an indigenous young woman who appears as a young Mary. This image has been indicated, by Ernesto de la Torre Villar and Ramiro Navarro de Anda, to relate to the description of Mary referenced in the book of Revelation in the New Testament of the Bible:[28] "A great sign appeared in heaven: a woman clothed with the sun, and the moon under her feet, and on her head a crown of twelve stars and she was with child; and she cried out, being in labor and in pain to give birth."[29] In the image of the Lady of Guadalupe, a halo surrounds her as the "woman clothed with the sun." Allegorically, the light rays can be interpreted, from a depth-psychological perspective, as referring to a solar god, the new sun that is born in the winter solstice announcing a new birth, a new cycle, a renovation of the establishment. The Lady is in prayer, indicating devotion, an attitude of deference that I interpret as a model of submission to a hierarchical structure, subordinate to the solar god. This subservience also appears in another mention of Mary in the Bible, in Acts 1:8. The angel Gabriel tells her that she will bear "the Son of the Most High" and that "The Holy Spirit will come upon [her], and the power of the Most High will overshadow [her]." Does this denote an action of divine creation that alludes to the imminent subservient disposition the Virgin should render? In similar terms, in Luke 1:26–38 Mary responds by indicating her obedience to Jesus Christ: "Let it be with me according to your word." To me, this version of the mother figure supports a patriarchal religion. According to Christian cosmology, Jesus Christ is a symbolic personification of the cosmic principles of creation,[30] which I see translated as representing a new belief system.

The red border around the sun's rays can, thus, be interpreted as a sign of the rising solar influence of the new royal heir and of the transition of power.

Similarly and as I mentioned above, the rays of the sun would have been recognized by indigenous people as a symbol of their highest solar god, Huitzilopochtli. Pre-Hispanic traditions also followed a patriarchal foundation of solar gods. The myth in the *Leyenda de los Soles*[31] is a token of this bias. Not surprisingly, the Nahuatl narrative also has been suggested to be about domination.[32] However, the difference between the Christian myths and the Nahuatl myths is that the latter characterizes the feminine figure as an equal in divine status; both mother and solar son are divine in origin. This difference is extremely important, contrasting the Nahuatl faith with the Christian faith, in which women are discriminated against. That is, in the Christian tradition the female figure remains of a lower status and under the domination of the male figure.

Fig. 25. Unknown artist, Nuestra Señora de Guadalupe [Our Lady of Guadalupe], also known as the Virgin of Guadalupe, shown in the Basilica of Our Lady of Guadalupe in México City, painting, presented by Juan Diego in 1531. Photograph by Wikimedia Commons contributors, "File:1531 Nuestra Señora de Guadalupe anagoria.jpg," Wikimedia Commons.

The image of the Lady of Guadalupe exhibits many aspects of the established Marian iconography of the 17th century that referred to basic Christian dogmas, such as perpetual virginity, the Immaculate Conception, the Assumption, and the Virgin as *Theotokos* (Mother of God) (*Figure 25*).[33] From the perspective of depth psychology, a reading of some of these symbols makes reference to the shadow aspect of the mind. For example, the illustration of the crescent moon under the Lady's feet is usually interpreted as a feminine symbol denoting the internal physical and psychic energies of the shadow aspect. These energies are, as mentioned earlier, the repressed instinctual forces that manifest unconscious behavior. On the other hand, the compassionate qualities that characterize the Virgin Mary, and hence the Lady of Guadalupe, are interpreted as a force to overcome the aggressive nature of the mind, which is the shadow or unconscious. The Lady can be said to represent reflective consciousness at the dawn of solar awareness, the solar god, which is Jesus Christ. The depiction of her standing on the moon, therefore, would be an ascension over the instinctual tendencies—that is, an assimilation of the shadow aspect.[34] This quality points toward integration.

Moreover, for the Nahuatl cultures the moon was the celestial symbol of the god of night and the underworld, which represents the unconscious. The psychic energies were assigned to the lord of the shadows, the lord of the dead, Mictlantecuhtli. Moreover, during the time of the colonization of Latin America, the Catholic Church dismissed polytheist beliefs as savage, so that standing on the moon could also indicate a triumph over those pagan indigenous convictions.

As mentioned above, the colors in the image of the Lady of Guadalupe have meaning for both Christian traditions and Nahuatl traditions. The mantle is blue-green or turquoise, which is the color with which the gods are depicted in Nahuatl culture and the color of the natural forces of water.[35] Members of the elite class wore mantles made of garments interwoven with exquisite jewels, feathers and threads, and for special ceremonies the emperor wore a mantle of fiber net studded with turquoise beads.[36] Further, in the Hebrew tradition blue is the color of the robe worn by the high priests, and in Christian symbolism the robe of the cardinal is purple.[37] The stars on the Lady's mantle also indicate royalty in her position as Mother of God. The color of the stars is gold, indicating solar qualities and an association with the royal family. All of these symbols indicate that the Lady is portrayed as a sovereign.

Continuing with the explorations of possible meaning of the image of the Lady, we see that she carries a cross, a pre-eminent Christian symbol. Based on depth-psychological interpretations, I see the cross as the intersection of opposing forces meeting at the heart—that is, the conciliation of opposites that I mentioned earlier.[38] The symbols found in the image indicate a tension of opposites that brings creation. Therefore, the Lady is a symbol of fecundity, the creation of new life, or the establishment of a new order that is to be accepted as a cycle of transformation that brings psychic integration. This quaternity of the cross also is present in the four-petaled flower girdle around the Lady's waist, which may have been intended as a motif of perpetual virginity, also referencing to Immaculate Conception ("she who is about to give birth").[39]

This cross or flower motif was also recognized by the native population. The motif is the preeminent Aztec Glyph 4 Movement, which represents the fifth sun or *nahui ollin*.[40] This glyph not only represents the current Fifth Age but also is a symbol of life, transformation and the recreation of the universe. Enrique Florescano noted the following:

From the chaos and darkness appears again the new order: the collapsed sky is lifted and returned to its place; the earth and water, furnished with their generative powers, surge froth again from the chaos; the gods create humans anew, along with the necessary gifts (fire, foods so that they can reproduce and people the earth.[41]

An interesting contrast to indigenous iconography is the way in which the eyes of the Lady of Guadalupe are depicted. Aztec gods have large, bulky, prominent eyes that look straight out in a manner of threat and power. For such a violent, war-driven society as the Aztecs, this empowering feature must have served to induce the passion needed in battle. Even more, perhaps a *participation mystique* took place and the devotee experienced the divine force as a power being created from within. (*Participation mystique* is a term derived from Lucien Lévy-Bruhl and which denotes a psychological association of a subject with the objects of his or her experience, as if the subject cannot clearly distinguish experience from the object itself.[42]) Conversely, the eyes of the Lady of Guadalupe look down, discreet and humble. One could certainly argue that this humility is a characteristic of kindness, but I would contend that the downward cast of the

Lady's eyes also could have been used as a model for submission for the subjugated population, a call for the native people not to challenge the system in power.[43]

The Dessert: Forgiveness, Unity and Reconciliation

In conclusion, the mixture of traditions is an organic process. It happens physically and psychically. When the process is a forceful, coercive one, scars remain. Intergenerational trauma manifests in the indigenous populations, as noted by Brave Heart and Debruyn ("The American Indian Holocaust: Healing Historical Unresolved Grief") and Brave Heart, Chase, Elkins and Altschul ("Historical Trauma Among Indigenous Peoples of the Americas: Concepts, Research, and Clinical Considerations").[44] Equity, dignity, freedom and respect are inalienable rights that the indigenous populations still struggle to access.[45] Their sacred landscapes are constantly desacralized for economic and political interests, leaving these populations even more vulnerable, and rarely are the people taken into account in the decision-making process.[46] Just as the first churches in Mexico were built from the rubble of Nahuatl temples that had been destroyed, the first spiritual foundations were constructed from the blood of Nahuatl goddesses. Over time, these combinations resulted in a hybrid tradition that has the Lady of Guadalupe as its pre-eminent icon. In symbol and in essence, the Lady of Guadalupe represents the *mestizaje* (racial and/or cultural mixing) of today's Mexican identity.

As I see it, the trinity of mother goddesses has returned as one: Tonantzin Coatlicue Guadalupe. She is an interdependent, relational, enriched figure composed of different, varied elements, in a whole complexity and fertility. She is the compassionate, the devouring, the tender, the young, the mother, the wise, the furious and the fearsome. She is the love-giving wise woman. She is the fierce warrior ready to fight for her people. She encourages truth making through relationality, enhancing our capacity for unity and respect, which can be achieved only through comprehension of the complexity of human nature.

A case of shadow-facing that I propose in this article has come to be manifested: Recently, the Catholic Church has taken unprecedented steps to adapt to an inclusive, nondiscriminatory world. The first-ever Latin American Pope, Pope Francis, has publicly acknowledged the abusive crimes committed against indigenous peoples during the colonization of Latin America. In July 2015, during a meeting in La Paz, Bolivia, with leaders of indigenous groups from the Amazon, led by indigenous Bolivian president Evo Morales, Pope Francis pleaded forgiveness for the abuse carried out in the name of the Christian faith.[47] Following suit, in his February 2016 visit to Mexico, Pope Francis spoke before a crowd of indigenous people and mestizos in San Cristobal de las Casas, Chiapas and offered another apology: "How worthwhile it would be for each of us to examine our conscience and learn to say, 'Forgive me!'"[48] More recently, he insisted for the rights of indigenous peoples over their lands.[49]

Pope Francis's recent public stance shows an unquestionable disposition toward openness and reconciliation. Furthermore, he is not only looking for the reunification of the indigenous peoples but going further, to take in account the whole of our planet. His public position is one of awareness and of working together in joint measures to address urgent matters that involve the people and the planet, bringing topics such as climate change and social justice to the conversations with those involved in political decision making. Pope Francis declared, "Working for a just distribution of the fruits of the Earth and human labor is not mere philanthropy. It is a moral obligation."[50] Indeed, our moral obligation is to nourish a sense of community and belonging so that an imperative sense of justice is established. But before a sense of community can be achieved, a process of atonement must take place. The atonement process starts by recognizing our own human shadow and the unconscious attitudes of exploitation that we as cultural societies have imposed on others and that have been imposed on us.

Political considerations aside, Pope Francis's apologetic attitude seems a courageous commencement of the process of shadow-facing by the Catholic faith. It certainly is a restitution of hope and a renewal of the nourishing archetype of a goddess mother figure. Perhaps, this time of intensely manifesting opposing forces signals the coming of a new order. Independently of a specific faith, we are being called to a renewal of a belief system based on ethical principles.

We are entering a moment in which the qualities of compassion, collaboration, courageous action and protection for our fellow human beings and for the environment will bring the change we need in order to better the quality of life. I emphasize that, as we acknowledge the shadow side, we also should praise the conscious side that takes responsibility for our choices and the effects we have on the rest of the world. Consciousness means taking action to change the conditions that perpetuate the vicious cycle of abuse. Awareness entails relating to others and embracing our rich diversity. Compassion involves understanding the causes and conditions of our confusion and regarding the other as being as important as oneself. It is essential to cultivate these new global narratives that nurture altruistic interactions among humans. It is imperative that we encourage ourselves to act as caregivers of one another and of the Earth. This is a time of transition, indeed, and a new sun for the betterment of human interactions with the world may be dawning.

References

Aguilera, Carmen. "Of Royal Mantles and Blue Turquoise: The Meaning of the Mexica Emperor's Mantle." *Latin American Antiquity* 8, no. 1 (1997): 3–19. doi:10.2307/971589.

Arnold, Philip P. "Colors." In *Encyclopedia of Religion*. 2nd ed., vol. 3. Edited by Lindsay Jones. Detroit, MI: Macmillan Reference USA, 2005. Accessed January 21, 2016. Gale Virtual Reference Library (go.galegroup.com/ps/i.do?id=GALE%7CCCX3424500622&v=2.1&u=-carp39441&it=r&p=GVRL&sw=w&asid=f6d7433c8fd202c3f5cedc6e-c854a9ee).

Barnett, Ronald A. "Mesoamerican Religious Concepts: Aztec Symbolism, Part Three." *MexConnect*, March 1, 2008. Accessed July 3, 2017. www.mexconnect.com/articles/2895-mesoamerican-religious-concepts-aztec-symbolism-part-three.

BBC News. "Mexico Indigenous People: Pope Francis Asks for Forgiveness." BBC News website, February 16, 2016. Accessed February 16, 2016. www.bbc.com/news/world-latin-america-35584031.

Bierhorst, John. *History and Mythology of the Aztecs: The Codex Chimalpopoca*. Tucson, AZ: University of Arizona Press, 1992.

Brading, D. A. *Mexican Phoenix: Our Lady of Guadalupe: Image and Tradition across Five Centuries*. New York: Cambridge University Press, 2001.

Brave Heart, Maria Yellow Horse, and Lemyra DeBruyn. "The American Indian Holocaust: Healing Historical Unresolved Grief." *American Indian and Alaska Native Mental Health Research* 8, no. 2 (1998): 56–78.

Brave Heart, Maria Yellow Horse, Josephine Chase, Jennifer Elkins, and Deborah B. Altschul. "Historical Trauma Among Indigenous Peoples of the Americas: Concepts, Research, and Clinical Considerations." *Journal of Psychoactive Drugs* 43, no. 4 (2011): 282–90. doi: 10.1080/02791072.2011.628913.

Brown, Jonathan. *Images and Ideas in Seventeenth Century Spanish Painting.* Princeton, NJ: Princeton University Press, 1978.

Burrus, Ernest J. *The Oldest Copy of the Nican Mopohua.* Vol. 2, no. 4, Cara Studies on Popular Devotion. Washington, D.C.: Center for Applied Research in the Apostolate, Georgetown University, 1981.

Cantú, Norma E. "Virgin of Guadalupe." In *Encyclopedia of Women's Folklore and Folklife,* edited by Liz Locke, Theresa A. Vaughan, and Pauline Greenhill, 682–83. Vol. 2. Westport, CT: Greenwood, 2008. Accessed May 15, 2015. go. galegroup.com/ps/i.do?id=GALE%7CCX2444500264&v=2.1&u=carp39441&it =r&p=GVRL&sw=w&asid=6ee5707926e8471345b1758d1a88568d.

Castillo, Ana, ed. *Goddess of the Americas: Writings on the Virgin of Guadalupe.* New York: Riverhead, 1996.

Chan, Román Piña. *Una visión del México prehispánico* [A vision of pre-Hispanic Mexico]. Mexico City: Instituto de Investigaciones Históricas, Universidad Nacional Autónoma de México, 1967.

Chauvet, Fidel de Jesús. *El culto guadalupano del Tepeyac: Sus orígenes y sus críticos en el siglo XVI* [The Guadalupe cult of Tepeyac: Its origins and its critics in the sixteenth century]. Mexico: Centro de Estudios Bernardino de Sahagún, 1978.

Cirlot, J. E. *A Dictionary of Symbols.* Translated by Jack Sage. London: Routledge, 1971.

Códice Chimalpopoca: Anales de Cuauhtitlan y leyenda de los soles [Annals of Cuauhtitlan and legend of the suns]. Mexico City: Instituto de Investigaciones Históricas, Universidad Nacional Autónoma de México, 1975.

Davidson, Linda Kay, and David M. Gitlitz. *Pilgrimage: From the Ganges to Graceland, an Encyclopedia.* Santa Barbara, CA: ABC-CLIO, 2002.

de la Torre Villar, Ernesto, and Ramiro Navarro de Anda, eds. *Testimonios históricos guadalupanos* [Guadalupan historical testimonials]. Mexico City: Fondo de Cultura Económica, 1982.

Fideler, David. *Jesus Christ, Sun of God: Ancient Cosmology and Early Christian Symbolism.* Wheaton, IL; Chennai, India: Quest Books, 1993.

Florescano, Enrique. *Memory, Myth, and Time in Mexico: From the Aztecs to Independence*. Translated by Albert G. Bork with the assistance of Kathryn R. Bork. Austin, TX: University of Texas, 1994.

Frank, McLynn. *Villa and Zapata: A History of the Mexican Revolution*. New York: Jonathan Cape, 2000.

Gambro, Luigi. In *Mariology: A Guide for Priests, Deacons, Seminarians, and Consecrated Persons*, edited by Mark Miravelle, 142–45. Goleta, CA: Seat of Wisdom Books, 2007.

Garibay, Angel María. *Historia de la literatura Náhuatl* [History of Náhuatl literature]. Vol. II. Mexico City: Porrúa, 1954.

Gibellini, Rosino. "Ecclesiology in Latin America." In *The Challenge of Basic Christian Communities*. New York: Orbis, 1981.

———. *Liberation Theology Debate*. London: SCM-Canterbury Press, 1987.

Graulich, Michel. *Myths of Ancient Mexico*. Civilization of the American Indian, vol. 222. Translated by Bernard R. Ortiz de Montellano and Thelma Ortiz de Montellano. Norman, OK: University of Oklahoma Press, 1997.

Greenberg, Yudit K., ed. *Encyclopedia of Love in World Religions*. Vol. 2. Santa Barbara, CA: ABC-CLIO, 2008.

Harrington, Patricia. "Mother of Death, Mother of Rebirth: The Mexican Virgin of Guadalupe." *Journal of the American Academy of Religion* 56, no. 1 (1988): 25–50.

Indian Country Media Network staff. "Pope Francis Apologizes to Indigenous Peoples for 'Grave Sins' of Colonialism." *Indian Country Today*, July 10, 2015. Accessed February 14, 2016. www.indiancountrymedianetwork.com/news/indigenous-peoples/pope-francis-apologizes-to-indigenous-peoples-for-grave-sins-of-colonialism.

Indian Country Media Network staff. "Pope Francis: Consult Indigenous Peoples." *Indian Country Today*, February 15, 2017. Accessed February 20, 2017. www.indiancountrymedianetwork.com/news/indigenous-peoples/pope-francis-indigenous-lands.

Instituto Nacional de Estadística y Geografía (INEGI). *Estructura porcentual de la población que profesa alguna religión por tipo de religion* [Percentage structure of the population that professes any religion by type of religion], 2010. Accessed July 2017. www.beta.inegi.org.mx/temas/religion.

Jung, C. G. *Symbols of Transformation*. Collected Works of C. G. Jung, vol. 5. 2nd ed. London: Routledge, 1956.

———. *Aion: Researches into the Phenomenology of the Self.* Collected Works of C. G. Jung, vol. 9, part 2. Princeton, NJ: Princeton University Press, 1959.

———. *Psychological Type*s. Edited and translated by G. Adler and R. F. C. Hull. Collected Works of C. G. Jung, vol. 6. Bollingen Series . Princeton, NJ: Princeton University Press, 1971.

———. *Aion: Researches into the Phenomenology of the Self.* Edited and translated by G. Adler and R. F. C. Hull. Collected Works of C. G. Jung, vol. 9, part 2. Bollingen Series . Princeton, NJ: Princeton University Press, 1974.

———. *The Structure and Dynamics of the Psyche.* Edited and translated by G. Adler and R. F. C. Hull. Collected Works of C. G. Jung, vol. 8. Bollingen Series . Princeton, NJ: Princeton University Press, 1975.

Kawakami, Holly Siebert, and Avinash Thombre. "The Evolving Genre of 'Our Lady of Guadalupe': A Feminist Analysis." *Texas Speech Communication Journal* 30, no. 2 (2006): 121–33.

Kirkwood, Burton. *The History of Mexico.* Westport, CT: Greenwood Press, 2000.

Lafaye, Jacques. *Quetzalcoatl and Guadalupe: The Formation of Mexican National Consciousness, 1531–1813.* Translated by Benjamin Keen. Chicago: University of Chicago Press, 1976.

Laso de la Vega, Luis, et al. *The Story of Guadalupe: Luis Laso de la Vega's Huei Tlamahuiçoltica of 1645.* Edited and translated by Lisa Sousa, Stafford Poole, and James Lockhart. UCLA Latin American Studies, vol. 84. Stanford and Los Angeles: Stanford University Press and UCLA Latin American Center Publications, 1998.

León-Portilla, Miguel. *Tonantzin Guadalupe: Pensamiento Náhuatl y mensaje Cristiano en el "Nican Mopohua"* [Náhuatl thought and Christian message in the Nican Mopohua"]. Mexico City: El Colegio Nacional, Fondo de Cultura Económica, 2000.

———. "Mesoamerican Religions: Pre-Columbian Religions." In *Encyclopedia of Religion.* 2nd ed., vol. 9. Edited by Lindsay Jones. Detroit, MI: Macmillan Reference USA, 2005. Accessed April 1, 2014. Gale Virtual Reference Library. (go.galegroup.com/ps/i.do?id=GALE%7CCX3424502033&v=2.1&u=carp3944 1&it=r&p=GVRL&sw=w&asid=b910047076d701bb0c966aa7a7d45e89).

Miller, David L. *The New Polytheism: Rebirth of the Gods and Goddesses.* 2nd. ed. Dallas: Spring Publications, 1981.

Monaghan, Patricia. "Nephthys." In *Africa, Eastern Mediterranean, Asia*. Vol. 1 of *Encyclopedia of Goddesses and Heroines*. Santa Barbara, CA: Greenwood Press, 2010. Accessed July 20, 2015. Gale Virtual Reference Library (go. galegroup.com/ps/i.do?id=GALE%7CCX2443600106&v=2.1&u=carp39441&it =r&p=GVRL&sw=w&asid=aabf2f376d42575210400f9140d806bc).

Noguez, Xavier. "De Tonantzin a la Virgen de Guadalupe: El culto prehispánico en el Tepeyac" (From Tonantzin to the Virgin of Guadalupe: The pre-Hispanic cult in Tepeyac]. *Arqueología Mexicana* 20 (1996): 50–55.

Nolasco, Manuel Olimón. *La búsqueda de Juan Diego* [The search for Juan Diego]. Mexico City: Plaza y Janés, 2002. Accessed January 13, 2016. www. olimon.org/manuel/libros/juandiego.htm.

O'Gorman, Edmundo. *Destierro de sombras: Luz en el origen de la imagen y culto de Nuestra Señora de Guadalupe del Tepeyac* [Exile of shadows: Light in the origin of the image and cult of Our Lady of Guadalupe of the Tepeyac]. 2nd ed. Mexico City: Universidad Nacional Autónoma de México, 1991.

Orcutt, April. "World's Most-Visited Sacred Sites." BBC web-site, January 25, 2012. Accessed July 22, 2015. www.bbc.com/travel/story/20120124-worlds-most-visited-sacred-sites.

Padden, R. C. *The Hummingbird and the Hawk: Conquest and Sovereignty in the Valley of Mexico, 1503–1541*. Columbus, OH: Ohio State University Press, 1967.

Phelan, John Leddy. *The Millennial Kingdom of the Franciscans in the New World*. 2nd ed. Berkeley, CA: University of California Press, 1970.

Poole, Stafford. *Our Lady of Guadalupe: The Origins and Sources of a Mexican National Symbol, 1531–1797*. Tucson, AZ: University of Arizona Press, 1995.

Pope Francis. *Encyclical Letter Laudato Si of the Holy Father Francis on Care for our Common Home*. Vatican, May 24, 2015. Accessed May 24, 2015. w2.vatican.va/content/francesco/en/encyclicals/documents/papa-fran-cesco_20150524_enciclica-laudato-si.html.

Pope John Paul II. *Canonization of Juan Diego Cuauhtlatoatzin, Homily of the Holy Father John Paul II* at the apostolic visit to Mexico City, July 31, 2002. Accessed March 15, 2016. w2.vatican.va/content/john-paul-ii/en/homilies/2002/documents/hf_jp-ii_hom_20020731_canonization-mexico.html.

Proceso 1332. "La mentira y la fe" [The lie and the faith]. *Proceso*, May 21, 2002. Accessed March 21, 2016. www.proceso.com.mx/241963/la-mentira-y-la-fe.

Ricard, Robert. *The Spiritual Conquest of Mexico: An Essay on the Apostolate and the Evangelizing Methods of the Mendicant Orders in New Spain, 1523–1572*. Translated by Lesley Byrd Simpson. Berkeley, CA: University of California Press, 1966.

Rodriguez, Jeanette. *Our Lady of Guadalupe: Faith and Empowerment Among Mexican-American Women*. Austin, TX: University of Texas Press, 1994.

Rodriguez, Jeanette, and Ted Fortier. *Cultural Memory: Resistance, Faith, and Identity*. Austin, TX: University of Texas Press, 2007.

Rojas, Mario Sánchez, and Juan Homero Hernández Illescas. "Las estrellas del manto de la Virgen de Guadalupe" [The stars of the mantle of the Virgin of Guadalupe]. Mexico City: Francisco Méndez Oteo, 1983.

Sahagún, Bernardino de. *The Origin of the Gods*. Translated by Arthur J. O. Anderson and Charles E. Dibble. Book 3 of *Florentine Codex: General History of the Things of New Spain*. Salt Lake City, UT: University of Utah Press, 2012.

Siegel, Daniel J. *The Developing Mind: How Relationships and the Brain Interact to Shape Who We Are*. 2nd ed. New York: Guilford Press, 2012.

Torres, Yolotl González. "Mesoamerican Religions: History of Study." In *Encyclopedia of Religion*. 2nd ed., vol. 9. Edited by Lindsay Jones. Detroit, MI: Macmillan Reference USA, 2005. Accessed April 1, 2014. Gale Virtual Reference Library (go.galegroup.com/ps/i.do?id=GALE%7C-CX3424502040&v=2.1&u=carp39441&it=r&p=GVRL&sw=w&asid=d 68e7996b25d23e13ea0675165b51b64).

United Nations, Economic and Social Council, Permanent Forum on Indigenous Issues. "Indigenous Speakers in Permanent Forum Decry Governmental Abuse of Traditional Lands, Natural Resources, Urge Respect for Self-Governing Systems." United Nations website, April 26, 2017. Accessed May 3, 2017. www.un.org/press/en/2017/hr5353.doc.htm.

———. "Informed Consent Critical to Protecting Survival, Human Rights of Indigenous Peoples, Speakers Tell Permanent Forum." United Nations website, May 1, 2017. Accessed May 3, 2017. www.un.org/press/en/2017/hr5356.doc.htm.

Endnotes

1 Instituto Nacional de Estadística y Geografía (INEGI), *Estructura porcentual de la población que profesa alguna religión por tipo de religion* [Percentage structure of the population that professes any religion by type of religion], 2010, accessed July 2017, www.beta.inegi.org.mx/temas/religion.

2 C. G. Jung, *Aion: Researches into the Phenomenology of the Self*, ed. and trans. G. Adler and R. F. C. Hull, Collected Works of C. G. Jung, vol. 9, part 2, Bollingen Series (Princeton, NJ: Princeton University Press, 1974), 423.

3 Daniel J. Siegel, *The Developing Mind: How Relationships and the Brain Interact to Shape Who We Are*, 2nd ed. (New York: Guilford Press, 2012), 28.

4 Patricia Harrington, "Mother of Death, Mother of Rebirth: The Mexican Virgin of Guadalupe," *Journal of the American Academy of Religion* 56, no. 1 (1988): 25–50.

5 Linda Kay Davidson and David M. Gitlitz, *Pilgrimage: From the Ganges to Graceland, an Encyclopedia* (Santa Barbara, CA: ABC-CLIO, 2002), 213.

6 Jeanette Rodriguez and Ted Fortier, *Cultural Memory: Resistance, Faith, and Identity* (Austin, TX: University of Texas Press, 2007).

7 Jeanette Rodriguez, *Our Lady of Guadalupe: Faith and Empowerment Among Mexican-American Women* (Austin, TX: University of Texas Press, 1994), 150.

8 Holly Siebert Kawakami and Avinash Thombre, "The Evolving Genre of 'Our Lady of Guadalupe': A Feminist Analysis," *Texas Speech Communication Journal* 30, no. 2 (2006): 121–33.

9 Burton Kirkwood, *The History of Mexico* (Westport, CT: Greenwood Press, 2000), 83.

10 McLynn Frank, *Villa and Zapata: A History of the Mexican Revolution* (New York: Jonathan Cape, 2000), 264.

11 Jonathan Brown, *Images and Ideas in Seventeenth Century Spanish Painting* (Princeton, NJ: Princeton University Press, 1978), 222–23.

12 Jacques Lafaye, *Quetzalcoatl and Guadalupe: The Formation of Mexican National Consciousness, 1531–1813*, trans. Benjamin Keen (Chicago: University of Chicago Press, 1976), 34.

13 R. C. Padden, *The Hummingbird and the Hawk: Conquest and Sovereignty in the Valley of Mexico, 1503–1541* (Columbus, OH: Ohio State University Press, 1967), 143.

14 Rosino Gibellini, *Liberation Theology Debate* (London: SCM-Canterbury Press, 1987).

15 John Leddy Phelan, *The Millennial Kingdom of the Franciscans in the New World*, 2nd ed. (Berkeley, CA: University of California Press, 1970), 42.

16 Phelan, *Millennial Kingdom of the Franciscans*, 92.

17 Harrington, "Mother of Death, Mother of Rebirth," 29.

18 Xavier Noguez, "De Tonantzin a la Virgen de Guadalupe: El culto pre-hispánico en el Tepeyac" (From Tonantzin to the Virgin of Guadalupe: The pre-Hispanic cult in Tepeyac], *Arqueología Mexicana* 20 (1996): 50–55.

19 Fidel de Jesús Chauvet, *El culto guadalupano del Tepeyac: Sus orígenes y sus críticos en el siglo XVI* [The Guadalupe cult of Tepeyac: Its origins and its critics in the sixteenth century] (Mexico: Centro de Estudios Bernardino de Sahagún, 1978), 65.

20 Lafaye, *Quetzalcoatl and Guadalupe*.

21 Bernardino de Sahagún, *The Origin of the Gods*, trans. Arthur J. O. Anderson and Charles E. Dibble, Book 3 of *Florentine Codex: General History of the Things of New Spain* (Salt Lake City, UT: University of Utah Press, 2012).

22 John Bierhorst, *History and Mythology of the Aztecs: The Codex Chimalpopoca* (Tucson, AZ: University of Arizona Press, 1992), 149.

23 Miguel León-Portilla, "Mesoamerican Religions: Pre-Columbian Religions," in *Encyclopedia of Religion*, 2nd ed., vol. 9, ed. Lindsay Jones (Detroit, MI: Macmillan Reference USA, 2005), accessed April 1, 2014, Gale Virtual Reference Library (go.galegroup.com/ps/i.do?id=GALE%7CCX-3424502033&v=2.1&u=carp39441&it=r&p=GVRL&sw=w&asid=b9100470 76d701bb0c966aa7a7d45e89); Edmundo O'Gorman, *Destierro de sombras: Luz en el origen de la imagen y culto de Nuestra Señora de Guadalupe del Tepeyac* [Exile of shadows: Light in the origin of the image and cult of Our Lady of Guadalupe of the Tepeyac], 2nd ed. (Mexico City: Universidad Nacional Autónoma de México, 1991); Ernest J. Burrus, *The Oldest Copy of the Nican Mopohua*, vol. 2, no. 4, Cara Studies on Popular Devotion (Washington, D.C.: Center for Applied Research in the Apostolate, Georgetown University, 1981); Robert Ricard, *The Spiritual Conquest of Mexico: An Essay on the Apostolate and the Evangelizing Methods of the Mendicant Orders in New Spain, 1523–1572*, trans. Lesley Byrd Simpson (Berkeley, CA: University of California Press, 1966), 223.

24 Pope John Paul II, *Canonization of Juan Diego Cuauhtlatoatzin, Homily of the Holy Father John Paul II* at the apostolic visit to Mexico City, July 31, 2002, accessed March 15, 2016, w2.vatican.va/content/john-paul-ii/en/homilies/2002/ documents/hf_jp-ii_hom_20020731_canonization-mexico.html.

25 *Proceso* 1332, "La mentira y la fe" [The lie and the faith], *Proceso*, May 21, 2002, accessed March 21, 2016, www.proceso.com.mx/241963/ la-mentira-y-la-fe.

26 Angel Maria Garibay, *Historia de la literatura Náhuatl* [History of Náhuatl literature], vol. II (Mexico City: Porrúa, 1954); León-Portilla, "Mesoamerican Religions."

27 C. G. Jung, *The Structure and Dynamics of the Psyche*, ed. and trans. G. Adler and R. F. C. Hull, Collected Works of C. G. Jung, vol. 8, Bollingen Series (Princeton, NJ: Princeton University Press, 1975), 342.

28 Ernesto de la Torre Villar and Ramiro Navarro de Anda, eds, *Testimonios históricos guadalupanos* [Guadalupan historical testimonials] (Mexico City: Fondo de Cultura Económica, 1982).

29 Revelation 12:1 (New American Standard Bible).

30 David Fideler, *Jesus Christ, Sun of God: Ancient Cosmology and Early Christian Symbolism* (Wheaton, IL; Chennai, India: Quest Books, 1993).

31 *Códice Chimalpopoca: Anales de Cuauhtitlan y leyenda de los soles* [Annals of Cuauhtitlan and legend of the suns] (Mexico City: Instituto de Investigaciones Históricas, Universidad Nacional Autónoma de México, 1975); Michel Graulich, *Myths of Ancient Mexico*, Civilization of the American Indian, vol. 222, trans. Bernard R. Ortiz de Montellano and Thelma Ortiz de Montellano (Norman, OK: University of Oklahoma Press, 1997), 63–69.

32 Roman Piña Chan, *Una visión del México prehispánico* [A vision of pre-Hispanic Mexico] (Mexico City: Instituto de Investigaciones Históricas, Universidad Nacional Autónoma de México, 1967), 208.

33 Luigi Gambro, in *Mariology: A Guide for Priests, Deacons, Seminarians, and Consecrated Persons*, ed. Mark Miravelle (Goleta, CA: Seat of Wisdom Books, 2007), 142–45.

34 C. G. Jung, *Symbols of Transformation*, Collected Works of C. G. Jung, vol. 5, 2nd ed. (London: Routledge, 1956), 357, 375.

35 Philip P. Arnold, "Colors," in *Encyclopedia of Religion*, 2nd ed., vol. 9, ed. Lindsay Jones (Detroit, MI: Macmillan Reference USA, 2005), 1860–62, accessed April 1, 2014, Gale Virtual Reference Library (go. galegroup.com/ps/i.do?id=GALE%7CCCX3424500622&v=2.1&u=-carp39441&it=r&p=GVRL&sw=w&asid=f6d7433c8fd202c3f5cedc6e-c854a9ee).

36 Carmen Aguilera, "Of Royal Mantles and Blue Turquoise: The Meaning of the Mexica Emperor's Mantle," *Latin American Antiquity* 8, no. 1 (1997): 3–19, doi:10.2307/971589.

37 Arnold, "Colors."

38 J. E. Cirlot, *A Dictionary of Symbols*, trans. Jack Sage (London: Routledge, 1971), 69ff.

39 Revelation 12.

40 Ronald A. Barnett, "Mesoamerican Religious Concepts: Aztec Symbolism, Part Three," *MexConnect*, March 1, 2008, accessed July 3, 2017, www.mexconnect.com/articles/2895-mesoamerican-religious-concepts-aztec-symbolism-part-three.

41 Enrique Florescano, *Memory, Myth, and Time in Mexico: From the Aztecs to Independence*, trans. Albert G. Bork with the assistance of Kathryn R. Bork (Austin, TX: University of Texas, 1994), 3–9.

42 C. G. Jung, *Psychological Types*, ed. and trans. G. Adler and R. F. C. Hull, Collected Works of C. G. Jung, vol. 6, Bollingen Series (Princeton, NJ: Princeton University Press, 1971), parr. 781.

43 Maria Yellow Horse Brave Heart and Lemyra DeBruyn, "The American Indian Holocaust: Healing Historical Unresolved Grief," *American Indian and Alaska Native Mental Health Research* 8, no. 2 (1998): 56–78; Maria Yellow Horse Brave Heart, Josephine Chase, Jennifer Elkins, and Deborah B. Altschul, "Historical Trauma Among Indigenous Peoples of the Americas: Concepts, Research, and Clinical Considerations," *Journal of Psychoactive Drugs* 43, no. 4 (2011): 282–90, doi: 10.1080/02791072.2011.628913.

44 Brave Heart and DeBruyn, "The American Indian Holocaust;" Brave Heart, Chase, Elkins, and Altschul, "Historical Trauma Among Indigenous Peoples of the Americas."

45 United Nations, Economic and Social Council, Permanent Forum on Indigenous Issues, "Informed Consent Critical to Protecting Survival, Human Rights of Indigenous Peoples, Speakers Tell Permanent Forum," United Nations website, May 1, 2017, accessed May 3, 2017, www.un.org/press/en/2017/hr5356.doc.htm.

46 United Nations, Economic and Social Council, Permanent Forum on Indigenous Issues, "Indigenous Speakers in Permanent Forum Decry Governmental Abuse of Traditional Lands, Natural Resources, Urge Respect for Self-Governing Systems," United Nations website, April 26, 2017, accessed May 3, 2017, www.un.org/press/en/2017/hr5353.doc.htm.

47 Indian Country Media Network staff, "Pope Francis Apologizes to Indigenous Peoples for 'Grave Sins' of Colonialism," *Indian Country Today*, July 10, 2015, accessed February 14, 2016, www.

indiancountrymedianetwork.com/news/indigenous-peoples/
pope-francis-apologizes-to-indigenous-peoples-for-grave-sins-of-colonialism.

48 BBC News, "Mexico Indigenous People: Pope Francis Asks for Forgiveness." BBC News website, February 16, 2016, accessed February 16, 2016, www.bbc.com/news/world-latin-america-35584031.

49 Indian Country Media Network staff, "Pope Francis: Consult Indigenous Peoples," *Indian Country Today*, February 15, 2017, accessed February 20, 2017, www.indiancountrymedianetwork.com/news/indigenous-peoples/
pope-francis-indigenous-lands.

50 Pope Francis, *Encyclical Letter Laudato Si of the Holy Father Francis on Care for our Common Home*, Vatican, May 24, 2015, accessed May 24, 2015, w2.vatican.va/content/francesco/en/encyclicals/documents/papa-francesco_20150524_enciclica-laudato-si.html.

SECTION 2

INQUIRY INTO THE ART
OF EXPERIENCING THE GODDESS

LITHA

She had been climbing, climbing. She
had reached the place beyond which is nothing
but sky and descent.

At the summit, no fanfare, no balloons,
no celebration. One step like all the other
steps, and she was there. One more step,
and the descent would begin.

As she climbed, she did not think of
the summit. She watched her hands, her
feet, her balance, as she rose high,
high, higher.

Suddenly, she had taken the last
upward step.

Do you think she made camp and
slept? Do you think she stopped moving? Do
you think she lives there still, at the height
she sought and won?

No. What would life be without movement,
without struggle? How can a clutched
hand hold freedom?

She stood for a moment, entranced
with the beauty of the world beneath her feet.
Then she took another step.

~ *Patricia Monaghan*

ABUNDANT EMBODIMENT IN AN ANICONIC TRADITION: NATURE, TRANCE AND ART IN YORUBA RELIGIONS

MEI-MEI SANFORD

Dedicated to Akinsola Akiwowo, of blessed memory, and to the Iyalaase Osun of Iragbiji, Osun mi toto.

"If you want to know about Osun, go study fish."
—Osun Priestess Luisah Teish

"It is during the scarcity of water that we seek abundant water."
—Babalawo Professor Akinsola Akiwowo, Ifa divination verse

Introduction

West African Yoruba religions are religions of continual embodiment. The *orisa* deities, female and male, appear to and interact with their devotees through trance, in nature and in ritually prepared images. They speak through the dolls, cowries and palm nuts of diviners and appear in dreams and apparitions. Yet the images of the orisa, with a few specific exceptions, do not portray the deities themselves but rather their devotees in the moment of trance or animal messengers called *iko*. The orisa are visible everywhere—in lightning, water, peacocks and crocodiles, metals and colored cloth, numbers, elderly priestesses and priests, the beautiful or terrible stranger in the market—and yet they are invisible

Fig. 26. The source of the Osun River, Igede, Nigeria. Photograph by Mei Mei Sanford, 1992.

105

in the sense of lacking a consistent identifiable shape (*Figure 26*). The orisa are protean in nature. What is constant is their changing form and continual appearance. Their forms of embodiment are endless. What orisa images make visible is not the likeness of the deity but rather the moment of embodiment itself, the orisa's descent into human being or animal or other elements of the tangible world. In this essay, I examine forms of Yoruba trance, aniconic images of the divine, and iconic exceptions to the rule in traditional Yoruba religions, their diasporic descendent Santería, and a contemporary Yoruba priestly artist's depiction of the goddess Osun.

The Aniconic Tradition in Yoruba Art

The Yoruba of southwestern Nigeria and the Republic of Benin have been urban for more than nine hundred years. They are the creators of a consummate tradition of carving, including *ere*, images made for and about the orisa deities. Yet, with certain exceptions, these images do not depict the deities but rather their priestesses and priests.

Why is this? In an example of a dance wand for the god Sango by carver Lamidi Olonade Fakeye (*Figure 27*), the figure is a priestess of Sango, kneeling in the position of childbirth, opening the conduit to the other world. The shape above her head is the emblem of Sango, twin meteoric stones that carry his presence. The emblem's placement is a clue. The *olorisa* priestesses and priests—the word *olorisa* has no gender in Yoruba and simply means "the ones who 'have' the orisa,"; the orisa, too, are female and male—have their heads prepared when they are initiated, in order to receive their deities in trance. Slits are made in the skin between the forehead and the crown and then substances are introduced to facilitate trance and the entrance of the deity. *Olorisa* enter trance to bring the deities into their communities to teach, heal, admonish, comfort, council and transform.

Fig. 27. Lamidi Olonade Fakeye, *Ose Sango*, wood carving, 1991.

In this carving, ("Ose Sango") the double emblem rests on the kneeling priestess's head. The emblem's position is how we know that she is in trance. Her face is composed in intense concentration. In some carvings, her eyes are open wide; Robert Farris Thompson has suggested that those eyes are pressing outward, pushed outward by the deity's presence.[1] The emblems on the priestess's head have no fixed form, and carvers carve them in many ways: simple lozenges, shapes inscribed with the *gbere* (cheek scarifications indicating the group to which the patron belongs) and even faces or drums. The faces refer to Sango's "children" or followers and to *ibeji* (twins) who are orisa in their own right and under Sango's special protection. The drums depicted are bata drums, which belong to Sango. Only the emblems' doubleness and position signal that they are the twin meteoric thunderstones that rest on the devotee's altar. The carving, then, is not a picture of an orisa but a picture of a moment of trance.

In slavery-era Cuba, Yoruba people encountered Catholicism and created the hybrid religion of Santería (the way of the Saints). Chromolithic images of the saints were matched with orisa with whom they shared characteristics: Osun with *La Caridad del Cobre* (Our Lady of Charity of Copper), because they shared characteristics of water, maternal care and copper, and Sango with Santa Barbara, because they shared lightning, the martial sword, sovereignty and the colors red and white. Notice that quality, not gender, determined the match. Cuban folklorist Lydia Cabrera reported that Afro-Cubans called the *orichas* (the Spanish spelling of *orisa*) *caminos de los negros* (the way of the blacks) and the chromolithic saints *caminos de los blancos* (the way of the whites).[2] Religious studies scholar Joseph Murphy believed that Yoruba in Cuba saw the saints as avatars or embodiments of the *orichas*. More exactly, he stated that Yoruba saw the saints in the chromoliths as white people embodying the *orichas* in moments of trance.[3] Catholic religious images were conceptualized by Yoruba people in the same way they conceptualized their own religious carvings: depicting the protean orisa by depicting their entranced devotees.

Art historian Marilyn Houlberg identified "More is more" (the opposite of the Bauhaus principle of "Less is more") as a central aesthetic principle of the Yoruba.[4] I contend that it also is a central religious principle of the Yoruba. While the world is full of the orisa presence, that presence can always be intensified by the spontaneous actions of the orisa or by ritual. People become more intensely orisa in initiation, in trance, and in the subtle form of trance that infuses priestesses and priests in everyday life. Art, clothing, jewelry, medicines and divining materials are placed on an altar not only to praise the orisa but also to be recharged, to soak up the orisa's potency.[5] The core of the altar—*fundamentos* (foundations) such as Sango's meteoric stones and Osun's river stones—must be periodically refreshed by ritual washing. Even Osun's sweet water, her element, is more potent in some places than in others and can be ritually intensified by offerings, the presence of certain objects, prayer and the deity's spontaneous appearance. Sabine Jell-Bahlsen, in her film *Mammy Water: In Search of the Water Spirits in Nigeria,* presented astounding footage, unique to my knowledge, of a water deity in aquatic form, roiling up the river to receive offerings.[6]

Iko: Messengers of the Orisa

The animals that belong to specific orisa and appear in art dedicated to them are no exception to the rule of intensification. Although some animals are offerings to the deity, many are *iko* (messengers). A friend of mine remembers that her family's compound in Ibadan, Nigeria, of a lineage dedicated to Osun, had crocodiles living in a pit in the center of the courtyard. The crocodiles were carefully tended as embodiments of Osun. Fish belong to Osun, as do ducks, snakes, snails, frogs and other aquatic creatures. This is why Osun Priestess Luisah Teish said, "If you want to know about Osun, go study fish."[7] Yet certain fish, snakes or snails become more Osun when they appear to deliver a gift: They become messengers of the orisa.

The story of the founding of Osogbo, Nigeria, is that Osun made a pact with the first inhabitants, agreeing to be the town's tutelary deity and protect the town forever. As part of the pact, she sent a piscine *iko* every year, during the town festival, to leap from her river to the sovereign's hand and spray him with water infused with her blessing. This act is the core of the sovereignty of the ruler, whose title, Ataoja, means "the one who stretches forth a hand to grasp a fish." People remember witnessing this event as recently as the 1950s, and in 1957 Ulli Beier wrote of it as current practice.[8] The Iyalaase Osun, the senior priestess of Osun in Iragbiji, Nigeria, told me that the *iko* still exists but has hidden itself away because foreigners have tried to steal it.[9] Such stealing can take many forms: religious persecution, wildlife killing and international trade in antiquities.

Human Messengers in Trance

Osun's messengers, animal and human, may be her spontaneous creations, like the apparitions that fill the stories of Osun's devotees: the beautiful woman on a lonely road who gives a gift to a child and then disappears and the woman and child who appear with a message in the waters flooding Ibadan. Or they may be the analog of human trance.

At the time of the creation of the new Osun state, a newspaper article titled "Unbelievable, Osun Comes Out Live, Out of the River and Speaks"[10]

(*Figure 28*) reported that a person who was both a deity who could walk out of the river in dry clothes and a young married woman with a difficult life came to the residents of the new state with a message from Osun. If they behave properly, she said, "I will make this state great."[11] The speech, as recorded, moved back and forth between the divine speaker and the human speaker who inhabited the same physical body. The young woman said that she was delivering a message and praying that Osun would reward her with children and peace with her in-laws, and Osun made a pact with the city. A priestess of the Osogbo city shrine confirmed that the event was an authentic appearance of Osun. As an example of trance,

Fig. 28. Jimmy Babalola and Tunde Bolatiti, "Unbelievable, Oshun Comes Out Live, Out of the River and Speaks," *The People's Voice* (Osogbo, Nigeria), August 29–September 11, 1991. Photograph of the article by Mei-Mei Sanford.

the young woman was both herself and more (Osun) than herself, in a kind of undulating shifting of identities. She was a human *iko*. An *iko* animal messenger, as the fish who jumps into the Ataoja's hand during the Osun festival is itself and more (Osun) than itself: an animal in trance.

Iko in Art

Batik artist and Ogun and Sango priest Adeleke Sangoyoyin has created a series of works called "Blessing from Iko *(Figures 29a and 29b)*." An art movement in Nigeria in the early 1960s, led by Kenneth Murray and Ulli and Georgina Beier, encouraged a generation of painters to paint the life that they saw around them. Their work on ritual subjects resembled their work on other subjects. It was illustrative and physically descriptive. These artists painted people, animals, things and events. The resulting art included snapshots, country scenes, and ethnographic recordings.

In contrast, a metal panel by Osogbo artist Asiru Olatunde achieves a ritual purpose, that of *oriki*. In the panel, an Osun priestess appears in procession, a sovereign makes an offering at the river, drummers drum

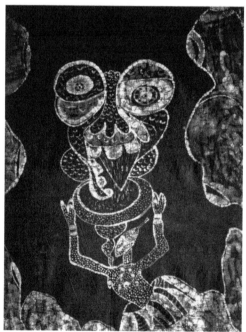

and fish swim nearby. The panel shows images of Osun worship as a visual *oriki*, with the praise poetry enumerating the powers and attributes of the deity. *Oriki*, verbal or visual, simultaneously praises and invokes the deity. The purpose and achievement of *ere*, shrine sculpture, such as Lamidi Olonade Fakeye's "Ose Sango," does this and something more.

The subject is not only the priestess and the shrine objects—in this case, the drum and the doubleness of the meteoric stones and the twins—but also the moment

Fig. 29a. Adeleke Sangoyoyin, *Blessing from Iko I*, batik, n.d. of transformation, trance and embodiment. In Yoruba terms, the *ere* is carved with the *oju inu* (inner eye) as well as the *oju ode* (outer eye). It is concerned with the inner reality as well as the outer reality. The double lozenge on the head of the priestess is an emblem of the deity Sango being connected to the priestess in this moment of trance. The lozenge has no particulars other than its twoness and its placement. That is why carvers carve it, like Sango's embodiments, in a profusion of forms.

Adeleke Sangoyoyin's first "Blessing from Iko" (*Figure 29a*), though created by painting in the medium of batik, is in the tradition of Yoruba shrine sculpture. Painted by a priest, it concerns the moment of trance and embodiment. Painting in Yoruba, especially on the walls of shrines, was traditionally the province of women and priestesses. "Blessings of Iko" is also new and innovative. In Sangoyoyin's batik, embodiment becomes visible. The priestess tilts her head and body in a gesture of trance as she holds a calabash over her head. The *iko*—a crocodile or perhaps a serpent—rises from behind the priestess, perhaps from her own body, to spit water of blessing into the calabash. The priestess has ritually prepared herself with medicines beneath a molded indigo protrusion of hair, with brass bracelets on her arms and the brass insignia of the society of elders and the Earth hanging from her neck. The figure is surrounded by the great granite outcroppings of the artist's own landscape, rounded like breasts and pregnant bellies.

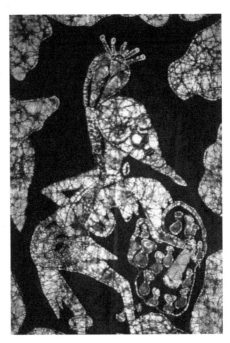

The moment shown in the second "Blessing from Iko" (*Figure 29b*) is similar. This time, red color indicates the elements of particular *ase* (potency), Osun's most intense embodiment. We can see that the *iko*, shown in the strongest red, begins as a spiral in the priestess's groin, moves up her spinal column, and then, with a face that may be

Fig. 29b. Adeleke Sangoyoyin, *Blessing from Iko II*, batik, n.d.

a duck's or a serpent's—with the crowning horns of a snail or five (Osun's number) red parrot feathers—gazes over her head. Her mouth is red, with Osun's incantations on her tongue, as is her beard, a sign not of gender but of age and otherworldly potency. Her brass anklets, *jinwinjinwin*, are red, as are her fingertips. Tiny red gourds of medicine surround the water container she holds, infusing it with Osun's potency.

In both batiks, Sangoyoyin innovated to make the moment of epiphany more visible. He linked animal and human messenger, even showing *iko* rising out of the priestess's body. As in the *ere*, the focus is on the moment of embodiment, not the face of the deity. Both the *ere* Sango and the batiks show us two actors: thunderstones and priestess or *iko* and priestess. Sangoyoyin shows us a third embodiment as well: the gift of blessed water. The deity is either multiply manifested or invisible, jumping like a spark between poles of divine current.

Exceptions to the Rule:
Intermediaries, Ancestors and Twin Spirits

There are some exceptions to the rule that *ere* do not depict the Orisa: the orisa Esu, ancestors and the *ibeji*. These three have in common that they are messengers, infinitely multiple, and close to the individual and the family. The orisa Esu is the messenger and connector between human beings and the other orisa. It is also said that every orisa has his or her own *esu* to communicate with devotees. Some even say that each human being has his or her own *esu*.[12]

In Yoruba thought, ancestors have continuing interest in the affairs of the living, sending messages and gifts from the other world. We, their descendants, have some of their selves (*ori*) in us, and that is why, even from infancy, we behave like them. *Egungun*, the ancestor masquerades of individual lineages, are a way in which ancestors council and protect their children. The masquerades are distinct, individual and built up from layer upon layer of cloth. Their appearance is a spectacle. Women of the family dance in their honor. Rowland Abiodun identifies the face on the Ifa divination tray as Esu, while *babalawo* (diviner) and scholar Akinsola Akiwowo says that it is the ancestor Ajagumale, a chief diviner from ancient times who continues to give assistance to diviners.[13] The face on a crown is the ancestor of the lineage of the monarch's royal family.

Finally, *ibeji* are carvings meant to house the spirits of twins who have died, so that they can continue to be honored by the family with food, clothing and dancing. The Yoruba have the world's highest birth rate of twins. Their traditional belief is that every human being has a twin in the other world. When twins are born, the otherworldly one comes through into this world. If one or both of the twins dies, the links—both otherworldly and familial—are nurtured carefully. As family members, parts of the self and messengers from the other world, all of these divine beings are close, familiar and easily encountered, imagined and depicted.

Conclusion: Reverberations

In contrast, the variety of the modes in which most orisa appear to us is more vast. Their appearance can be human, animal, geographical, elemental, meteorological, numerical, chromatic, temperamental or gastronomical. The orisa are present, every day, in profusion. Walt Whitman could have been describing them when he wrote the following:

> Why should I wish to see God better than this day?
>
> I see something of God each hour of the twenty-four, and each moment then,
>
> In the faces of men and women I see God, and in my own face in the glass,
>
> I find letters from God dropped in the street, and every one is signed by God's name,
>
> And I leave them where they are, for I know that others will punctually come forever and ever.[14]

With so many reverberations of the orisa, how could we fix on one?

My last argument for multiple embodiment of orisa is personal testimony. I have visited and lived in Nigeria off and on for twenty-five years. Iragbiji is my hometown. I have been a priestess of Osun for twenty-two years. when I think of the face of Osun, I see the Iyalaase Osun, my ritual mother who initiated me (*Figure 30*). Or the Jagun Osun okunrin, the Osun priest who also initiated me. Or the Osun priest who invited me into his home with great kindness, gave me the first new yam of the season and showed me his new kitten. When I knelt at his shrine, I felt a little warm weight against my leg, and there was a kitten, curled up asleep on the edge of my wrapper. Or the woman in a Nigerian church, who danced with me, fed me and looked after me during service one afternoon. Or a woman in a New York subway, wearing a gold sequined cap and an amorous smile. Or a samba dancer, dressed in copper and surrounded by Bahianas on the streets on New York City's East Village. I also see sunlight on water, taste honey and remember a golden orb spider on my porch.

Fig. 30. Iyalaase Osun of Iragbiji, Nigeria. Photograph by Mei Mei Sanford, 1992.

My mother heard Osun laugh once, in a dream. It was a deep rich laugh, she said, and then she heard Osun say, "Honey, don't you know I've been with you all your life?" In a film about South American religions, called *The Southern Cross*, a Brazilian priestess of Osun was interviewed. She said, "In so many religions, people are waiting for God to come. We're not waiting for anybody. Everyone is already here!"[15]

References:

Abiodun, Rowland. "Ifa Art Objects: An Interpretation Based on Oral Traditions." In *Yoruba Oral Tradition: Poetry in Music, Dance and Drama*, edited by Wande Abimbola, 421–69. Ile-Ife, Nigeria: University of Ife, 1975.

Babalola, Jimmy, and Tunde Bolatiti. "Unbelievable: Osun Came Out Live, Out of the River, and Speaks." *The People's Voice* (Osogbo, Nigeria), August 29–September 11, 1991.

Beier, Ulli. "Osun Festival." *Nigeria Magazine* 53 (1957): 170–87.

Guzman, Patricio. *La cruz del sur* [*The Southern Cross*]. Directed by Patricio Guzman. Spain: Quasar Films and Radio Televisión Española, 1991.

Jell-Bahlsen, Sabine. *Mammy Water: In Search of the Water Spirits in Nigeria*. Directed by Sabine Jell-Bahlsen. New York: Ogbuide Films, 1989. Available from University of California Extension Media Center, Berkeley, CA, catalog no. 38097, VHS.

Murphy, Joseph M. *Santeria: African Spirits in America*. Boston: Beacon, 1988, 1993.

Sanford, Mei-Mei. "Powerful Water, Living Wood: The Agency of Art and Nature in Yoruba Ritual." PhD diss., Drew University, 1997.

Thompson, Robert Farris. *Flash of the Spirit: African and Afro-American Art and Philosophy*. New York: Random House, 1983.

Whitman, Walt. *The Portable Walt Whitman*. Edited by Mark Van Doren. New York: Viking, 1974.

Endnotes

1 Robert Farris Thompson, *Flash of the Spirit: African and Afro-American Art and Philosophy* (New York: Random House, 1983), 87.

2 Joseph M. Murphy, *Santeria: African Spirits in America* (Boston: Beacon, 1988, 1993), 124.

3 Murphy, *Santeria*, 121.

4 Marilyn Houlberg, personal communication to the author.

5 Rowland Abiodun, "Ifa Art Objects: An Interpretation Based on Oral Traditions," in *Yoruba Oral Tradition: Poetry in Music, Dance and Drama*, ed. Wande Abimbola (Ile-Ife, Nigeria: University of Ife, 1975), 421–69.

6 Sabine Jell-Bahlsen, *Mammy Water: In Search of the Water Spirits in Nigeria*, directed by Sabine Jell-Bahlsen (New York: Ogbuide Films, 1989), available from University of California Extension Media Center, Berkeley, CA, catalog no. 38097, VHS.

7 Luisah Teish, personal communication to the author.

8 Ulli Beier, "Oshun Festival," *Nigeria Magazine* 53 (1957): 187.

9 Mei-Mei Sanford, "Powerful Water, Living Wood: The Agency of Art and Nature in Yoruba Ritual" (PhD dissertation, Drew University, 1997), 197.

10 Jimmy Babalola and Tunde Bolatiti, "Unbelievable: Osun Came Out Live, Out of the River, and Speaks," *The People's Voice* (Osogbo, Nigeria), August 29–September 11, 1991.

11 Babalola and Bolatiti, "Unbelievable."

12 Sanford, "Powerful Water, Living Wood," 130.

13 Akinsola Akiwowo, personal communication to the author.

14 Walt Whitman, "Song of Myself," in *The Portable Walt Whitman*, ed. Mark Van Doren (New York: Viking, 1974), stanza 48.

15 Patricio Guzman, *La cruz del sur* [*The Southern Cross*], directed by Patricio Guzman (Spain: Quasar Films and Radio Televisión Española, 1991).

SANCTUARY: FEMININE CENTERED DWELLINGS AS AREAS OF SACRED PROTECTION

TONI TRUESDALE

Fig. 31. Toni Truesdale, *Grandmother's House*, acrylic painting, 2012.

Historically, the homes of women are spiritual places of prayer, safety and sustenance. The female-centered house, with the kitchen as the apex of feminine activity, has always held sacred symbology.

Throughout time, women's altars within the house, often set inside the kitchen, reflect a relationship to the ancestors, protective spirits, saints and household deities. From generation to generation, women's hands have carefully chosen material images and made offerings. They continue to pass on these traditions, within households, from mother to daughter, for all mothers are the first teachers of culture, language and tradition. And these simple practices of honoring link us not only to our maternal ancestors but also to one another as women across human migrations, into all civilizations and through

116

time itself, creating a common culture of women. Because I am an artist, my honoring takes the form of sharing my own paintings (*Figures 31-42*) and words that explore these sacred, female-centered spaces.[1]

> *The culture of women exists with each prayer; centered*
> *in the hearth with our daily bread.*

> *The family is sheltered within the home, protected with*
> *feminine presences,*

> *Shrines to ancestors, and beautifully evolving altars*
> *evoke the art of the household.*[2]

Embellishments to altars can take on many forms: flowers, candles, votives, food, figures, seashells, seasonal representations, small, meaningful objects and photos of loved ones. All are symbolic gestures that show thought, emotion and devotion. In this way, the home can become a shrine in itself, filled with sacred objects and offered prayers that transcend the mundane. Some indigenous households, as well as contemporary Western households, make use of symbolic art forms as visual spiritual practice. Women of all cultures appear to share a love of the beauty that emerges in the preparation and presentation of food, as well as hospitality, decoration and festive adornments. Everyday life is celebrated in what is still the domain of women. This is the legacy of the hearth, the central fire, the altar within the home.

The hearth, fire, food and altars are metaphorical examples of the importance that women have placed on their daily life-sustaining routines. According to Jungian Erich Neumann, even the village is a symbol of the feminine "natural nourishing principle," for "great round" is the center of the circle of life that is dominated with female mysteries.[3] The hearth, signifying warmth, food and love, is the original altar. Here too we find the timeless practice of sacred protection and invocation.

Fig. 32. Toni Truesdale, *House Shrine*, oil painting, 2012.

The construction of a house can be undertaken with intentional consciousness. This intent is reflected in the dwellings of matrilineal cultures, such as the Diné (Navajo) hogan, which is dedicated to the four directions, and the structure by the Turkanoans of Columbia that evokes the very cosmos itself.[4] The structures of the Dogon people of West Africa inspired architect Aldo van Eyck in his search for sacred architecture. Meaningful even to the smallest item, an object has the potential to transform the mundane into spiritual connections.[5]

Fig. 33. Toni Truesdale, *Basket-House-Village-Universe*, acrylic painting, 2013.

Baskets of women
Reflect nourishment
Physical as well as spiritual
Object to concept
Keeping sacred the spirit of everyday life;

Within the home
Utilitarian to universal
Dwelling to village
Community to cosmos
Each human passage
Through 140 thousand years...

Birth to death
The finite to consummation
End to beginning. . .[6]

We can draw a timeline of women's practices across millennia, beginning with ancient Canaanite rites approximately 8,000 years ago in the Middle East and crossing those years and many continents to modern multicultural traditions. The seeds of female folk religion—or house religion, as it is sometimes called by academics—connect diverse women in the act of creating sacred spaces for the same essential purpose. That purpose is protection against all that would harm their children and loved ones. "They placed figurines that represented and invoked protective deities in front kitchens or courtyards near doorways that provided access to the roof and interior living and work areas."[7]

Archeology has uncovered evidence to support a devotional purpose for the kitchens and households of ancient women. Various cultures had similar practices; in both Çatal Hüyük and Crete, the feminine sphere was exalted with the use of protective goddesses. But in early Palestine the finds are quite stunning. Evidence has been discovered of Israelite households, as early as the 8th century BCE, worshipping with the forms of votive candles, small female figures, incense and lamps juxtaposed with looms, needles vessels and bowls in situ with feminine implements.[8] Alongside cooking bowls found in domestic cult rooms, amulets were discovered that depict objects of devotion. Prayer was probably invoked on a daily basis to combat the many uncertainties of life, as demonstrated in this prayer to Ishtar.

Fig. 34. Toni Truesdale, *Ancient Kitchen*, watercolor painting, 2017

Fig. 35. Toni Truesdale, *Clay Prayers*, watercolor painting, 2017.

Oh, Ishtar, merciful Goddess, I have come to visit you,
I have prepared for you an Offering: pure milk,
A Cake baked in ashes,
I stood up for you a vessel for libations,
Hear me and act favorably towards me.[9]

In *Did God Have A Wife? Archaeology and Folk Religion in Ancient Israel*, William G. Dever wrote about the overwhelming archaeological evidence that the worship of Asherah—probably connected to the archaic goddesses Ishtar, Hathor and Astarte—in ancient Israel continued well into patriarchal religions and beyond.

Some of the historical household goddesses invoked by women are well known through written myth and oral tradition: Greek Hestia of the hearth, sacred fire and home; Roman counterpart Vesta (virtually every home contained a statute of her sacred central fire, which was never to be extinguished); Ishtar of the ancient Middle East; Asherah of Israel; Celtic Morrigan, in one of her many aspects; Callileach of the pre-Celtic United Kingdom; Pachamama of Central America; Arani, Hindu goddess of the hearth; Ayaba of the African Fon; Brigid of the sacred fire (both Celtic and Catholic traditions); Esta, the Etruscan goddess of the household; Huchi of the hearth, in the cosmology of the indigenous Ainu of Japan; and many, many more across the continents. These goddesses are various representations of the eternal fire, the hearth, the sacred center in the feminine divine.[10]

Fig. 36. Toni Truesdale, *Callileach*, oil painting, 2013.

Early Christianity, too, harbored the divine feminine; the church went through many changes before finally sublimating womanhood into the symbolic wisdom of Sophia. To further that end, the medieval Christian church began a feminization of the Christ figure to include the sphere of the household, most notably, intellectually and aesthetically, in the mystical works of Hildegard of Bingen, Julian of Norwich and Bernard of Clairvaux. Christ symbolically became the house of God, which Christians entered through the metaphorical door of his wound. The body of Christ became the church. Christ gave the milk of nourishment.[11] Healing and miracles were attributed

Fig. 37. Toni Truesdale, *Sacred Writing*, oil painting, 1996.

to holy shrines and reliquaries; 6th century work about the life of Saint Symeon the Stylite, the younger, refers to a woman who set up an image of him, in her house, that worked miracles, including curing people of diseases.[12]

In the many traditions of household, women have invoked practices of blessings that create and permeate sacred spaces. They rely on the help of guardians in the form of icons, to invoke ancestors, deities and saints, in performing heritage rites of protection for both their loved ones within the home and those who are crossing into the outer, more dangerous world. These practices of prayer span virtually every race and era. This commonality is part of the culture of women that has always existed secretly but in sight, and, in many instances, separate from male-dominated society and religion.

Little Blessings

Each and every daybreak;
We ask the spirits to watch over us
As we go about a busy day.
For our children to be well,
Healthy and thrive;
And our loved ones;
Sometimes far away,
To be protected please.
And for angels to smile upon this beautiful day,
We ask for our
Little Blessings.[13]

The formal, institutional religions of the patriarchs build huge fixed structures that are ordered, authoritarian and static and that rise high to proclaim dominance. Through these structures they claim to be the gatekeepers of knowledge, social mores, aesthetics, history and the very structure of the world.

Yet women have enshrined their homes, gardens and nature with icons and offerings to a spirit world that evoke prayers of peace, health and safety for family, community and even the world through the entire history of organized religions. For each household embellishment has an iconic value that flows and changes with seasons, passages and feasts. Even the daily bread has an intrinsic value created with love served with beauty. Textiles are created to reflect sacred images passing through each generation,

Connected by the hands of women;

Stories are told, language and traditions are learned, songs are sung in celebration of

The mythologies of imagery that encircle loved ones and celebrate ancestry.

In commonality, all women have brought comfort within the loving walls

That holds who is dear. To nourish with food, warm by fire, and clothe in our handmade legacy.

Each day is a sacred exercise in timeless feminine spirituality.[14]

Both Westernized and indigenous cultures hold the seeds of original civilizations within the rites of women in the household. Multiple sources refer to traditions associated with the sacredness of the home. For the N'Debele of South Africa, decorative elements inside the house and external murals both represent abstractions of the natural world. The Basotho, also of South Africa, have constructed their homes with beautiful paintings rich with vivid designs that reflect the vegetal world and natural environment as well as the cosmos. According to Roann Barris, "the Basotho house becomes the womb; the Basotho woman becomes the house."[15]

Fig. 38. Toni Truesdale, *Daily Bread*, oil painting, 2012.

"Within those interior house spaces, ceremonial healings also happen. All houses are healed periodically and fed cornmeal. Traditionally, some burials occurred in the floor of the houses. Houses are deemed to be alive and have energies which can bring harmony if recognized and treated with proper respect."[16]

In her signature work *From the Milk River: Spatial and Temporal Processes in Northwest Amazonia*, Christine Hugh-Jones wrote, "They construct their houses to represent the universe" and this "universe is a womb."[17] Kay Turner, in *Beautiful Necessity*, emphasized that a modern woman's altar is "a different altar, one that is not male-dominated or dogma-bound. It is an intimate altar, a home altar, made by a woman and dedicated for her own personal devotion to the deities she chooses."[18] She went on to explain that "cultures of the Goddess and her domestic altars were transformed and diminished but never fully obliterated."[19]

Fig. 39. Toni Truesdale, *N'Debele Woman*, gouache painting, 2015.

In *Face of the Gods*, Robert Farris Thompson documented altars of the African diaspora that link West African traditions, which survived slavery, to the modern trans-Atlantic world.[20] In "The Matrifocal Household: Santeria Religious Practice and Gender Relations Explored," Carin Tunaker wrote about Hispanic house traditions of "the Mother as giver of food (and, symbolically, the giver of life)," quoting Stener Ekern: This not only locates the mother (or women) at the center of the household but also "epitomizes how life in Nicaragua's barrios revolve around this institution . . . the household is where the stream starts, is sustained and also eventually ends."[21]

Women's rituals in the home have remained constant even under the most repressive of cultures, where inside the house may be compromised. Dever wrote about Muslim households today that re-create ritual outside the house: "Located in external sacred spaces, meetings of women and children join together in 'joyful' gatherings with food and music away from Muslim orthodoxy."[22]

Women have always found ways to rejoice in time-honored feminine rites. From the table decorated with flowers and candles to the photos of loved ones set beside memorabilia, feminine values are celebrated outside the sanctified church.

Fig. 40. Toni Truesdale, *The Culture of Women*, oil painting, 2013.

Fig. 41. Toni Truesdale, *Feast Day*, gouache painting, 2012.

Fig. 42. Toni Truesdale, *The Return*, oil painting, 2013.

Dever described how archeology has brought to light "folk religion," which is feminine, fluid and personal, as opposed to "book religion," which fixed, literal and authoritarian.[23] We can see now the unbroken chain of the simple, everyday practices of women. We can call them sacred acts that still take place in the sanctuary of women-centered dwellings all over the world.

House Shrines, Feminine Spaces and Women's Altars

The body of the home is a woman;
Within, we build shrines to our family and ancestors decorating
Constantly changing altars; in the act of sanctifying.
Archaic houses too contained
The arts of women.
Stones, shells, bones, votives and clay goddesses were
Placed for prosperity, health and protection;
Evolving into dwellings with flowers, candles and
Photos of loved ones with small objects;
Images to keep, memories to honor;
Purposely and unconsciously evoking
Female divinity honoring spiritual bridges to
Peace, hearth and womb, with neither beginning nor end.
Nourishment is at the eternal center of the house;
Sustenance from the body or hands of mother and wife.
Clothing and utensils lovingly crafted or chosen
for their beauty;
With archetypal images passed through the generations
To connect genetically to our primordial Mother.
As we continue women's prayers to our children,
In every culture, on all days, in so many ways.[24]

References

Ahituv, Shmuel. "Did God Really Have a Wife?" *Biblical Archaeology Review*, Sept/Oct 2006.

Barris, Roann. "Metaphors and Meanings of House: African Painted House Traditions," Eastern Illinois University, February 15, 2004. Accessed November 25, 2008. www.ux1.eiu.edu/-rbarris/paintedhouses.htm.

Bledsoe, Jenny. "Feminine Images of Jesus: Later Medieval Christology and the Devaluation of the Feminine." *Intermountain West Journal of Religious Studies* 3, no. 1 (2011). Accessed March 15, 2016. http://digitalcommons.usu.edu/imwjournal/vol3/iss1/4.

Dever, William G. *Did God Have a Wife? Archaeology and Folk Religion in Ancient Israel*. Grand Rapids, MI and Cambridge, UK: Eerdmans, 2008.

Ekern, Stener. *Street Power: Culture and Politics in a Nicaraguan Neighborhood.* Bergen, Norway: Norse, 1998.

Heathcote, Edwin. "Home Is Where the Heart Is." *Financial Times,* January 30, 2009.

Hugh-Jones, Christine. *From the Milk River: Spatial and Temporal Processes in Northwest Amazonia.* Cambridge Studies in Social and Cultural Anthropology, no. 26. First paperback edition. Cambridge, UK: Cambridge University Press, 1988.

Killebrew, Ann, and Steven Fine. "Qatzrin: Reconstructing Village Life in Talmudic Times." *Biblical Archaeology Review* 17, no. 3 (May/June 1991).

Lent, Rev. Frederick. *Journal of Oriental Society* (New Haven, CT) 35 (1915). Translation of Syrian text "The Life of Simeon Stylites," in *Bedjan Acta Martyrum et Sanctum,* vol. IV. Accessed August 14, 2017. www.tertullian.org/fathers/simeon_stylites_vita_00_intro.htmjan.

MacMorrigan, Wade. "Hearth Goddesses," Accessed December 30, 2015, www.merciangathering.com/silverwheel/hearth_goddesses.htm.

Naranjo, Tito, and Rina Swentzell. "Healing Spaces in the Tewa World." *American Indian Culture and Research Journal* 13, nos. 3 and 4 (1989), 257–65.

Neumann, Erich. *The Great Mother: An Analysis of the Archetype.* 2nd ed. Princeton, NJ: Princeton University Press, 1974.

Oliver, Paul. *Dwellings: The House Across the World.* University of Texas Press edition. Austin, TX: University of Texas Press, 1987.

Rogers, Eugene F. *After the Spirit: A Constructive Pneumatology from Resources Outside the Modern World.* Radical Traditions. Grand Rapids, MI and Cambridge, UK: Eerdmans, 2005.

Thompson, Robert Farris. *Face of the Gods: Art and Altars of Africa and the African Americas.* African Art. New York: Prestel, 1993.

Tunaker, Carin. "The Matrifocal Household: Santeria Religious Practice and Gender Relations Explored." *Graduate Journal of Social Sciences 8,* no. 2 (2011).

Turner, Kay. *Beautiful Necessity: The Art and Meaning of Women's Altars,* New York: Thames & Hudson, 1999.

Willett, Elizabeth. "Women and House Religion." The Bible and Interpretation website, 2001. Accessed April 17, 2007. www.bibleintrep.com/articles/Housereligions.shtml.

Endnotes

1 All poems by the author have been published on Tonitruesdale.blogspot.com

2 T. Truesdale, "The Culture of Women."

3 Erich Neumann, *The Great Mother: An Analysis of the Archetype*, 2nd ed. (Princeton, NJ: Princeton University Press, 1974), 283.

4 Paul Oliver, *Dwellings: The House Across the World*, University of Texas Press edition (Austin, TX: University of Texas Press, 1987), 158–60.

5 There are many resources about the groundbreaking architect Aldo van Eyck, but Edwin Heathcote's summary is particularly well stated: "At one time, objects defined us far more clearly. Every 'thing' had a purpose and its centrality to the rituals of everyday life made it a vessel for containing meaning. Architect Aldo van Eyck once described the phenomenon of 'basket-house-village-universe,' in which everything, even the smallest receptacle, expresses ideas about our being in the world, our picture of the cosmos. Now we have so much more 'stuff' and so many technological devices for which no deeper cultural language of meaning has developed, that the individual items have lost their symbolic potency. This makes the image of the house even more important." See Edwin Heathcote, "Home Is Where the Heart Is," *Financial Times*, January 30, 2009.

6 Toni Truesdale, "Basket-House-Village-Universe."

7 Elizabeth Willett, "Women and House Religion," The Bible and Interpretation website, 2001, accessed April 17, 2007, www.bibleintrep.com/articles/Housereligions.shtml.

8 Ann Killebrew and Steven Fine, "Qatzrin: Reconstructing Village Life in Talmudic Times," *Biblical Archaeology Review* 17, no. 3 (May/June 1991).

9 Mesopotamian text quoted in William G. Dever, *Did God Have a Wife? Archaeology and Folk Religion in Ancient Israel* (Grand Rapids, MI and Cambridge, UK: Eerdmans, 2008), 238.

10 Wade MacMorrigan, "Hearth Goddesses," December 30, 2015, www.merciangathering.com/silverwheel/hearth_goddesses.htm.

11 Eugene F. Rogers, *After The Spirit: A Constructive Pneumatology from Resources Outside the Modern World*, Radical Traditions (Grand Rapids, MI and Cambridge, UK: Eerdmans, 2005), 124.

12 Rev. Frederick Lent, *Journal of Oriental Society* (New Haven, CT) 35 (1915), translation of Syrian text "The Life of Simeon Stylites," in *Bedjan Acta Martyrum et Sanctum*, vol. IV, accessed August 14, 2017, www.tertullian.org/

fathers/simeon_stylites_vita_00_intro.htmjan. The archaic Syrian text is in an exhibit at the Metropolitan Museum of Art in New York, metmuseum.org/exhibitlistings/2012/byzantium-and-islam/blog/charactors/posts/symeon.

13 Toni Truesdale, "Little Blessings."

14 Truesdale, "The Culture of Women."

15 Roann Barris, "Metaphors and Meanings of House: African Painted House Traditions," Eastern Illinois University, February 15, 2004, 13, accessed November 25, 2008, www.ux1.eiu.edu/~rbarris/paintedhouses.htm.

16 In this statement, Santa Clara Pueblo architect Rina Swentzell was referring to the adobe dwellings that are often many generations old. See Tito Naranjo and Rina Swentzell, "Healing Spaces in the Tewa World," *American Indian Culture and Research Journal* 13, nos. 3 and 4 (1989): 264.

17 Christine Hugh-Jones, *From the Milk River: Spatial and Temporal Processes in Northwest Amazonia*, Cambridge Studies in Social and Cultural Anthropology, no. 26, first paperback ed. (Cambridge, UK: Cambridge University Press, 1988), 325.

18 Kay Turner, *Beautiful Necessity: The Art and Meaning of Women's Altars* (New York: Thames & Hudson, 1999), 7.

19 Turner, *Beautiful Necessity*, 14.

20 Robert Farris Thompson, *Face of the Gods: Art and Altars of Africa and the African Americas*, African Art (New York: Prestel, 1993).

21 Tunaker, Carin, "The Matrifocal Household; Santeria Religious Practice and Gender Relations Explored.", Graduate Journal of Social Sciences, 8, no. 2 (Oct. 2011)

22 Dever, *Did God Have a Wife?*, 245.

23 Dever, *Did God Have a Wife?*, 314.

24 Toni Truesdale, "House Shrines, Feminine Spaces and Women's Altars."

DREAMS OF EARTH: MYTH AND PLANETARY PRESENCE WHILE CONVENING A VIRTUAL HYGEIAN DREAM TEMPLE

Marna Hauk

In ancient Greece, Hygeian dream temples were alternate medicine centers, retreat spaces in natural settings where those seeking healing meditated and made sacred contact with earth to incubate healing dreams. A current-day researcher convened two dozen participants to incubate dreams for earth healing in a virtual Hygeian dream temple. Sparked by the desire to directly interview the earth, this research extended women's dream research infused with Gaian and arts methods to explore diverse modes of co-evolutionary contact with the numinous. The depth dimension of international dreamers birthed more than eighty earth dreams, constellating into themes such as the living land, matriarchy, interspecies collaboration, earth superpowers, and disaster and sanctuary. Muddying the question of whether the dreams surfaced from individual women, emergent dreamtime collectives, and/or from the planetary supersystem, the pathways of these dream pilgrimages suggest effective practices for much-needed presence, healing and regeneration.

The Matrix of Earth Dreaming: A Theoretical Convergence

The planetary living system is in a time of healing and regeneration. Some imagine a resurgence of the matrix cultures or mother cultures as a remedy to deepen humans' relationship within the collaborative matrix of place. Bracha Ettinger's work on the matrixial borderland[1] focused on the co-being of the fetus with the pregnant mother as an alternate model of co-presencing. Carol Flinders imagined matrix cultures as cultures of belonging: woven within, embedded and generative.[2] Evolutionary microbiologist Lynn Margulis studied the collaborative nature of evolution articulated as a "symbiotic planet."[3] Marija Gimbutas emphasized the third core role of the Goddess of Old Europe as not only life-giving and death-bringing but also "transformational...self-renewing...regeneration," immanent and physically manifest as nature itself.[4] My research extends matrixial theory and culture, mythopoetic regenerative earth cultures and planetary symbiotic evolution to theorize humans as matrixially implicated and co-presencing within place, ecosystem and planet. Movements toward Gaia theory,[5] naturecultures,[6] relational reality,[7] and the Ecozoic era[8] offer alternate paths through an age of domination, patriarchal cultural threats and industrial-caused challenges to global living systems. My intention in this study[9] was to make use of the patterns of these ancient dream healing practices combined with shared and social dreaming methods to serve as a way of interviewing women and the Earth system directly and collectively to actively foster and participate in Earth's regeneration.

Herstorical Precedents: Dream Healing

In ancient Greece, Hygeian dream temples were alternative medicine centers, retreat spaces in natural settings where those who were seeking healing meditated and made sacred contact with earth to incubate healing dreams. This study arose from dream healing practices and traditions from deep history, including the Hygeian and Asklepian traditions of earth dream healing. In these healing traditions, querents meditated in nature healing sanctuaries and contemplatively entered a space carved into the earth. There they incubated healing dreams that were understood to come directly from the earth and could include what today would be considered spontaneous healings or guidance on curative regimens.[10] The rituals around incubating such a healing dream included rest, meditation, preparation and the feeding of honey cakes to nonvenomous tree snakes before descending into the earthen spaces within the dreaming temple to incubate the dream. Often the dreams themselves were curative via the appearance of a healing deity and direct healing occurring during the dreamtime. At other times, dreams offered prescriptions or regimens for cures. Upon waking, the dreamer shared the dream with a temple scribe, who inscribed the dream on a clay tablet. These clay tablets were then placed on the walls of the healing sanctuary.[11]

Imaginally, Asclepius held a staff on which snakes twined, with the snakes symbolizing closeness to the earth and healing. This is the image from which the caduceus, the symbol of modern medicine, originates. Hygeia, the goddess of healing and Asclepius's daughter, needed no mediation through a staff; instead, the snakes coil directly around her healing body.[12] Snakes are particularly potentized as symbols of healing. Gimbutas described the "dynamic energy of the snake as a symbol of regeneration . . . exud[ing] regenerative force."[13] These dream-healing practices have precedents in the practices of Egyptian curative dream healing,[14] and they correlate with other cultural traditions, including indigenous, earth-based and Chinese, Islamic, Indian, Japanese and Hebrew cultural traditions.[15]

Planetary Dreaming

The design of this study was to extend this inspiration from the ancients and mix it with the praxis of modern earth dreaming, which attends to planetary healing and regeneration, to create a shared earth dreaming temple with a virtual repository for the dream scribings. Current-day conceptualizers of earth dreaming include depth ecotherapists such as Meredith Sabini,[16] Karen Jaenke[17] and Laura Schneider,[18] who mix social dreaming approaches, connections with planetary presence, plunges into the depths of ecotherapeutic connection and the cultivation of earth dreams as a way in which the earth and other species may be cultivating bidirectional communication, expression and healing. Also incorporated are healing dream approaches, such as those suggested by Marc Barasch.[19]

For example, Sabini's approach to earth dreaming is applied, immersive, embodied, multidisciplinary, arts-based, evolutionary and depth-oriented. She viewed the earth and dreaming as "universally available source[s] of guidance"[20] and argued that "dreaming itself is a natural resource, abundant and self-renewing."[21] She described dreaming as "a 140-million-year-old survival function in all mammals" and dreams related to the earth as reaching a planetary presence, including "a nature god, the Great Mother, on whose body we are mere dots," and she has reminded us that "the life force extends beyond our species' reach."[22] Sabini's Dream Institute offers monthly programs "in which dreams are explored for their larger sociocultural implications rather than for their personal meaning to the dreamer,"[23] which she has connected with the social dreaming work of W. Gordon Lawrence (in the '80s, at the Tavistock Institute).[24] She imagines that these kinds of dreams and the intercultural, artistic relationship and re-ritualizing of them will help to "restore the living connection between spirit and matter."[25]

Karen Jaenke suggested that "impending environmental collapse presents humanity with the necessity of a collective initiation, along with renewal of ways of knowing and being more attuned to nature, the earth, the body, matter and the deep feminine."[26] She contended that connection with dreams and embodiment can increase connection and respect for the earth:

> Cultivating respect for the natural mind present in the dreaming self and for the sensitivities and intelligence suffused within the body offers a doorway into renewed respect for the earth body.[27]

Jaenke further suggested that earth dreaming can be curative: "We must plummet the depths of our psyches in order to heal the human–earth split, outwardly manifested as our ecological crisis."[28] She also offered earth dreaming as reconnective, a gateway to "reconnect to our essential relatedness," because dreams "pull back the veil, revealing the hidden energies into which our lives are cast . . . transport[ing] us into this seamless fabric of being."[29] She went further, saying that "dreams labor to heal the fragmented breaks with our relationships with our deep nature . . . and the entire web of earthly life." Jaenke viewed earth dreaming as reconnective and revelatory, mending the web of life.

She identified several kinds of earth dreams and pointed out how earth dreaming can be restorative and catalytic: "earth communing dreams also inspire and enliven, bestowing infusions of numinous psychic energy."[30] Earth dreams can further nurture parts of ourselves that have lacked mothering and reconnect us to place and earth: "Mirroring, mothering, and mending the isolated and wounded soul, earth communing dreams generate in the dreamer deep feelings of kinship between person and place."[31] Earth dreams give energy and lead to "the recovery of psychic kinship with the earth . . . bath[ing] the dreamer in the same bath of animating energy that washes over the planet."[32] Earth dreams not only increase the aliveness and animation of being in the presence of elemental forces (such as those in earth destruction dreams), but also psychically open humans to "the vital guidance from beyond the life-and-death moment,"[33] cultivate reverence, connection and respect and heal humans' relationship with the living earth. Schneider[34] echoed these insights, particularly the cross-species possibilities, in her scholarship on ecodreaming.

Methods

This study has leveraged the extensive insight and depth/ecotherapeutic earth dreaming research of Sabini, Jaenke and Schneider; studies by the leading researchers of women's dreaming, Patricia Garfield,[35] Connie Kaplan[36] and Karen Signell;[37] and the dreaming practices of many wisdom and indigenous cultures (for example, the Senoi[38]). I positioned this inquiry as an extension of my previous work in practical methods for cultivating earth empathy.[39] At the beginning of this study, a participant shared an earth dream that captured the possibility to articulate what I have termed Earthvox, the prophetic, polyvocal voice of the planetary system:

> When I first heard about this project, I had a dream about a standing stone which wanted to speak. Next to the stone was a room-sized depression in the grass, which began to form a sort of spiral, then it changed into a vulva-like opening . . . with a stairway going down. Voices were coming out of the Earth, and the standing stone was vibrating in resonance-like frequencies.[40]

Fig. 43. Marna Hauk, 2017. "Stone Portalway and Earth Spiral Opening" dream montage from initial participant Survey 1. Composite digital image by Hauk, 2017, used with permission.

I convened two dozen participants to incubate dreams for earth healing in a virtual Hygeian dream temple. Over a six-month period, the participants shared their incubated earth dreams in a virtual *temenos* (dream sanctuary), virtually inscribing their dreams and their impressions via a private electronic wiki and commenting on one another's dreams. The qualitative methods of data synthesis included the creation and visual sorting of image mandalas from the dreams (*Figures 43-45*). These mandalas were created by the researcher, for the purpose of qualitatively coding the dreams.[41] Methods also included member checking. Sparked by the desire to directly interview the earth, in this study I extended women's dream research, infusing it with Gaian and arts methods to explore diverse modes of co-evolutionary contact with the numinous.

Findings and Discussion

The depth dimension of dreamers from Arizona to Africa birthed more than eighty earth dreams. The findings included health- and hope-giving possibilities for cross-species collaborations, experiences of the living land, transformative supercapabilities of earth and women (e.g., flight, submersion and reclamation) and sanctuary from earth disaster.

Cross-Species Collaborations That Heal

Many women in this study reported dreams of snakebites or spider bites with transformative effects. Other earth dreamers collaborated with bears to save lives from earth catastrophes such as tsunamis or glacial melt caused by climate change. Sometimes the dreamers themselves became cross-species hybrids, sprouting butterfly wings, flying as birds or breathing underwater. These impossible possibilities were hope-giving if chimaeric. One participant described merging with avian and Terran elements, with vivid effects (see the account in the next section).

Living Land

For some participants, the merging with or as other elements of the natural world brought fresh perspective, shared presence and healing sense of aliveness:

> When I think about how the Earth is alive, and how dream
> and reverie take me out of my smallbuzzing brain into

the larger aliveness, I think about a dream I had a long while back that stays with me, about flying. In a way, the dream feels like earth connection in that it's like I'm in a bird body. I can see acutely down into the landscape that's going by. I feel the air buoying my body and also whizzing past my face, it's exhilarating. I am particularly connected with the trees, I can see/sense their large green presences far out from their physical branches. Also, my sense of "I"-ness is different than in my waking human body. It's almost like if I put my attention to something, I go down into it, into its center and also see/sense from its perspective. Each part of the aliveness has a different signature/feel/way of see/sensing. —I also get this feeling sometimes while gardening, tuning into a particular plant, I can feel its ?aura? ?energy body? ?presence?, also from its being, its aliveness/wholeness.—In the fragment of the dream of flying, I go down to sit/sense/rest am in a large tree, inside of its greenness, both physically and in that feltsense extending beyond the tree body form. That's it, like many dreams, it's not a story, it's just a moment that stays, that felt sense, that different way of being. When I think of your question about how it feels to connect with the larger Earth, that's what comes to me, these bird-being tree-presence senses and feelings. In good, whole moments of waking, I also feel inklings or moments like this. And when I arrive/arise/realize that's where I am, I feel renewed, deepened, fresh, alive. Something else, almost covered, underneath, but which is tingling and alive, surfaces. My senses widen. I know I am whole while also being dissolved/merged/thrummed/extended into everything else, and that too feels whole.[42]

Another participant described an earth dream of her family's ancestral home, offering an alternative to the construct of land ownership by returning it to shared access, tearing down fences and creating an unseen ribbon of connection: "to hold the land: lightly, not with our hands but with our eyes and hearts. This creates a tie to the land which cannot be severed."[43]

Perhaps these imaginal mergings and uncoverings of "something underneath but which is tingling and alive [that] surfaces"[44] can be construed as the resurgence of the older ways of co-presencing that are offered by matrix/mother cultures.

Matriarchal Dreams

Some women in the study dreamed of matriarchy. In the following earth dream, attention brightens the world and places come back to life, through women in community offering movement and ceremony and attending to place presence:

> Then we are walking back down from the (north/up) point we had been walking before, to the first of the three side points of the triangle canyon. As we walk back, yes, that's when there are waterfalls being lit up.
>
> It is tawny desert with scrub and trees. Also, though, there are these vortex portalways that have waterfalls or other painting/altar/magic made to cross between. The altars aren't static placements of objects. They are more like weave-painting new realities (the waterfalls) with our arms, and from the imagination the new terrain/feature/ beauty springs—*but like it was always there in the landscape, it was just not lit up yet. As we bring our attention to it, the world brightens. The inherent natural beauty that was in that place awakens/comes alive/is catalyzed/ activated, and colors enrich and water/life sparkles.*
>
> There are dozens of dozens of women in various places, communing with the earth/the land/a tree/a crook of rock, a particular place and each other. There is a sense of calm, meditative enchantment, something being made, something coming alive.
>
> . . . Afterwards is when D. shows me how the walls and terrain awaken in collaboration with the priestesses/women all around.

I awake with the final images of walking with D. and the waterfall making and a holistic/synergistic/epiphanic/totalistic/gestaltic ah-hah understanding in body depth of how the land can wake up, the earth-land-women complex can awaken with colorful, verveful, artful, alive attention. Splendid. (emphasis added).[45]

Fig. 44. Marna Hauk, 2014. "Triangle Canyon of the Goddesses Dream" dream montage from Dreamthread 36. Composite digital image by Hauk, 2014, used with permission.

Earth dreaming can envision possibilities, perhaps sourced from the generative, collaborative ecomind,[46] ecological intelligence,[47] or Gaian intelligence[48] of planet and people. The revivification of land via prophetic/projective movement, the world-brightening power of attention and the lively "earth-land-women complex" are moving, ecocommuning, mutualistic collaborations suggested by these earth dreams. Earth dreaming is a current option for reaching underneath the grid culture overlay of (post) modernity and recontacting the primary biocultural matrix.

Sanctuary and Disaster

Perhaps related to the treasure tradition in wisdom lineages and the seed pattern and possibly connected with the nest pattern of convergent radiance, sanctuary and cavern also arose as a meta-pattern in the study. The refuge concept was often the regenerative counterpoint in earth dreams related to earth disaster or catastrophe. At least twenty of the eighty earth dreams (twenty-five percent) related to earth disaster, destruction or catastrophe. The metapattern of sanctuary and cavern recurred repeatedly, especially in the disaster dreams. This metapattern was exemplified by getting to high ground during tsunamis, discovering a nest or a puppy litter at the base of an uprooted tree,[49] retreating to an earth cavern for healing after violation,[50] and getting to the safety of a kayak, raft, rock or shore during flooding caused by global warming (e.g., Dreamthread 20 and 50, P-01-019).

The Earth itself was often the sanctuary. Gardens, walking and hiking in wild nature all became forms of sanctuary held within the larger, healing matrix of earth.[51]

Fig. 45. Marna Hauk, 2014. "Traveling Tsunami Bear Dream" dream montage from Dreamthread 1. Composite digital image by Hauk, 2014, used with permission.

This sanctuary theme reflects how the earth metapattern of sanctuary is a form of emergent ecosocial regenerative, collaborative creativity. Together, women in the study dreamed of earth–culture collaborations that modeled Margulian symbiotic and mutualistic possibilities featuring nurture, caring, heightened creativity and what R. Keith Sawyer has termed collaborative emergence.[52]

Conclusions

Connecting the questions of whether the dreams surfaced from the individual women, emergent dreamtime collectives, or a planetary super-system, the pathways of these dream pilgrimages suggest effective practices for much-needed presence, healing and regeneration.

Dreaming has been typified as the "hyper-connective" end of the creative spectrum,[53] related to thin boundary states.[54] For millennia and across cultures, earth dreaming and ecodreaming have been used as methods for direct healing with the numinous and communication of healing regimens. The results of this study suggest that the collaborative co-evolution of the human-naturecultural matrix and life-on-earth-enhancing mother cultures can be regenerated in shared healing and earth dreaming. Earth dreaming can catalyze earth healing, including at greater scales than the individual life. It is possible these shared circles of intentional social dreaming serve as omphali (navels) of the living earth, generating polyvocal spaces for Earthvox, the earth's voices, to communicate across, through and with human collectives and collective consciousness. It is possible that this communication initiates emergent properties of Gaian knowing and intelligence. The resonance of the superinfused, supraordinary states of dream, earth dreaming and what are termed big dreams or extraordinary dreams resonate with other forms of mythological material that also convey a depth of meaning and supraordinary content for expanded possibility, as was revealed in the data generated by this study. Gimbutas confirmed this conclusion:

> These symbols remain the only real access to this invigorating, earth-centered, life-reverencing worldview . . . a symbol of the unity of all life in Nature. Her power was in water and stone, in tomb and cave, in animals and birds, snakes and fish, hills, trees, and flowers. Hence the holistic

and mythopoeic perception of the sacredness and mystery of all there is on Earth.[55]

As we cogenerate prophetic, nurturing, healing, strength-giving processes of earth regeneration that make space for a fuller range of individual and collective intelligence and creativity, including the imaginal and mythological dimensions, we step into new possibilities of presence, connection and capability. Layers of presence elide and merge.[56] It is possible that the dream visitations from superpowered deities or numinous entities and the superpowers revealed in this study and rife in current culture offer a return to meta-conscious possibilities and Gaian knowing/being/presencing beyond our current conceptions of what is humanly possible. Perhaps earth dreaming can return us to our larger and emergent co-presencing and matrixial, earth-embedded powers. Confronted by the seeming impossibility of recovering from the current life system threats from industrial growth society, we see no better time to shift our sense of what is possible. Physician Michael Kearney emphasized that incubating healing dreams is a practice of returning to a state of "wholeness [that] is already there. . . . Wholeness and interconnectedness are a priori."[57] Earth dreaming practices cultivate reconnection with these larger states of planetary systemic intelligence and wholeness. Joanna Macy and Chris Johnstone described practices for active hope: "We belong to this world / The web of life is calling us forth at this time."[58] Gimbutas affirmed that view:

> Human alienation from the vital roots of earthly life ensued, the results of which are clear in our contemporary society. But the cycles never stop turning, and now we find the Goddess reemerging from the forests and mountains, bringing us hope for the future, returning us to our most ancient human roots.[59]

Because we are actually embedded and embodied within Gaia E/mergent,[60] this thinking suggests possible avenues for future research, the cultivation of earth dreaming temples, and the sharing of the material from many earth dreaming temples. One of my colleagues has noted that within this study the dream temple was not virtual; rather, the dream repository was.[61] Ancient dream sanctuaries, *temenos*, were located in places of great natural beauty. The results of this study suggest that earth dreaming awakens heightened states of sensory awareness such that the beauty of wherever we find ourselves awakens and shines. In this understanding, the entire Earth becomes a shared dreaming temple for incubating earth dreams, regenerating capacities and embodying expanded, planetary-curative states. Whether through setting intention for incubating earth dreams,[62] group appreciation of dreams[63] or active development of physical or virtual earth dreaming temples,[64] we are birthing a renewing world from the dreaming matrix, becoming imaginal, oracular portals and instantiations of the voice(s) of the Earth while re-embodying regenerative and life-giving wholeness.

References

Barasch, Marc Ian. *Healing Dreams: Exploring the Dreams That Can Transform Your Life*. New York: Riverhead/Penguin, 2000.

Barrett, M. J. "Doing Animist Research in Academia: A Methodological Framework." *Canadian Journal of Environmental Education* 16 (2011): 123–41.

Bickel, Barbara. *Dream Scroll Journey: Releasing the Dreams* (online multi-layered artwork video companion to nap-in and dream-scroll research), 2013. Accessed August 10, 2017. http://vimeo.com/74959744.

Bowers, Chet A. *Transitions: Educational Reforms that Promote Ecological Intelligence or the Assumptions Underlying Modernity*. Portland, OR: Ecojustice, 2010.

de la Bellacasa, María Puig. "Ethical Doings in Naturecultures." *Ethics, Place and Environment* 13, no. 2 (2010): 151–69. doi:10.1080/13668791003778834.

Ettinger, Bracha L. *The Matrixial Borderspace*. Theory Out of Bounds, bk. 28. Minneapolis: University of Minnesota Press, 2006.

Flinders, Carol Lee. *The Values of Belonging: Rediscovering Balance, Mutuality, Intuition, and Wholeness in a Competitive World*. San Francisco, CA: Harper, 2002.

Gimbutas, Marija. *The Language of the Goddess*. San Francisco, CA: Harper, 1989.

Garfield, Patricia. *Creative Dreaming*. New York: Ballantine, 1974.

———. *Pathway to Ecstasy: The Way of the Dream Mandala*. New York: Holt, Rhinehart, and Winston, 1979.

———. *The Healing Power of Dreams*. New York: Simon and Schuster, 1991.

Goleman, Daniel, Lisa Bennett, and Zenobia Barlow. *Ecoliterate: How Educators Are Cultivating Emotional, Social, and Ecological Intelligence*. San Francisco, CA: Jossey-Bass and the Center for Ecoliteracy, 2012.

Hartmann, Ernest. *The Nature and Functions of Dreaming*. New York: Oxford University Press, 2011.

Hauk, Marna. "En-earthing." *Earth Empathy: Planetary Connecting* (website). Institute for Earth Regenerative Studies, 2010. http://www.earthregenerative.org/earth-empathy/homepage.html. http://www.earthregenerative.org/earth-empathy/body-cat3b.html.

———. "Gaia E/mergent: Earth Regenerative Education Catalyzing Empathy, Creativity, and Wisdom." PhD diss., Prescott College, 2014.

———. "Dreams of Earth: Earth Dreaming as Eco-Resilience Practice for the Long Emergency." *Ecopsychology* 7, no. 4 (December 2015): 258–65. doi:10.1089/eco.2015.0039.

Jaenke, Karen. "Earth Dreaming." In *RebEarths: Conversations With a World Ensouled*, edited by Craig Chalquist, 187–202. Walnut Creek, CA: World Soul, 2010.

———. "Earth, Dreams, Body." *ReVision* 30, nos. 1 & 2 (2008): 10–12.

Kaplan, Connie C. *The Woman's Book of Dreams: Dreaming as a Spiritual Practice*. Hillsboro, OR: Beyond Words, 1999.

Kearney, Michael. *A Place of Healing: Working with Nature and Soul at the End of Life*. New Orleans, LA: Spring Journal Books, 2009.

———. "Healing the Soul in a Culture of Fear." In *Imagination and Medicine: The Future of Healing in an Age of Neuroscience*, edited by Stephen Aizenstat and Robert Bosnak, 35–44. New Orleans, LA: Spring Journal Books, 2009.

———. "Working with the Body, Working with Nature." Presentation at the Conference on Healing and Medicine II: The Body in Depth Psychology— Healing in an Age of Neuroscience, Pacifica University, Santa Barbara, CA, January 30, 2010.

Krippner, Stanley, Fariba Bogzaran, and André Percia deCarvalho. *Extraordinary Dreams and How to Work with Them*. Albany, NY: State University of New York Press, 2002.

Lappé, Francis Moore. *EcoMind: Changing the Way We Think to Create the World We Want*. New York: Nation Books, 2011.

Lawrence, W. Gordon. *The Creativity of Social Dreaming*. London: Karnac, 2010.

Macy, Joanna, and Chris Johnstone. *Active Hope: How to Face the Mess We're in Without Going Crazy*. Novato, CA: New World Library, 2012.

Margulis, Lynn. "Gaia by Any Other Name." In *Scientists Debate Gaia: The Next Century*, edited by Stephen H. Schneider, James. R. Miller, Eileen Crist, and Penelope J. Boston, 7–12. Cambridge, MA: MIT Press, 2004.

———. *Symbiotic Planet: A New Look at Evolution*. New York: Basic Books, 1998.

Minati, Gianfranco, and Eliano Pessa. *Collective Beings*. New York, NY: Springer, 2006.

Monaghan, Patricia. *Encyclopedia of Goddesses and Heroines*. Vol. II. Santa Barbara, CA: Greenwood/ABC-CLIO, 2010.

Patton, Kimberley C. "Ancient Asklepieia: Institutional Incubation and the Hope of Healing." In *Imagination and Medicine: The Future of Healing in an Age of Neuroscience*, edited by Stephen Aizenstat and Robert Bosnak, 3–34. New Orleans, LA: Spring Journal Books, 2009.

Sabini, Meredith. "Dreaming a New Paradigm." In *Ecotherapy: Healing with Nature in Mind*, edited by Linda Buzzell and Craig Chalquist, 211–18. San Francisco, CA: Sierra Club, 2009.

———. "Dreams of the Earth." *DreamTime* 25, no. 1 (2008): 29, 39. Accessed August 10, 2017. http://dream-institute.org/articles/dreams-of-the-earth/.

Sawyer, R. Keith. "Individual and Group Creativity." In *The Cambridge Handbook of Creativity*, edited by James Kaufman and Robert Sternberg, 366–80. New York: Cambridge University Press, 2010.

Schneider, Laura Z. "Eco-Dreaming: The Whale's Tale." In Ecotherapy: Healing with Nature in Mind, edited by Linda Buzzell and Craig Chalquist, 116–22. San Francisco, CA: Sierra Club Books, 2009.

Signell, Karen A. *Wisdom of the Heart: Working with Women's Dreams*, 2nd ed. New York: Fromm International, 1998.

Spretnak, Charlene. *Relational Reality: New Directions of Interrelatedness That Are Transforming the Modern World*. Topsham, ME: Green Horizon, 2011.

Swimme, Brian, and Thomas Berry. *The Universe Story: From the Primordial Flaring Forth to the Ecozoic Era—A Celebration of the Unfolding of the Cosmos*. San Francisco, CA: HarperCollins, 1992.

Endnotes

1 Brache Ettinger, *The Matrixial Borderspace*, bk. 28, *Theory Out of Bounds* (Minneapolis: University of Minnesota Press, 2006). An alternate construction for matrixial is *porosity*, as theorized in M. J. Barrett, "Doing Animist Research in Academia: A Methodological Framework," *Canadian Journal of Environmental Education* 16 (2011): 128, 130: "Porosity is a state of being open and attuned to communication with an animate earth."

2 Carol Lee Flinders, *The Values of Belonging: Rediscovering Balance, Mutuality, Intuition, and Wholeness in a Competitive World* (San Francisco, CA: Harper, 2002), 56–57.

3 Lynn Margulis, *Symbiotic Planet: A New Look at Evolution* (New York: Basic Books, 1998).

4 Marija Gimbutas, *The Language of the Goddess* (San Francisco, CA: Harper, 1989), 316.

5 Lynn Margulis, "Gaia by Any Other Name," in *Scientists Debate Gaia: The Next Century,* ed. Stephen H. Schneider, et al. (Cambridge, MA: MIT Press, 2004), 7–12.

6 María Puig de la Bellacasa, "Ethical Doings in Naturecultures," *Ethics, Place and Environment* 13, no. 2 (2010): 151–69, doi:10.1080/13668791003778834.

7 Charlene Spretnak, *Relational Reality: New Directions of Interrelatedness That Are Transforming the Modern World* (Topsham, ME: Green Horizon, 2011).

8 Brian Swimme and Thomas Berry, *The Universe Story: From the Primordial Flaring Forth to the Ecozoic Era—A Celebration of the Unfolding of the Cosmos* (San Francisco, CA: HarperCollins, 1992), 240–60.

9 This work adapts passages from my doctoral dissertation account of the study, particularly Marna Hauk, "Gaia E/mergent: Earth Regenerative Education Catalyzing Empathy, Creativity, and Wisdom" (PhD diss., Prescott College, 2014). Accessed August 10, 2017,https://pqdtopen.proquest.com/doc/1563382491.html?FMT=ABS

10 Michael Kearney, "Working with the Body, Working with Nature" (presentation, Conference on Healing and Medicine II: The Body in Depth Psychology—Healing in an Age of Neuroscience, Pacifica University, Santa Barbara, CA, January 30, 2010). See also Michael Kearney, *A Place of Healing: Working with Nature and Soul at the End of Life* (New Orleans, LA: Spring Journal Books, 2009); Kimberley C. Patton, "Ancient Asklepieia: Institutional

Incubation and the Hope of Healing," in *Imagination and Medicine: The Future of Healing in an Age of Neuroscience*, ed. Stephen Aizenstat and Robert Bosnak (New Orleans, LA: Spring Journal Books, 2009), 17–29.

11 Patton, "Ancient Asklepieia," 20–21.

12 Kearney, "Working with the Body, Working with Nature." See also Patricia Monaghan, *Encyclopedia of Goddesses and Heroines*, vol, II (Santa Barbara, CA: Greenwood/ABC-CLIO, 2010), 412–13.

13 Gimbutas, *Language of the Goddess*, 121.

14 Stanley Krippner, Fariba Bogzaran, and André Percia deCarvalho, *Extraordinary Dreams and How to Work with Them* (Albany, NY: State University of New York Press, 2002), 67.

15 Patricia Garfield, *Creative Dreaming* (New York: Ballantine, 1974), 23.

16 Meredith Sabini, "Dreaming a New Paradigm," in *Ecotherapy: Healing with Nature in Mind*, ed. Linda Buzzell and Craig Chalquist (San Francisco, CA: Sierra Club, 2009), 211–18.

17 Karen Jaenke, "Earth, Dreams, Body," *ReVision* 30, nos. 1 & 2 (2008): 10–12. See also Karen Jaenke, "Earth Dreaming," in *RebEarths: Conversations With a World Ensouled*, ed. Craig Chalquist (Walnut Creek, CA: World Soul Books, 2010), 187–202.

18 Laura Z. Schneider, "Eco-Dreaming: The Whale's Tale," in *Ecotherapy: Healing with Nature in Mind*, ed. Linda Buzzell and Craig Chalquist (San Francisco, CA: Sierra Club, 2009), 116–22.

19 Marc Ian Barasch, *Healing Dreams: Exploring the Dreams That Can Transform Your Life* (New York: Riverhead/Penguin, 2000), 167–69.

20 Sabini, "Dreaming a New Paradigm," 211.

21 Sabini, "Dreaming a New Paradigm," 212.

22 Sabini, "Dreaming a New Paradigm," 216.

23 Sabini, "Dreaming a New Paradigm," 217.

24 W. Gordon Lawrence, *The Creativity of Social Dreaming* (London: Karnac, 2010).

25 Sabini, "Dreaming a New Paradigm," 218.

26 Jaenke, "Earth, Dreams, Body," 11.

27 Jaenke, "Earth, Dreams, Body," 12.

28 Jaenke, "Earth Dreaming," 189.

29 Jaenke, "Earth Dreaming," 188.

30 Jaenke, "Earth Dreaming," 192.

31 Jaenke, "Earth Dreaming," 192.

32 Jaenke, "Earth Dreaming," 196–97.

33 Jaenke, "Earth Dreaming," 198–99.

34 Schneider, "Eco-Dreaming," 116–22.

35 Patricia Garfield, *Pathway to Ecstasy: The Way of the Dream Mandala* (New York: Holt, Rhinehart, and Winston, 1979), 4–20.

36 Connie Kaplan, *The Woman's Book of Dreams: Dreaming as a Spiritual Practice* (Hillsboro, OR: Beyond Words, 1999), 6–8, 76–88.

37 Karen A. Signell, *Wisdom of the Heart: Working with Women's Dreams*, 2nd ed. (New York: Fromm International, 1998), 13–47.

38 Garfield, *Pathway to Ecstasy*, 12.

39 Marna Hauk, "En-earthing," *Earth Empathy: Planetary Connecting* (website), Institute for Earth Regenerative Studies, 2010, http://www.earthregenerative.org/earth-empathy/body-cat3b.html.

40 Participant P-01-012, dream scribing from the pre-survey of this study.

41 Hauk, "Gaia E/mergent," 222–28. This is a technique for which I have coined the term *SIMage*, meaning synthesis with image mandalas for resonant visual sorting and coding and for surfacing of themes.

42 Participant P-01-041, Dreamthread 29.1 from this study, June 14, 2012. Spelling and punctuation as in the original.

43 Participant P-01-023, Dreamthread 01.07 from this study, March 11, 2012.

44 Participant P-01-041, Dreamthread 29.1 from this study, June 14, 2012.

45 Participant P-01-041, Dreamthread 36 from this study, July 14, 2012.

46 Francis Moore Lappé, *EcoMind: Changing the Way We Think to Create the World We Want* (New York: Nation Books, 2011).

47 Ecological intelligence is an emergent construct that includes emotionally and ecologically intelligent ecoliteracy. Research in this field includes Daniel Goleman, Lisa Bennett, and Zenobia Barlow, *Ecoliterate: How Educators Are Cultivating Emotional, Social, and Ecological Intelligence* (San Francisco, CA: Jossey-Bass and the Center for Ecoliteracy, 2012). Ecological intelligence suggests the expansion toward emergent and collective intelligence based on cultural commons. See Chet A. Bowers, *Transitions: Educational Reforms that*

Promote Ecological Intelligence or the Assumptions Underlying Modernity (Portland, OR: Ecojustice, 2010). In addition, the idea of complex collaborative emergence was articulated in R. Keith Sawyer, "Individual and Group Creativity," in *The Cambridge Handbook of Creativity*, ed. James Kaufman and Robert Sternberg (New York: Cambridge University Press, 2010), 366–80. That idea also has been supported by the findings of complexivists Gianfranco Minati and Eliano Pessa, *Collective Beings* (New York: Springer, 2006).

48 Hauk, "Gaia E/mergent, 477."

49 Participant P-01-004, Dreamthread 07 from this study, April 18, 2012.

50 Participant P-01-010, Dreamthread 01.08 from this study, March 12, 2012.

51 See, for example, participant P-01-023, Dreamthread 08 from this study, April 18, 2012.

52 Sawyer, "Individual and Group Creativity," 368.

53 Ernest Hartmann, *The Nature and Functions of Dreaming* (New York: Oxford University Press, 2011), 43.

54 Hartmann, *Nature and Functions of Dreaming*, 105–6.

55 Gimbutas, *Language of the Goddess*, 321.

56 Barbara Bickel. "Dream Scroll Journey: Releasing the Dreams" (online multilayered artwork video companion to nap-in and dream-scroll research), 2013. Accessed August 10, 2017, http://vimeo.com/74959744.

57 Michael Kearney, "Healing the Soul in a Culture of Fear," in *Imagination and Medicine: The Future of Healing in an Age of Neuroscience*, ed. Stephen Aizenstat and Robert Bosnak (New Orleans, LA: Spring Journal Books, 2009), 37.

58 Joanna Macy and Chris Johnstone, *Active Hope: How to Face the Mess We're in Without Going Crazy* (Novato, CA: New World Library, 2012), 35.

59 Gimbutas, *Language of the Goddess*, 321.

60 Hauk, "Gaia E/mergent," 456–57.

61 Denise Mitten, personal conversation with the author, August 7, 2014.

62 Patricia Garfield, *The Healing Power of Dreams* (New York: Simon and Schuster, 1991), 247–49.

63 Kaplan, *Woman's Book of Dreams*, 76–88. For more on social dreaming and earth-dreaming-circle practices, see Lawrence, *Creativity of Social Dreaming* and Meredith Sabini, "Dreams of the Earth," *DreamTime* 25, no. 1 (2008): 29, 39.

64 Hauk, "Gaia E/mergent," 471–75, 478–79.

SECTION 3

HONORING OUR
ARTIST-SCHOLAR FOREMOTHERS

I GIVE YOU TO THE ANCESTORS

How will I teach you
to love the world even when
the world may not love?

How will I show you
that you are a being of
consequence, a gift?

How will I give you
my strength, my courage,
my fierce grace,
to wear like . . .
. . . A sheltering cloak?

How will I honor your
gentle spirit growing
in my ardent embrace?

I will give you to
the ancestors, remember
the love of thousands.

They remember you.
They will teach you, show you,
give you strength and courage
. . . Fierce grace.

You remember them
when you walk in this world
with heart,
Sit in the forests.

You remember them
when you swim in rivers and
hike the far mountains.

You remember them
when you bury me, ashes
among the love of thousands.

~ Gina Belton

LYDIA RUYLE:
A PERSONALIZED BIOGRAPHY
(1935 - 2016)

JOAN M. CICHON

Lydia Ruyle, M.A., is an artist, author, scholar emerita of the Visual Arts faculty of the University of Northern Colorado in Greeley, Colorado. Her research into sacred images of women has taken her around the globe. Ruyle creates and exhibits her art and does workshops through-out the U.S. and internationally. Her Goddess Icon Spirit Banners have flown in over forty countries. Her art is in more than thirty books.

Lydia wrote the above in February 2016, when I asked her to contribute a brief biography to the information about our panel for the 2016 Matriarchal Studies Day. Much has been said about Lydia's career, but I would like to elaborate on her biography here, filling in the blanks from the perspective of our twenty-year friendship.

As attendees of ASWM conferences, many of you are aware of one of Lydia's great artistic achievements: more than 340 images of goddesses of the world as portrayed in her Goddess Icon Spirit Banners. Lydia travelled the globe, studying these icons first-hand and learning all that she could about the cultures that produced them, before re-creating them in

Fig. 46. Lydia Ruyle, Self Portrait: Ancient Mother, glowing edges, digital manipuation of drawing, 2005.

her unique banner form. Lydia's beloved niece, Katie Hoffner, who often traveled with her, has told wonderful stories about the adventures that she and Lydia had in the pursuit of studying goddess images firsthand. Because those adventures provide a great deal of insight into Lydia's character, I recount some of them here:

- Sitting under the Wesak full moon at Machu Picchu, in a sacred drum circle with a small group of women surrounded by Lydia's goddess banners dancing in the breeze.

- Getting stuck in a river—not once, but twice—in a "hippie" Volkswagen van that Lydia had hired in the depths of the jungle so that she and Katie could see rare Mayan temples and the Mexican goddesses that had been etched into the steles of the temples. Lydia demanded that the driver get out and let Katie drive, since Katie "grew up on a farm" and could help them get unstuck. Luckily, Katie prevailed!

- Sleeping in hammocks in a treehouse, where they were served dinner and serenaded by howler monkeys.

- Katie driving Lydia around the English countryside and hoisting her over fences so that she could visit crop circles.

- Multiple visits to Turkey, with Resit Ergener, including one in October 2015 to the land of the Mother Goddess and the ancient Neolithic site of Çatal Hüyük, where Lydia not only repeatedly chided the archeologists for not including goddess stories in their documentation but also made sure that the site stayed open early on when it ran out of funds. It's now a UNESCO site.

- Convincing Katie to travel to Saint Petersburg, Russia, in the middle of December for a Women & Earth conference. Katie, who had never been so cold in her life, thought for sure she'd find Lydia's tiny frame frozen mid-stride in the street.

- Almost getting arrested in front of the *David* statue in Florence but only getting fined $3,000 each for illegal tour guiding. (Thank the goddess for the esteemed lawyers in their family—Lydia's husband, Katie's Uncle Robert, and Lydia's daughter, Robin— because they got Lydia and Katie out of that one.)

- Being chased off a rancher's land in Albuquerque, New Mexico, by the rancher pointing a shotgun at them, because Lydia had insisted on seeing a piece of rock art on his land.
- Their almost annual pilgrimage to the Glastonbury Goddess Conference in England.

Lydia was incredibly generous with the loan of the goddess banners. As her brief statement reveals, they have flown in more than forty countries, including Australia, Canada, Britain, France, Luxembourg, Italy, Greece, Serbia, Bulgaria, Germany, the Czech Republic, Poland, Russia, Turkey, Ghana, Brazil, Mexico, Peru, Japan, Nepal, Bhutan, Tibet, China and the U.S., spreading the energy of the female divine everywhere they went. The "girls," as Lydia sometimes lovingly referred to her banners, regularly graced the Glastonbury Goddess Conferences, ASWM Conferences, the World Congresses of Matriarchal Studies, and other conferences and symposia too numerous to mention—including a meeting of the World Parliament of Religions in September 2015. When I asked Lydia to send me twelve banners for several talks I was giving locally, she graciously did so. When it came time for me to defend my dissertation, Lydia suggested that she might send several banners that were related to the topic of my dissertation so that I could use them as part of my presentation.

In her fifty-plus-year career as an artist, Lydia created other forms of art in addition to the Goddess Icon Spirit Banners: landscapes, self-portraits, sculptures, collages and prints. At the Columbia College of Chicago's Center for Book and Paper she even produced the paper on which she printed her collection of crop circle images. She loved to work at the Santa Reparata International School of Art in Florence, Italy, probably because Florence (in addition to Turkey) was one of the places on earth that she loved most dearly. I only became fully aware of all the media in which Lydia worked when, shortly before her death, I visited her home and saw her sculptures, collages and paintings on display there. I remember marveling at the breadth and the scope of her work. In her presentations, Lydia often told the story of how as a young mother she again took up art (a subject that she had abandoned as a young woman in favor of political science) to help her cope with the demanding task of raising four young children close in age. I think that in the telling of that story Lydia sought not only to share with us the story of her life but to encourage women to begin working at something they love no matter what the obstacles might appear to be.

Lydia was a scholar and teacher on the faculty of the University of Northern Colorado (UNC) for many years. One of her early achievements there was to weave the story of women artists into the art history courses she taught. Lydia did this at a time when women artists were totally ignored by the discipline; she researched the information so she could bring the herstory of women's contributions to art to her students and to public consciousness. In more recent years, Lydia taught "HERstory of the Goddess," another pioneering course, this time bringing the female divine to public consciousness. In April 2013, she received the Century of Scholars Lifetime Achievement Award at the UNC graduate school's 100-Year Commemorative Celebration. In 2010, the Lydia Ruyle Room of Women's Art was dedicated. I believe that Lydia was especially thrilled with this last honor. The naming of that room in her honor and in honor of women's contributions to world art seems to me a beautiful symbol and culmination of Lydia's work at the university. She had brought things full circle—from the exclusion of women artists from the university's curriculum to the naming of a room for them and the woman who had reclaimed their herstory.

Lydia not only taught courses at the university but also presented workshops throughout the U.S. and internationally. In addition, over a seven-year period, she took more than 200 women on spiritual journeys to sacred sites in Britain, Turkey, France, Germany, Greece, Italy, Sicily, Malta, the Czech Republic, Russia, Mexico, Peru, the Himalayas, Hawaii and the southwestern United States. Lifelong friendships were forged on those trips, and for many women those sacred journeys were life-changing events.

Lydia's scholarship was not limited to teaching. She also wrote several books about her goddess banners, further spreading divine female energies and re-introducing goddesses into the world. See *Goddess Icons: Spirit Banners of the Divine Feminine* (Boulder, CO: Woven Word Press, 2002) and *Goddesses of the Americas: Spirit Banners of the Divine Feminine* (Albuquerque, NM: Goddess Ink, 2016).

Before she died, I asked Lydia what I might do for her. One of her responses was that I could work for the election of Hillary Clinton, who was then the Democratic candidate for President of the United States. Lydia had always been active in politics. Indeed, I think political involvement was a part of her upbringing. Her involvement began at a young age and then showed itself continually throughout the rest of her life: in her election to the Greeley school board in the 1970s, on which she fought for, among other things, the inclusion of art programs in the curriculum, and in more recent years, when she participated in the marches for women's right to abortion. In those marches, she was joined by her daughters, granddaughters, and members of the larger tribe of her family and friends.

Lydia always ended her presentations by showing pictures of her family. She expressed great love of and gratitude for her husband and life partner of more than fifty years, Bob Ruyle. She was proud of being the matriarch of a large clan: three children, a son and two daughters, and their spouses, grandchildren, and nieces and nephews. I was continually amazed at how frequently and how far Lydia and her husband Bob would travel to attend the graduations, recitals, swim meets, high school debates, and birthday parties of their family members. Lydia was always available for her loved ones.

I was happy to call Lydia Ruyle my friend. Generous, enthusiastic, full of life, empathetic, encouraging, supportive, extremely wise, funny and fun, she possessed all of the qualities we could wish for in a friend and in ourselves. Lydia concluded some of her presentations with this quotation: "One day, you'll be just a memory for some people. Do your best to be a good one." Lydia left us with so many good memories. I miss her very much.

AN APPRECIATION OF MARY B. KELLY
(1936–2016)

JOAN MARLER

Fig. 47. Mary B. Kelly. Photograph by
Ann Frutkin, n.d.

On March 16, 2016, the dedicated scholar, artist, author and beloved teacher Mary B. Kelly passed into the realm of the ancestors at her home on Hilton Head Island, South Carolina. She is gravely missed by her close family and countless friends, students and colleagues throughout the world who treasured her indomitable spirit and shared her love for spinning, weaving, embroidery and painting. Mary is especially honored for her tireless research on ancient textiles and the sacred imagery they transmit (See appendix for a complete list of her scholarly publications). She was a keynote speaker for the Association for the Study of Women and Mythology (ASWM) and a member of its advisory board.

For four decades, Mary traveled the world nearly every year to research and document folk textiles. That travel was made possible by research grants and fellowships. Her intensive investigations resulted in numerous

Fig. 48. Mary B. Kelly, *Berehina,
Ukranian Goddess of Vegetation*, oil
painting on canvas, 2010.

published works, including her trilogy composed of *Goddess Embroideries of Eastern Europe* (1989), *Goddess Embroideries of the Balkan Lands and the Greek Islands* (1999) and *Goddess Embroideries of the Northlands* (2007). She also published five volumes (1992–2008) for needleworkers in which she introduced the history and use of goddess imagery on ritual cloths and costumes from Ukraine, Russia, Slovakia, the Greek Isles and Old Norway, the book *Making and Using Ritual Cloths* (2002), and the book *Goddess, Women, Cloth: A Worldwide Tradition of Making and Using Ritual Textiles* (2011). Mary published more than thirty articles, in the United States and abroad, about her ongoing pioneering research and she lectured internationally in museums and universities. She also is celebrated as a masterful visual artist.

Mary Florence Berger, the eldest of six children, was born in 1936 in a suburb of Cincinnati. She was surrounded by a close-knit extended family. Her parents, Florence and Alfred Berger, were idealistically motivated to raise their children according to creative, humanitarian principles. Florence had earned graduate degrees in English and early childhood education, while Alfred was a scientist with a doctorate in chemistry. They believed in democracy and nonviolence, demonstrated active concern for social and economic justice and have been described as "masters of cross-cultural and multicultural understanding."[1]

In 1940, as World War II was expanding in Europe, Mary's parents bought a dilapidated farmhouse on sixteen acres of ruined land overlooking the beautiful Ohio Valley, with its gracefully winding river. Their goal was to create a generative environment for their children, away from the growing insanity of the world at war. Over the years, they gradually rebuilt the farmhouse, installed indoor plumbing, planted hundreds of trees to prevent erosion and restored the ecological integrity and fertility of the land. The children learned to garden, gather eggs and care for the various collections of barnyard animals.

Florence and Alfred raised their children—five girls and one boy—with freedom and flexibility. The farm functioned as a laboratory where they designed a learning curriculum that expressed their progressive values and the egalitarian nature of their leadership. Mary's sister Ann recalled that the children's chores were interspersed with singing, drawing and sewing. "Except for naptime, everyone was always busy."[2] Both parents were "able, tough and excellent teachers. . . . The ideals that they fostered and had us practice made us strong, creative and resilient."[3] On Saturdays, all of the children took classes at the Cincinnati Art Museum, where Mary's talent for art began to blossom. "Mary inherited her mother's determination to try new things and her dad's optimistic outlook and, from both, curiosity and a will to work hard."[4]

After graduating from a twelve-year Catholic school, Mary attended St. Mary-of-the-Woods College in Indiana, where she earned a bachelor of fine arts degree in 1958. She received commissions for mosaic murals and book illustrations and began her teaching career in primary schools, secondary schools and colleges. In 1960, she married. Over the next few years, she gave birth to three beautiful children and devoted herself to child rearing and the domestic arts.[5] By 1968, she had earned a master's degree from the Rhode Island School of Design in Providence, Rhode Island, and in 1973 she was hired as an assistant professor at Tompkins Cortland Community College in Dryden, New York.

Mary had learned spinning and weaving from her mother, so while she was living in upstate New York, after having renovated an abandoned farmhouse there, she raised dozens of sheep whose wool she sheared, spun, dyed and wove into cloth. She also continued to paint, and she was active throughout her life as an exhibiting artist. Her paintings (*Figures 48-56*) have been featured in more

Fig. 49. Mary B. Kelly, *Dordona, Hungarian Goddess of Harvests*, oil painting on canvas, 1996.

Fig. 50. Mary B. Kelly, *Guan Yin, Chinese Goddess of Mercy*, oil painting on canvas, 2010.

than thirty-five exhibitions, including twenty-five solo and two-person shows.

Florence and Alfred Berger saved their modest resources for traveling, especially with their children, which they considered essential for developing an open mind.[6] In 1974, they invited Mary to join them on a trip to Scandinavia and Poland so that Florence and Mary could study weaving while Alfred enjoyed the sights. After obtaining the proper visas, they crossed the Atlantic Ocean, by boat, to Sweden. There, Florence and Mary studied Swedish double-weave before taking a plane to Poland, behind the Iron Curtain. In Krakow, mother and daughter studied Polish double weave and were introduced to contemporary Polish textiles. It was there that Mary became aware of traditional solar symbols and other ancient motifs rendered on textiles, wood, stone and cut paper. She returned to Poland in three consecutive summers, with those trips made possible by foundation grants and fellowships, to further her study of Polish techniques and designs. In 1976, between her summer travels, she earned a master of fine arts degree at Syracuse University in Syracuse, New York.

Mary continued a full schedule of teaching at Tompkins Cortland Community College, where she developed the art program and served as a tenured professor of art until her retirement in 2008. One day, while looking through a catalogue from the Ukrainian Museum in New York City, she noticed a remarkable female figure called Berehinia. She knew that she had seen the image before, but she didn't know where. "This question," she wrote, "led me on a three-year quest for the answer."[7] In 1980, after having made elaborate arrangements to be away from her family and teaching duties, she departed for the Soviet Union to spend nine months doing research on folk symbolism sponsored by a State University of New York–Moscow State University exchange grant. That journey launched her lifelong dedication to uncovering sacred female imagery transmitted

160

through the weaving and needlework of countless generations of women throughout the world.

When she arrived in the Soviet Union, Mary met her research advisor, the Russian art historian V. M. Vasilenko, at the University of Moscow. He was prepared to reject her research proposal out of hand until he realized that her aim was to study textile evidence of Berehinia. Suddenly, his attitude changed. He announced to her that he was one of very few scholars in all of the Soviet Union who understood her subject and that he had been researching that goddess for nearly thirty years. Professor Vasilenko introduced Mary to the major specialists in the fields of traditional textiles and ancient Slavic symbolism and made it possible for her to have privileged access to major museum collections in Moscow and throughout the Soviet Union.[8] During her months of total immersion, including intensive study of the Russian language, Mary studied hundreds of Russian images of Berehinia and other goddess figures and related imagery on ritual cloths and Easter eggs, as well as Ukrainian images of Berehinia in a different style with upraised arms and open legs. While she often was not allowed to photograph the treasures she was seeing, she usually was allowed to draw them. She was glad to have the skills of an artist, and she sometimes made full-scale paintings of the images.[9]

Mary traveled throughout the Soviet territories. In Romania, abundant female figures and imagery from the Neolithic and later prehistoric periods are preserved in national museums. She recognized similarities between these early designs and traditional patterns in Eastern European textiles. Continuing on to Hungary, she found numerous examples of the goddess "as the embodiment of all life, the Female, the 'moist Mother Earth,' the Berehinia."[10] "Thus, with camera and watercolors," Mary wrote, "I traveled throughout Eastern Europe, the Carpathian basin, through Russia and Ukraine, down the Adriatic, and across the Hungarian plain. . . . By the time I left Russia, I had what amounted to a whole

Fig. 51. Mary B. Kelly, *Hecate, Triple Goddess of the Crossroads,* oil painting on canvas, 1998.

Fig. 52. Mary B. Kelly, *Kali, Black Virgin* series, oil painting on canvas, 1995.

encyclopedia of motifs and variations. I could begin to categorize the images and recognize the more abstract designs."[11] Mary used these images to create a major exhibition sponsored by the National Endowment for the Arts, *Goddess Embroideries of Eastern Europe,* which was displayed at the Roberson Center in Binghamton, New York, and the Cleveland Museum of Art (1986). Later, Mary published "A Walk with Berehinia: Goddess of Ukraine and Russia" in *Goddesses in World Culture* (2010), the second volume of the three-volume set edited by Patricia Monaghan.

During her months in the Soviet Union, Mary was introduced to the most prominent ethnologists, art historians and archaeologists who recognized analogies between Neolithic imagery and the symbolism preserved on traditional embroideries. Their approach confirmed the validity of her multidisciplinary orientation and her investigations. In 1983, Mary corresponded with Marija Gimbutas about the antiquity of the female images found in association with plants, animals, birds and various signs and symbols on traditional textiles. Gimbutas replied, "I have no doubt that these female figures are from prehistoric times, i.e., representations of the Old European Goddess."[12] As early as 1974, Gimbutas had emphasized that this Neolithic goddess represented the entire cycle of life— birth, death and regeneration.[13] She defined the Old European goddess, in all of her manifestations, as "a symbol of the unity of all life in Nature."[14]

Mary received a second SUNY-Moscow exchange grant in 1988, to complete her folk art research at Moscow State University. That research resulted in the publication of *Goddess Embroideries of Eastern Europe* in the following year. Each book she published, following her research travels, featured lengthy acknowledgments of textile specialists, museum curators, authors, colleagues, family members and, especially, village women who had brought out their treasured textiles, shared their special techniques and told irreplaceable stories. In August 1989, Mary inscribed a copy of *Goddess Embroideries of Eastern Europe* with gratitude to Marija

Gimbutas: "Without your pioneering research and inspiration this book would not have been written."[15]

In *Goddess Embroideries of Eastern Europe*, the first volume of her trilogy, Mary discussed the widespread replication of embroidered images on sacred cloths, their meanings and the related folklore. She explored the embroidered cloths in the context of their functions in village rituals and folk life in Russia, the Ukraine, Yugoslavia, Romania and Poland. She did not confine her investigations to museum collections but rather went to great lengths to visit remote villages to meet with the eldest textile artists and their daughters. Among those villages were the Carpathian villages of Poland, Transylvania, and beyond, where the goddess was depicted with the Tree of Life, sun symbols, birds, animals and plants.

From the beginning of her research, Mary found it necessary to grapple with the contrasts between realistic images and abstract images in an effort to make sense out of highly stylized patterns. The development of her investigations is reflected in her published work. In *Goddess Embroideries of Eastern Europe*, one of her early texts, she compared specific goddess motifs and their progressive stylization with specific signs and symbols, providing an initial key for recognizing the significance of complex schematic patterns and how their meanings may be decoded.[16]

After returning home, Mary received a Fulbright exchange grant to teach art and graphic design courses in the United Kingdom (1989–1990). She was recognized for her technical and artistic expertise, which she applied to the design and layout of her own publications. She received two additional Fulbright grants to study Czechoslovakia and Yugoslavia in Transition (1991) and to continue her ethnographic research in Bulgaria (1992). The outbreak of the Yugoslav Wars made it necessary for Mary to cancel the Yugoslavian part of the trip, but her travel in Czechoslovakia was uninterrupted, even during the Velvet Revolution. In Czechoslovakia, she found

Fig. 53. Mary B. Kelly, *Laima, Baltic Goddess of Spring and Renewal*, oil painting on canvas, 1988.

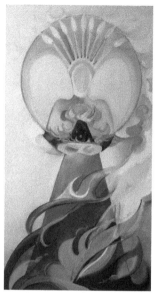

Fig. 54. Mary B. Kelly, *Lucina, Swedish Goddess of Light*, oil painting on canvas, 1989.

traditional houses still painted with ancient symbols, such as birds facing the Tree of Life, while goddesses with solar and horn symbols, animals and plants were expressed on textiles, wood and cut paper, linking the ancient past with the current reality unfolding around her. Her discussions with Czech and Slovakian textile artists gave her an intimate view of the continuity of their traditions. The Slovakian women, for instance, were still wearing symbolic horns on their heads and echoing the horned goddess in their embroidery.17 Interestingly, the women covered their horns with kerchiefs before entering Christian churches.18 In Bulgaria, she studied women's folklore and rituals and their direct relationship to textile motifs.

After the breakup of the Soviet Union, Mary was finally granted permission to visit the Carpathian region of the Ukraine, previously forbidden to Westerners, particularly Americans, due to its strategic military function during the Cold War. The Hutsul people, isolated high in the mountains, had escaped being collectivized by the Soviets and had been able to continue their traditional ways. Making the treacherous journey with Mary, not knowing what they would find, were two textile specialists, a mother–daughter team from New York. In a small remote village, they discovered several generations of women who were engaged in the entire process of textile production, from carded wool to completed cloth, replete with ancient symbols. Here the textile chain from great-grandmother to grandmother to mother to daughter had not been broken. "Not only the techniques of production were saved, but the precious motifs, the record of women's heritage, were never erased from their memory."19 The ancient motifs they had preserved contained "images of the Mother Goddess, her daughters, her sacred symbols—the sun, the rhomb, spiral horns, the Tree of Life, and her sacred animals, the snake and the bird."20 Mary and her colleagues had arrived at the last possible moment to find everyone still wearing hand-woven, embroidered costumes and continuing their unbroken traditions. On Mary's next visit to the village, people were wearing jeans and T-shirts, indicating that their world had begun to change.

Goddess Embroideries of the Balkan Lands and the Greek Islands (1999), the second book of Mary's trilogy, explored Bulgarian myths, rituals and early religious beliefs as reflected in Bulgarian embroideries; ancient traditions reflected in Romanian folk textiles; and stories of treasured continuity in the "changeless Carpathians," remarkable discoveries on remote Greek islands and Greek embroidery traditions. The appearance of each of Mary's books and articles chronicles the development of her discoveries and evolving perspective. A central thread is the recognition that ancient textile patterns are not simply decorative; they express deeply held sacred concepts that are inseparably entwined with domestic rituals and

Fig. 55. Mary B. Kelly, *Oshun, Black Virgin* series, oil painting on canvas, 1996.

cultural memory. Sacred images that carry deep symbolic meaning were replicated and preserved by means of tediously exacting techniques and the devotion of many generations of women.

> "In a sense," Mary wrote, the patterns of these ancient embroideries "resemble poetry, emphasizing ideas by repetition, duplication, and mirroring of images."[21]

> They evoke music in that there are refrains, motifs and variations. They are a religious litany of sorts, in that the cloth helps us visualize their prayers or wishes for those benefits most needed by their world—protection, fertility, good health, and holiness. . . . The beauty of life and of the earth is the source of the aesthetic beauty of the embroideries. Again and again . . . we see images surrounded by small "life signs," spirals or tendrils which cover much of the surface of ritual embroidery, repeating the message of life's primacy.[22]

Fig. 56. Mary B. Kelly,
Rozhanitza, Siberian Elk Goddess,
oil painting on canvas, 1988.

In *Goddess Embroideries of the Northlands* (2007), the third volume of Mary's trilogy, she took us on a cultural journey though Siberia, the Altai Mountains, Central Asia, Northern Russia, the Baltic region, Sweden and Old Norway.[23] In this masterful text, Mary drew together the results of broad research in the northern regions of Eurasia, weaving a wide range of visual, folkloric and historic evidence together with knowledge about the function of textiles in broadly separated communities. Her exploration linked past and present, deep history and personal recollections. It demonstrated the power of informed curiosity and embodied scholarship. In preparation for that multidimensional investigation, Mary revisited the ethnographic and archaeological collections in the Hermitage in Leningrad (St. Petersburg) multiple times. Most importantly, she trekked to remote regions to gather firsthand knowledge from such places as the open-air markets on the Silk Road and along the Volga River, where nomadic peoples arrive on camels to display their multicolored rugs, elaborate costumes and other handmade wares. Russian is their *lingua franca* (common language), which made it possible for Mary to converse with the women about their textile practices and to glimpse the living contexts of their nomadic cultural traditions.[24]

Mary acknowledged the influence of migrations and invasions on the relevance and continuity of goddess imagery and the influence of Christianization on the suppression of goddess imagery. After discussing Scandinavian traditions where home rituals in remote areas formed the basis of women's religion,[25] she expressed her appreciation for the two-hundred-year-old handcraft movement in Sweden, which has successfully conserved the textile techniques of the past. She noted, however, that the sacred motifs of earlier times, "having lost their religious/ritual value, have not been salvaged."[26]

While Mary successfully documented the continuity of traditional images in many locations, she recognized the progressive loss of their sacred meanings in the modern world. Her expressed intention was to not only encourage a wider appreciation for these exquisite textiles but also inspire present-day weavers and embroiderers to pick up the threads of what is being lost. She wrote the following:

> Like other folk arts, fabrics reflect a world inseparable from the idea of wholeness. . . . The Great Goddess was embroidered again and again by women artists because she protected, fertilized, sanctified and gave life to those who enfolded themselves in her fabrics. Following their example, may it be possible . . . to adapt their beauty of design to our own fabrics and to enhance our own lives with portions of their wisdom.[27]

A textile artist herself, Mary experienced how repetitive textile work induces contemplation, allowing spiritual beliefs and insights to arise. The process of creating sacred imagery becomes a prayer, reflecting women's ancient abilities to commune with divine powers in order to sustain the family, community and world. Just as the Old European goddess was honored as the sacred source of life, death and rebirth, the ritual use of cloths embroidered in her image have accompanied the phases of human lives for millennia.

In Mary's view, symbols accompany rituals by visually expressing the eternal order of the universe.[28] Therefore, she insisted that ritual cloth "must be used—for blessing, prayer, loving celebrations. It must affect and infect our friends, lovers, families, with joy and well-being. We must not be afraid to devise rituals ourselves. Our foremothers did."[29] Mary's 2002 publication, *Making and Using Ritual Cloths,* was created precisely to inspire this rediscovery.[30]

Mary continued to travel, expanding her research to include China and the Far East, Central and Southeast Asia, Africa, India and the Americas.[31] In 2009, she curated an exhibition of her textile collection "Sacred Symbols, Ceremonial Cloth" at the Vesterheim Norwegian-American Museum in Decorah, Iowa. That exhibition led to the publication of Mary's final book, *Goddess, Women, Cloth: A Worldwide Tradition of Making and Using Ritual Textiles,* in 2011. Mary began that book with a quotation by anthropologist Andrea Heckman that sums up its cross-cultural focus:

> Textiles, loaded with symbols, are active companions to all rituals. They are not still-life hangings, but rather moving, wrapped, layered forms used within ritual sequences, and

in these roles they join forces with rituals in the communication of culture.[32]

In the foreword to *Goddess, Women, Cloth*, the textile specialist Sheila Paine wrote, "The ethos of Kelly's work is that she never takes anyone else's word for granted but makes certain she has seen and decided for herself. This makes her books both original and authoritative."[33]

Mary stressed the importance of questioning established interpretations. She wrote, "Much of what was gathered and written about in the last hundred years was done by men who, while perfectly competent, were blinded by their own religious and cultural biases."[34] She considered a balanced gender interpretation to be a key component of her lens. Moreover, she valued cross-disciplinary research, using archaeology, mythology, art history, social history and other sources—an approach resembling archaeomythology—"in order to tease out a meaning which one discipline alone does not encompass."[35] She encouraged her students to be curious and courageous and to ask a lot of questions. "Listen to what people say and record it. This is especially important with women, who have suffered for millennia from lack of documentation concerning their art work and religious beliefs."[36]

Mary's sister Ann Berger Frutkin recalled, "Mary was a challenging and self-directed leader. She was focused, quick and always curious. She was a connector of ideas and people. She lured people to follow her. I should know!"[37] Mary did, indeed, lure friends, family members and colleagues to join her adventures of discovery. She also led formal study tours, including Textile Traditions of Old Europe (2003), sponsored by the Textile Museum, Washington, D.C., and a study tour to Norway and Finland (2013), sponsored by the Vesterheim Norwegian-American Museum in Decorah, Iowa.

Mary wrote that working with folk textiles is one of the greatest joys in life. "Seeing these beautiful hand-made objects, holding them lovingly in our hands now, years after their creators have died, reminds us of our profound responsibilities."[38]

> Folk textiles from a pre-literate world call out to us and communicate essential ideas about what human life is. If we fall in love with folk art, it is because it is essentially a mirror of our own humanness, our human predicament. If we fail to read that communication, if we forget those who

are communicating to us, we will forgo their secrets and our own enlightenment. Our thanks goes, finally, to those who made this work, our foremothers. Let us then make a commitment to them and to these beautiful and meaningful embroideries; and let us make it a joyful experience.[39]

Our deep gratitude goes to Mary Berger Kelly, whose spirited dedication to the creation, preservation and ritual use of sacred textiles honors countless generations of women throughout the world, whose devoted labors have fostered the transmission of ancient knowledge and the spiritual well-being of their communities. As she reminded us, "throughout the world, folk textiles shine with lustrous threads, speaking a symbolic language. Using this gift, we will continue to weave our wishes, embroider our prayers."[40]

My sincere gratitude goes to Mary's sister Ann Berger Frutkin for generously providing a wealth of information about Mary's life and work. Thanks also to Mary's daughter Susannah, her son Stephen, and his wife Kelly for providing access to Mary's CV and other important material. Without your vital assistance, this piece could not have been written
—Joan Marler

References

Frutkin, Ann Berger. *A Collaborative Memory of a Cincinnati Family.* Hilton Head Island, SC: Studiobooks, 2009.

———. "Ann's Memories of Mary," unpublished paper read at the funeral of Mary B. Kelly, 2016.

Gimbutas, Marija. *The Gods and Goddesses of Old Europe, 7000–3500 BC: Myths, Legends, and Cult Images.* Berkeley and Los Angeles: University of California Press, 1974. Republished in 1982 as *The Goddesses and Gods of Old Europe.*

———. *The Language of the Goddess.* San Francisco: Harper, 1989.

Heckman. Andrea M. *Woven Stories: Andean Textiles and Rituals.* Albuquerque, NM: University of New Mexico Press, 2003.

Kelly, Mary B. *Goddess Embroideries of Eastern Europe.* Exhibition sponsored by the National Endowment for the Arts. Binghamton, NY and Cleveland, OH: Roberson Center and the Cleveland Museum of Art, 1986.

————. *Goddess Embroideries of Eastern Europe.* Winona, MN: Northland Press of Winona, 1989.

————. *Embroidering the Goddesses of Russia.* Denver, CO: Counted Thread Press, 1992.

————. *Embroidering the Goddesses of Slovakia.* Denver, CO: Counted Thread Press, 1995.

————. *Embroidering the Goddesses of Ukraine.* Denver, CO: Counted Thread Press, 1997.

————. *Embroidering the Goddesses of the Greek Islands.* Denver, CO: Counted Thread Press, 1997.

————. *Goddess Embroideries of the Balkan Lands and the Greek Islands.* Hilton Head Island, SC: Studiobooks, 1999.

————. *Making and Using Ritual Cloths.* Hilton Head Island, SC: Studiobooks, 2002.

————. *Goddess Embroideries of the Northlands.* Hilton Head Island, SC: Studiobooks, 2007.

————. *Embroidering the Goddesses of Old Norway.* Hilton Head Island, SC: Studiobooks, 2008.

————. "Finding Sacred Symbols: A Life of Textile Travel." Recorded lecture at Bethania Lutheran Church at the Vesterheim Norwegian-American Museum, Decorah, IA, September 27, 2009.

————. "A Walk with Berehinia: Goddess of Ukraine and Russia." In *Eastern Mediterranean and Europe.* Vol. 2 of *Goddesses in World Culture,* edited by Patricia Monaghan. Santa Barbara, CA: Praeger, 2010.

————. *Goddess, Women, Cloth: A Worldwide Tradition of Making and Using Ritual Textiles.* Hilton Head Island, SC: Studiobooks, 2011.

Endnotes

1 Ann Berger Frutkin, *A Collaborative Memory of a Cincinnati Family* (Hilton Head Island, SC: Studiobooks, 2009), 48.

2 Ann Berger Frutkin, "Ann's Memories of Mary," unpublished paper read at the funeral of Mary B. Kelly, 2016.

3 Frutkin, *A Collaborative Memory of a Cincinnati Family,* v.

4 Frutkin, "Ann's Memories of Mary."

5 Frutkin, "Ann's Memories of Mary."

6 Frutkin, *A Collaborative Memory of a Cincinnati Family*, 21.

7 Mary B. Kelly, *Goddess Embroideries of Eastern Europe* (Winona, MN: Northland Press of Winona, 1989), 1.

8 Kelly, *Goddess Embroideries of Eastern Europe*, 3.

9 Kelly, *Goddess Embroideries of Eastern Europe*, 3.

10 Kelly, *Goddess Embroideries of Eastern Europe*, 4–5.

11 Kelly, *Goddess Embroideries of Eastern Europe*, 4–5.

12 Marija Gimbutas, letter to Mary B. Kelly, August 17, 1983, in Mary B. Kelly, *Goddess Embroideries of the Balkan Lands and the Greek Islands* (Hilton Head Island, SC: Studiobooks, 1999), 61.

13 Marija Gimbutas, *The Gods and Goddesses of Old Europe, 7000–3500 BC: Myths, Legends, and Cult Images* (Berkeley and Los Angeles: University of California Press, 1974), 152. Republished in 1982 as *The Goddesses and Gods of Old Europe*.

14 Marija Gimbutas, *The Language of the Goddess* (San Francisco: Harper, 1989), 321.

15 This inscribed copy of *Goddess Embroideries of Eastern Europe* was donated by Marija Gimbutas to the library of the Institute of Archaeomythology.

16 Kelly, *Goddess Embroideries of Eastern Europe*, 31–61.

17 Kelly, *Goddess Embroideries of Eastern Europe*, 125–26. See also the picture on the cover of the book, photographed by Helene Cincebox, which shows traditionally clad Slovakian women, some wearing horizontal horns.

18 The description of Slovakian women wearing horns is from Mary B. Kelly, "Finding Sacred Symbols: A Life of Textile Travel," recorded lecture at Bethania Lutheran Church at the Vesterheim Norwegian-American Museum, Decorah, IA, September 27, 2009.

19 Mary B. Kelly, *Goddess Embroideries of the Balkan Lands and the Greek Islands* (Hilton Head Island, SC: Studiobooks, 1999): 58–59.

20 Kelly, *Goddess Embroideries of the Balkan Lands and the Greek Islands*, 60.

21 Kelly, *Goddess Embroideries of the Balkan Lands and the Greek Islands,* 38.

22 Kelly, *Goddess Embroideries of the Balkan Lands and the Greek Islands*, 38.

23 Mary B. Kelly, *Goddess Embroideries of the Northlands* (Hilton Head Island, SC: Studiobooks, 2007).

24 Kelly, "Finding Sacred Symbols: A Life of Textile Travel."

25 Kelly, *Goddess Embroideries of the Northlands,* 205.

26 Kelly, *Goddess Embroideries of the Northlands,* 232.

27 Kelly, *Goddess Embroideries of Eastern Europe,* 170–71.

28 Kelly, *Goddess Embroideries of the Northlands,* 298.

29 Kelly, *Goddess Embroideries of the Northlands,* 170.

30 Mary B. Kelly, *Making and Using Ritual Cloths* (Hilton Head Island, SC: Studiobooks, 2002).

31 During her 2009 lecture, "Finding Sacred Symbols: A Life of Textile Travel," Mary commented that her visit to Guatemala during the 1990s took place toward the end of the protracted civil war, which she experienced as still somewhat dangerous.

32 Andrea M. Heckman, *Woven Stories: Andean Textiles and Rituals* (Albuquerque, NM: University of New Mexico Press, 2003). This quotation appears in Mary B. Kelly, *Goddess, Women, Cloth: A Worldwide Tradition of Making and Using Ritual Textiles* (Hilton Head Island, SC: Studiobooks, 2011), 1.

33 Sheila Paine, foreword to *Goddess, Women, Cloth: A Worldwide Tradition of Making and Using Ritual Textiles,* by Mary B. Kelly (Hilton Head Island, SC: Studiobooks, 2011), 32.

34 Kelly, *Goddess Embroideries of the Northlands,* xv.

35 Kelly, *Goddess Embroideries of the Northlands,* xv.

36 Kelly, *Goddess Embroideries of the Northlands,* xvi.

37 Frutkin, "Ann's Memories of Mary." For a remarkable description of one of Ann's journeys with Mary to the remote Greek island of Astipalia, see Mary B. Kelly, *Embroidering the Goddesses of the Greek Islands* (Denver: Counted Thread Press, 1997).

38 Kelly, *Goddess Embroideries of the Northlands,* vii.

39 Kelly, *Goddess Embroideries of the Northlands,* vii.

40 Kelly, *Goddess, Women, Cloth,* 175.

SECTION 4

ARTISTS, THEIR WORK
AND THEIR WORDS

A BLESSING ON THE POETS

Patient earth-diggers, impatient fire-makers,
Hungry word-takers and roving sound-lovers,
Sharers and savers, musers and achers,
You who are open to hide or uncover,
Time-keepers and –haters, wake-sleepers, sleep-wakers;
May language's language, the silence that lies
Under each word, move you over and over,
Turning you, wondering, back to surprise.

~ Annie Finch

COLORS AND FORMS SHIFTING INTO TIME AND PLACE

LAURA FRAGUA-COTA

My art is my voice. I use many languages of art to give dimension and depth to that voice. I create through the use of words, movement, or two- or three-dimensional forms. My art includes images of life in Pueblo Indian villages, faces sculpted in stone, words inspired by a sense of place, and movement with the community during ceremonies and dances throughout the cycles of the seasons. I had the privilege and honor of sharing my work at the Association for the Study of Women and Mythology's 2014 Conference in San Antonio, Texas. Here I share the pieces that I showed at that conference, in the order in which I presented them.

"Emergence" *(Figure 57)*

Creation stories speak of leaving one world and entering the next. This piece was made with that journey in mind. Perhaps those who walked had to use a ladder to leave the lower worlds. The red sand inside the bowl, from my village, symbolizes that we were made from the earth. All around the bowl are pictographs that represent animals, plant life and supernatural beings.

Fig. 57. Laura Fragua-Cota, *Emergence*, a bowl of white micaceous clay, wooden ladder, and red sand, with pictographs on the outside, 2007.

"Where the Spirit Goes" *(Figure 58)*

While I was at the Institute of American Indian Arts in Santa Fe, NM, I wanted to learn every art medium that was offered. Because I have worked with stone, I have learned a lot about the various stones and which ones work for the type of composition that I want. I like to work with limestone. Alabaster is a challenge, because of its natural cracks and variety of colors.

Fig. 58. Laura Fragua-Cota, *Where the Spirit Goes*, Indiana limestone on a wooden base, 1988.

When I visited a friend in another Pueblo village who also carves in stone, I saw a small piece of limestone that had a hole in it. I asked what my friend thought he might carve with that piece. He said he hadn't thought about it, and he asked me if I wanted the stone. I said, "Sure. I've never had a stone that had a hole in it. It will be a challenge to see what comes from it." This is an abstract depiction of a Pueblo Indian woman wearing a manta, a necklace and a shawl over her head. I left the hole, to symbolize the space that holds spirit. It cannot be felt or seen, but it is there. We all have that hole, where the spirit goes, but what is seen on the outside will vary.

"La Entrada Conquistadores en El Nombre de Jesus Christo" *(Figure 59)*

This oil painting is in remembrance of the 300-year anniversary of the Pueblo Indian Revolt. The scene depicted took place in the Southwestern landscape with a procession of Franciscan priests and Spanish conquistadors coming behind them. The first priest is carrying a large cross, and the group is entering new lands and

Fig. 59. Laura Fragua-Cota, *La Entrada Conquistadores en El Nombre de Jesus Christom*, oil painting, 1980.

176

forcing a new religion on those they meet. I thought of the priests saying, "We are here to care for your heathen souls!" When the Spanish colonists came to the Southwest, they enslaved or murdered many of the Indians they encountered.

"With No Eyes My Hands Feel What I See" *(Figure 60)*

Fig. 60. Laura Fragua-Cota, *With No Eyes My Hands Feel What I See*, white alabaster carving of an abstract head, 1990.

Most museums and galleries have DO NOT TOUCH signs posted, for good reason. But I have often wondered about those who cannot see. What is there that speaks to them about what is in front of them? There are three-dimensional pieces that draw my hands to touch them. They are made especially to be touched. Let fingers feel the nose, the lips and the eyes to truly get a feel for the entire piece. This is a piece that I intentionally made so that it could be touched.

"Beneath the Red There Were the Blues" *(Figure 61)*

There are times when I envision an art piece that needs to be shared regarding the history of the people indigenous to this land. This painting depicts an Indian man whose eyes speak volumes. Half of his face is blue and the other half is red. The way in which we now understand the term *the Blues* came about at a different time, but I am sure that he would have felt the blues at the thought of the history of the indigenous people of this land. I can feel the sadness in his eyes at all of the devastation that came upon his people.

Fig. 61. Laura Fragua-Cota, *Beneath the Red There Were the Blues*, pastel painting on velour paper, 2011.

Fig. 62. Laura Fragua-Cota, *My Cornmeal Bowl Full of Prayers*, line drawing of original sculpture carved out of Colorado pink alabaster, 1984.

"My Cornmeal Bowl Full of Prayers"*(Figure 62)*

This is one of the first stone carvings I made while at the Institute of American Indian Arts. I tried every medium they offered. Sculpture class was a very challenging class as I began to work in stone. When I started, I used a soft stone called alabaster; it has natural cracks, and it comes in many colors. The specific stone that I chose was a light pink one. I had an idea of what I wanted to create, but as I worked on it I couldn't get what I wanted.

178

My (male) teacher made some remarks about my piece, but they were not constructive. In fact, they were condescending. I felt like a woman in man's territory. Many of the tools were heavy, and so were many of the stones. But I kept, on even though I didn't like the teacher's tone. I think most women would have left!

In Pueblo Indian villages, the act of prayer seems unceasing. A bowl of cornmeal is always present in the home, accessible so that it can be given as a grain offering in prayer. Corn is a major crop in our village. Many fields of corn are planted, and every phase of the cycle of its growth and preparation is important. The corn image is prevalent in my work. Because of its many uses throughout its growth cycle, corn is a staple that feeds not only our bodies but also our souls. It has been and will always be one of many "Mothers" that care for and nurture their children. This piece shows a Pueblo Indian woman sitting on the floor and holding a bowl of cornmeal. She holds it as if she were a bit selfish for the bowl. She has many prayers for her family, her home, the village and all of the things she desires for the good of all. It is a beautiful piece, and I felt that it would make a beautiful bronze edition -- and here it is!

"Aboriginal Daughter with Great White Mom and Dad" (Figure 63)

I received a postcard from my husband when he traveled to Washington, D.C. for a meeting. On the front of the postcard is a picture of President Ronald Reagan and First Lady Nancy Reagan. I knew I had to save it and use it in my art sometime.

I heard when the indigenous people began their relationships with the U.S. government and often had to travel to Washington, D.C. to meet with the president, they called him Great White Father. This piece is a graphite drawing of a young Hopi Pueblo Indian maiden. She is wearing the traditional manta of the Pueblo Indians.

Fig. 63. Laura Fragua-Cota, *Aboriginal Daughter with Great White Mom and Dad,* graphite on drawing paper, with feathers and postcard, 1987.

Her hair is in the style called butterfly whorls, which signifies her young age. I placed the postcard to her right and at the top a line symbolic of land and from which hang feathers. For me, particular feathers symbolize prayer. To make this relationship a little more personal, instead of White Father I used "Mom and Dad" in the title.

"Aboriginal Son with Great White Father" *(Figure 64)*

When Bill Clinton was president of the United States, I had a postcard of only his image. I wanted to create a counterpart to "Aboriginal Daughter with Great White Mom and Dad." This piece is a picture of an Indian man holding a pipe, which is usually used during prayer. Below the postcard, I placed a cigar in a cigar holder. Many Native American tribes used tobacco during prayer. What might Clinton have used his tobacco for?

Fig. 64. Laura Fragua-Cota, *Aboriginal Son with Great White Father*, graphite, postcard, feathers, and cigar in cigar case, 1998.

"A Pathway of our future . . ." *(Figure 65)*

At a curio shop, I saw a piece of rawhide that reminded me of the map of the United States. I purchased it, knowing that someday I would use it in my art. My daughter calls me an art hoarder! Eventually, after many years, I was invited to submit a piece for an exhibit called *The Artist's Perspective of Columbus*. When I think of Christopher Columbus, I think of the things he brought when he "discovered" America. Such devastation occurred! All I can think of is the death and destruction of many innocent lives. In the painting, bodies strewn are along a path on the hide, which is shaped like the United States. At the top is a sword with a cross, and at the one end a spear is thrust into the first body on the path. As I prayed and pondered about what to create for the exhibit, the following poem came to me, which led me to the painting's title:

A Pathway of our future
born of unholy
sacrifice
in the name
of God
and GOLD
Blood
from hands
that already prayed
from feet
that danced
to a loving Creator

A symbol of guilt
never
to be redeemed
in the lives
of their descendents
numerous
as the stars

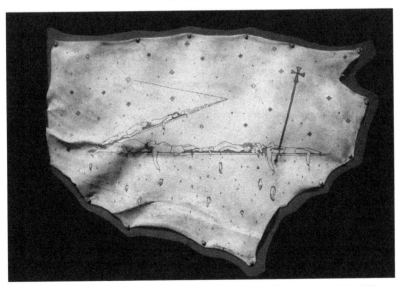

Fig. 65. Laura Fragua-Cota, *A Pathway of our future . . .*, painting of figures on rawhide, 1992.

"The Naming Ceremony"*(Figure 66)*

In Pueblo Indian villages, when a child is given a name the parents ask someone else to give the name. In the naming ceremony and blessing, an ear of corn from the garden is used. Family and friends are present. The corn is raised in the four directions and placed at the child's heart and forehead. When the corn is at the child's forehead, the name and then a blessing are said. Those who are present follow by saying the child's new name, and they too give the child a blessing. This sculpture depicts a Pueblo Indian woman dressed in the traditional style. Holding an ear of corn, she is praying and ready to name the child.

Fig. 66. Laura Fragua-Cota, *The Naming Ceremony*, Indiana limestone carving on a wooden base, 2012.

"Is it Just Makeup?"*(Figure 67)*

Eventually, some Native Americans found their place in the mainstream of America. The Indian Relocation Act of 1956 encouraged many to undergo vocational school training and take on employment far from their homelands. I have heard stories about Indian women who wanted their skin color to be light as that of the white people they lived and worked with. One story spoke of a child who was placed in a bath of bleach, in hope that the bath would lighten the child's skin. Another story spoke of an aunt who wore makeup

Fig. 67. Laura Fragua-Cota, *Is it Just Makeup?* oil painting, 1997.

three or four shades lighter that her own skin so that she would appear more white.

"Is It Just Makeup?" depicts a young contemporary woman sitting at her vanity. Mascara, powder makeup, and lipstick are on the vanity. She is wearing high heels, and her powwow dress is on a mannequin. Magazines are scattered on her dresser: The covers list articles such as "How Sexy Are You? Find Out," "10 Surefire Ways to Lose Weight While Eating Fry Bread," "Your Man, Your Lover, Your Snag—Will He Stay?" and "How to Save Your Relationship When He's a Tipi Creeper." The young woman is looking in the mirror, putting on makeup lighter than her own skin. Hanging on the wall are a cross and an eagle feather. As she looks up at the reflection of a picture of her grandmother wearing a buckskin dress, she thinks about her grandmother and the time when she lived. It's easier to be white these days, she may be thinking. It's not just makeup.

"Just Because You Put Feathers in Your Hair Don't Make You an Indian" *(Figure 68)*

Fig. 68. Laura Fragua-Cota, *Just Because You Put Feathers in Your Hair Don't Make You an Indian,* clay, ceramic stains, war bonnet with feathers, beaded "Indian belt," trading cards, rubber tomahawk, and white rock from Abiquiú, New Mexico, 1985.

I was inspired to create this piece by a show held in New Jersey during Columbus Day weekend. The state of New Jersey had given the Powhatan tribe some acres of land from a nature reserve area. The tribe used that land to present various activities to bring awareness that many Indian tribes exist. They planned to eventually build a museum on the land. One of the activities was an art show that brought in artists from Indian tribes from all across

America. The Powhatan tribe asked that the artists bring items that children could purchase, because the first three days of the art show they bussed in more than four thousand children from various school districts. The Cherokee tribe had a booth that sold rubber tomahawks, beaded belts and other things. There were hundreds of little white children wearing warbonnets and swinging rubber tomahawks at each other. For that moment, they were "Indian."

"Pueblo Indian Harvest Dance" *(Figure 69)*

Fig. 69. Laura Fragua-Cota, *Pueblo Indian Harvest Dance*, oil painting on canvas, 1996.

Not all dances in Pueblo Indian villages are open to the public. Some dances are closed, and only members of the tribe can attend. The harvest dance or corn dance is open to the public. In my village, the harvest dance is held during the special feast days. I painted this piece on a 3' 1/2 by 4' canvas. It shows the dancers coming down the plaza and the singers singing and the visitors watching from the side. The women wear waa-ha, or clouds, on their heads, and the men wear kilts and, across their bare chests, bands of shells. The women hold evergreens in their hands, and the men hold rattles and branches of blue spruce. The koshare is the striped character who is ever present during ceremonies. The men sing songs for the she-wah-na (cloud spirits) to water the fields. The entire dance is a prayer for our families, our village, our fields, our hopes and dreams and all people. This large painting took me nine years to finish.

"Who Made the Box?" *(Figure 70)*

How often have you heard people say, "We have to think outside the box"? Where did that term come from? Koshares are figures found in most Pueblo Indian villages. They help with almost all of the ceremonies. Sometimes they wear regular clothing, but sometimes they are painted in stripes and

Fig. 70. Laura Fragua-Cota, *Who Made the Box?* micaceous clay, cloth, corn husk, ceramic stains, and wooden box, 2007.

they wear loin cloths. Koshares help with the ceremonies and often entertain during breaks. People from the audience give them things to eat and drink. Watermelon is one of their favorites, and it is easy to share. Known as clowns, they often use humor to relay messages. For this piece, I asked the koshares to help me with these questions: Who put us in the box? What is the box made out of? What was in the box that we no longer need?

"The Blessing of the Animals" *(Figure 71)*

One of the winter dances that is open to the public is the Buffalo Dance. In this painting are three main figures—two male buffalo and one female—along with hawk, eagle, antelope, ram, and deer. The painting is in the early Southwestern style of Native American painting. It depicts the song that calls each of the animals to come forward to be blessed. The

Fig. 71. Laura Fragua-Cota, *The Blessing of the Animals*, gouache painting on watercolor paper, 2011.

little hawk is down on one knee looking up in awe of the Buffalo Woman as she touches an eagle feather to his head and blesses him.

"Mother Earth's Blessing"*(Figure 63)*

Fig. 72. Laura Fragua-Cota, *Mother Earth's Blessing*, acrylic painting on Masonite, 2013.

The opportunity to submit a proposal for art in public places came with the call for artwork from the University of New Mexico Sandoval Regional Medical Center. The call was for Native American artists from tribes that have lands in Sandoval County, which is served by the medical center. Five artists from Jemez decided to submit a proposal to do a collaborative project. We were a weaver, a woman who made clay figurines, one who made a wedding vase, a cabinet-maker who made the frames, and me. My contribution was a painting. After our proposal was accepted, we had several meetings to discuss our collaboration in more detail. We decided what each person would contribute and presented our plan to our tribal leaders. They approved.

My submission was a large acrylic painting on Masonite board. I wanted to depict the village dances, how hunting and agriculture are still strong in our village, and how prayer is always a part of our life. I painted Mother Earth praying with cornmeal and blessing the lands, the animals, the village and the people. My artist's statement, posted beside the painting, is as follows:

> In my painting, I depict a woman symbolic of "Mother Earth" praying as she gives us a grain offering of corn meal. She smiles upon all that the Creator has blessed us with. The water flowing from her onto the earth sustains all that grows on the earth, those that crawl or walk the earth and the abundance of the fields and plant life that nourishes

our bodies. She sees the clear blue skies that offer a home to those that fly and present the stars at night. She hears our songs and feels the pounding of the drum as dancers' feet move in unison, bringing their prayers in dance and song and giving thanks as the eagle carries our prayers to the heavens. We, as humans, must be guardians for all of this. It is through sustaining this balance that we can be nourished and healed. I believe Mother Earth's prayer is that we continue to care for and maintain that balance so we can walk in wellness as one with all of our brothers and sisters including both our human relatives and all other beings that share this world."

I am grateful to the Creator, who has placed me in this world at this time and place. I have been given so much to embrace through my family, my community and my culture. Our culture is kept alive through not only our children but also our prayers. In dance and song, we will continue to live the life we have been given.

Thay cone known pah! (Thank you!)

IN THE EYES OF MEDUSA

CRISTINA BIAGGI

Medusa is one aspect of the primordial dark goddess found in all cultures. She is that from which everything emerges and to whom everything returns. She is the goddess of the crossroads, of death and transformation, of transition and renewal. Because she contains all contradictions within herself, she is all powerful—hideous and beautiful at the same time. In her total state, she combines the old hag in one moment and the beautiful young girl in the next. She is cyclical continuity, embodying the past, present and future. She is the dark moon that precedes the shining sliver of the new moon in the night sky. She enfolds in her powerful velvet arms, consumes, regurgitates and transforms anew. We are living in the age of the dark goddess. To live with the dark goddess is to live with contradictions, with extremes, to live in a state of suspended animation while what is happening inside mirrors what is happening outside.

Medusa was one of the three Gorgons who dwelt in Libya: Stheno, the mighty one; Euryale, the wanderer; and Medusa, the great queen, ruler of the sea. The word *gorgon* is derived from the Greek word *gorgos*, which means "terrible, horrifying." According to the classical patriarchal myth, Medusa, the one mortal Gorgon, had been a beautiful maiden. She had been seduced by Poseidon, who appeared in front of her in the shape of a horse in one of Athena's temples. As a result, Medusa became pregnant with twins. Athena became incensed and turned Medusa into a hideous monster with snake hair, capable of turning into stone anyone who looked at her. Perseus, son of Danaë, was sent by King Polydectes on a mission that was considered impossible to complete. He was to kill Medusa and bring back her head. Armed with a sharp sickle, a cap to make him invisible, winged sandals given to him by the god Hermes, and a polished shield, a gift from Athena, Perseus completed the task. Inspired by Athena, he looked at Medusa's reflection in Athena's shield rather than directly at her and sliced off Medusa's head. From the decapitated body of Medusa, Pegasus was born. Athena later mounted Medusa's head on her breastplate, her aegis.

This is the patriarchal myth. But let us examine the myth more closely to glean its deeper roots, its matriarchal substratum. The myth that has come down to us is a classical overlay. The legend of Perseus beheading Medusa seems to suggest that patriarchal newcomers—the Hellenes—took over and dismantled the ancient shrines of the goddess. The names of the Gorgons and their number—three—are significant. The mighty one, Stheno; the wide roaming one, Euryale; and the queen, Medusa, are titles of the moon goddess. Priestesses in moon-worship rituals apparently wore Gorgon masks to gather power and frighten away strangers. These rituals included divination, healing magic and mysteries associated with death and rebirth. The snakes in Medusa's hair bespeak Medusa's ancient lineage. The snake is the terrestrial alter ego of the goddess, dating back to the Paleolithic era and still prevalent in the Neolithic. The snake was thought to possess regenerative powers, because it sheds its skin. Because the bite of certain snakes can induce hallucinogenic states, snakes were thought to possess oracular powers. Therefore, snakes were kept in temples, to facilitate priestesses' trances. Medusa's staring eyes are related to those of the earliest Neolithic eye goddess, whose eyes are depicted in temples throughout Mesopotamia. The eye is connected with the owl, an embodiment of the goddess of death—hence, the Wadjet eye of the Egyptian goddess Maat and the eye shown on the U.S. dollar bill. In some societies, women's eyes are considered dangerous—women create life and they were thought to be able to destroy it with a stare—hence, the belief in the *malocchio* (evil eye), which is prevalent in many parts of the world, including Southern Italy and Turkey.

Medusa is a complex figure with many prepatriarchal layers. Let us look at her genesis. According to Miriam Robbins Dexter in her brilliant article "The Ferocious and the Erotic 'Beautiful' Medusa and the Neolithic Bird and Snake," the patriarchal myth of Perseus slaying Medusa did not appear until 700 BCE, in Hesiod's *Theogony*.[1] Even though Perseus was mentioned in *The Iliad*, there was no reference to his decapitation of Medusa. In 500 BCE, when the Greek poet Pindar wrote about the Gorgons and Medusa, he was first to mention snakes in their hair. In 560 BCE, the Greek historian Herodotus placed Medusa and Perseus in Libya. The Roman poet Ovid also associated Medusa with Libya, attributing to her the origin of the multitude of Libyan snakes. That Perseus uses a mirror to look at Medusa, so that he does not have to look at her face directly and thus be killed by her stare, is interesting. Historically, the mirror was a priestess's or shaman's tool of divination.

What is the significance of Medusa's power to turn men into stone? Her power combines two symbols: the power of eyes and the turning of men into stones/megaliths/funerary monuments. To look at Medusa is to die.

Medusa's blood can cure as well as kill. From this, it is evident that she represents regeneration as well as death. Medusa's sacred blood has the power to create snakes and Pegasus. That Medusa's blood can both create and destroy life refers to menstrual blood, which early societies considered to have special powers. Men regarded menstrual blood with holy dread: Women bleed but do not die. To diminish women's power, patriarchal societies pronounced menstruating women unclean and therefore unworthy to enter sacred places such as mosques and temples.

Fig. 73. Cristina Biaggi, *Yew Medusa*, yew tree, 1976.

And, according to Dexter, Medusa's gaping mouth can be seen as the vulva, the cave through which we reach the underworld, which may be compared to the womb of the birth mother. In this sense, Medusa is a shaman, an arbiter between this world and the otherworld.[2]

Let me now talk about my own artistic history with Medusa. I created this wooden Medusa in 1980. At that point, I did not know much about

Medusa's lineage. I was merely intrigued by the personage and symbology of Medusa. I had cut down a dead yew tree. (Later I found out that the yew was sacred to Hecate, another dark goddess.) Its trunk and branches were lying in my driveway. My sister came along and exclaimed, "Oh, Cris! This tree is great! It looks just like a Medusa!" Bingo! My mind started racing with plans, and I imagined Medusa in the tree. It took me 108 hours of hard work to create this piece (*Figure 73*). The face is based on my face 35 years ago. Her eyes stare at the viewer, trying to get inside her or his soul, and her grin is crooked. She is fierce, but she is also laughing. By hook or by crook, she'll get to you—if not with vinegar, then with honey. I chose to exhibit her in a black alcove, to conceal her power. She appears to be float-ing in space, like a disembodied apparition, like a dream or a nightmare. Her sacred space, the black tent, is meant to be a place removed from time and space, a space where the viewer is asked to confront whatever she or he needs to face.

In the mid-1980s, I went through a very political phase of my life, during which I rediscovered the power of women. I actively took part in protests against the military–industrial complex. I visited women's encampments and took part in peaceful protests at such places as Seneca Falls in New York, Greenham Common in England and Comiso in Sicily. I had finished my doctoral dissertation about the Great Goddess and, therefore, was begin-ning to realize the deep connection between Medusa and the Great Goddess. The sculptures *Black Medusa* and *Red Medusa* are reflections of this period.

Black Medusa is based on my face (*Figure 74*). She is depicted with a sardonic grin—she laughs with her mouth but glares with her eyes. She is superimposed on a sea of supporting women who stare at the viewer. *Red Medusa*, a portrait of my daughter, depicts Medusa in her full power, her laughter (*Figure 75*). She is superimposed on a sea of laughing women. Laughter is a powerful tool for survival, change and health, hence the bumper sticker SHE WHO LAUGHS, LASTS.

Fig. 74. Cristina Biaggi, *Black Medusa*, collage and plaster on wood, 1983.

Raging Medusa (*Figure 76*) was created at the turn of the millennium. Here is Medusa in her full-blown anger. As a model of women's power, I used the face of Maria Callas hitting a high C during a performance of Bellini's *Norma* at the Metropolitan Opera in New York. Here Medusa represents the rage of women duped and enslaved by patriarchy and the deepest anger of the earth herself at having been so cataclysmically devastated.

Fig. 75. Cristina Biaggi, Red Medusa, collage and plaster on wood, 1983.

Fig. 76. Cristina Biaggi, *Raging Medusa*, fiberglass, 2000.

What can Medusa mean to modern women? Perseus decapitating Medusa is the patriarchal answer to women's full powers, which are not allowed to exist in a patriarchal structure. According to prehistorian Joan Marler, "to be decapitated is to be silenced."[3] The patriarchal myth is a teaching: If you women manifest your full powers, this is what will happen to you. To embrace the spirit of Medusa, of the dark goddess, we must resolve to be totally truthful with ourselves and to act from our inner core. To embrace Medusa is to resolve to change one's consciousness.[4]

How do we do that? We must not hide our heads in the sand. Rather, we must become aware of the injustices around us and try to change them, taking small steps but taking steps. Here are some doable suggestions. We must: keep ourselves informed about what is happening around us; write to our elected officials about injustices; take part in marches and demonstrations; boycott products that exploit other people, animals or plants; recycle; compost; join goddess-related or other consciousness groups; help the needy and downtrodden; help animals, children and seniors; create inspiring art and meaningful writing that reaches people; engage in public speaking about meaningful issues; and create life-affirming rituals. How we live our individual lives not only matters to ourselves, our immediate family and our friends, but also, by six degrees of separation, can affect the whole world. Finally, we need to consider ourselves not only as Americans, Chinese or Russians but also as citizens of the world.

Medusa has been depicted in art from the Neolithic era to the present. Examples abound, from the Neolithic era, and from Archaic and Classical Greece and Rome. A 1st century BCE fresco from Pompeii, depicts Perseus freeing Andromeda while he carries the severed head of Medusa in his left hand. From The Loggia dei Lanzi in Florence Benvenuto Cellini's gorgeous bronze statue, dating to 1554, shows the victorious hero Perseus holding aloft the recently severed head of Medusa. In 1597, Michelangelo Merisi da Caravaggio painted Medusa on a shield that echoes Athena's shield from Archaic and Classical Greece. In 1734, Gian Lorenzo Bernini created a sad-looking Medusa. In Archaic, Classical and Hellenistic times, Medusa was often used in breastplates, to scare off the enemy, black and red figure vases, shields, coins, door knockers, jewelry, and so forth.

Why this fascination for a supposedly monstrous character? I believe that Medusa was a particularly potent aspect of the Great Goddess, in her role as generatrix, that has been demonized by patriarchy. She represents the idea of accepting that if we are alive we cannot escape being killers.[5] Life lives on life. What should we do with that knowledge? We must resolve to kill respectfully, consciously and in a sacred manner.

Medusa is often depicted with a lolling tongue and the fangs of a wild boar. Her tongue is red, the color of blood. The wild boar is a corpse eater, the power of the underworld. There is a connection here with death and regeneration of the underworld. Medusa's protruding, staring eyes also say, "If you are not respectful of these mysteries, go away."

In writings from the Classical period, Medusa is decapitated and, thus, ferocity is separated from wisdom. It must be reconnected. Medusa is naturally connected to the Indian goddess Kali/Durga. Kali eats lies, corruption and anything that gets in the way of time, knowledge or enlightenment. She upsets the comfortable order of society. She makes us remember that "No matter what you do, Cosmo, you're gonna die," as the character Rose Castorini says in the movie *Moonstruck*.[6] Kali/Durga/Medusa cuts out everything that fosters the illusion that we are immortal. Finally, Medusa represents the full powers of women whose gifts are not allowed to exist in a patriarchal structure.

And now let us examine Taranto, the city of Medusa. Taranto, in the region of Puglia, the heel of Italy, has been inhabited since prehistoric times. The present city was founded in 706 BCE as a Spartan colony. A Doric temple to Hera, from the 6th century BCE, is located in the old port of Taranto. The temple's columns are nine meters tall. The Taranto museum has a vast collection of female statuary from the temple, including Hera, Persephone, Demeter and Aphrodite.

In ancient times, Taranto was the city of Medusa. Evidence for this statement can be amply seen in the National Archaeological Museum in Taranto, which has a vast collection of Medusa images, especially ante-fixes. An antefix is an architectural detail, usually made of terra-cotta, that decorates the roof of an archaic Greek temple. Terra-cotta was a popular medium for architectural details on Greek buildings in Southern Italy, and the carved details of this antefix would have been painted in bright colors at the time. The head of Medusa, a device frequently featured in antefixes, would have been appropriate along the façade of a building, warding off any approaching evil.

The antefixes on temples were distributed evenly at the edges of the roofs and had both a decorative function and an apotropaic function, especially those antefixes that depicted Medusa. The antefixes served to keep away or neutralize any evil or dangerous influences. The widespread occurance of the Tarantine antefixes suggest that they were used not only for important temples but also for more modest funerary structures and perhaps even habitations.

Approximately 1,000 terra-cotta antefixes have been found in and around Taranto. They were found in the countryside, sometimes in wells or cisterns, especially in places that had to do with necropolis, and in habitation sites. The architectonic antefixes of terra-cotta that were produced in Taranto between the end of the 7th century and the 3rd century BCE were manufactured from molds.

As one can see from these five antefixes (*Figures 77-81*),[7] there is an interesting evolution in the face of Medusa, from terrifying monster in the 6th century BCE to a beautiful and sometimes sad young woman in the 4th century BCE. This evolution would bear more thorough examination in subsequent research.

Fig. 77. Gorgoneion antefix, Etruscan or South Italian, terra-cotta, 6th–5th century BCE. Public domain image from the Metropolitan Museum of Art of New York, accession number 1991.171.44.

Fig. 78. Gorgoneion antefix roof tile, Greek, terra-cotta, circa 580–570 BCE. Public domain image from the Metropolitan Museum of Art of New York, accession number 10.210.44.

Fig. 79. Gorgoneion antefix roof tile, Greek, South Italian, Tarentine, terra-cotta, second half of the 5th century BCE. Public domain image from the Metropolitan Museum of Art of New York, accession number 20.215.

Fig. 80. Medusa head antefix, Greek, South Italian, 4th century BCE. Public domain image from the Metropolitan Museum of Art of New York, accession number 10.210.51.

Fig. 81. Medusa head antefix, Greek, South Italian, 4th century B.C. Public domain image from the Metropolitan Museum of Art of New York, accession number 10.210.92.

In conclusion, the character and depiction of Medusa in mythology, literature and art presents an incomparably multilayered and rewarding challenge to anyone who may wish to research her and write about her.

References

Dexter, Miriam Robbins. "The Ferocious and the Erotic: 'Beautiful' Medusa and the Neolithic Bird and Snake." *Journal of Feminist Studies in Religion* 26, no. 1 (Spring 2010): 25–41. doi: 10.2979/fsr.2010.26.1.25.

Jewison, Norman, dir. *Moonstruck*. 1987; Beverly Hills, CA: Metro-Goldwyn-Mayer, 2006. DVD.

Marler, Joan. Talk at the town hall in Tubingen, Germany, July 4, 1997.

Endnotes

1 Miriam Robbins Dexter, "The Ferocious and the Erotic: 'Beautiful' Medusa and the Neolithic Bird and Snake," *Journal of Feminist Studies in Religion* 26, no. 1 (Spring 2010): 25–41, doi: 10.2979/fsr.2010.26.1.25.

2 Dexter, "The Ferocious and the Erotic," 39.

3 Joan Marler, talk at the town hall in Tubingen, Germany, July 4, 1997.

4 Marler, talk at the town hall in Tubingen, Germany.

5 Marler, talk at the town hall in Tubingen, Germany.

6 The character Rose Castorini, played by Olympia Dukakis, says this toward the end of the movie *Moonstruck*, directed by Norman Jewison (Beverly Hills, CA: Metro-Goldwyn-Mayer, 1987).

7 The Metropolitan Museum of Art, images of artworks in the public domain, www.metmuseum.org/about-the-met/policies-and-documents/image-resources.

SPLASH: MERMAIDS

LYDIA RUYLE

Editorial Note: We are honored to include in this Proceedings Volume the lecture notes from recently passed goddess scholar and banner artist Lydia Ruyle. These are lecture notes from her 2012 Association for the Study of Women and Myth presentation at the San Francisco conference, "Splash: Mermaids," which she intended to submit for our proceedings. These notes reflect Lydia's artist-practitioner's autoethnographic voice and flow of meaning. This unfinished, archival notes convey general folklore and cultural background about mermaids from multiple cultures, and then provide context for several of the included color figures of her own mermaid-related Goddess Icon Spirit Banners. Other of her banners are featured in more detail in the recently published Goddess Ink volume by Ruyle (2016), "Goddesses of the Americas: Spirit Banners of the Divine Feminine." We hear in this piece the gathering insights of an artist-practitioner project in process. We hope these elder notes might inspire other artists to engage with this rich topic.

O, train me not, sweet mermaid, with thy note,
To drown me in thy sister's flood of tears:
Sing, siren, for thyself and I will dote.

--*Comedy of Errors,* William Shakespeare

Part I. Mermaids: Culture and Folklore

Mermaids have been part of folklore, literature and popular culture around the world since ancient times. They bring fresh questions to mind:

How did these mythological creatures come to be?
Are they real?
Do they have secret powers?
Are they friendly or dangerous?

According to modern folklore, a mermaid is "a mythological aquatic creature with a female human head, torso and the tail of a fish. The word is a compound of mere, the Old English word for sea, and maid, a woman."[1]

Mythological or not, mermaids are a recurrent figure in world cultures. Mermaids are very real to little girls. Walt Disney's *The Little Mermaid,* both on the screen and on Broadway, is beloved by adults and young alike, including our five granddaughters.

For adults the most famous "real" mermaid today is the Starbucks Coffee logo which has gone through several transformations in 40 years. She started out in 1987 at Seattle's Pike Street market as a twin tailed mermaid with definite connections to medieval images. In 1992, when Starbucks became a publicly traded company, she lost her twin tails and today the mermaid logo has been reduced to just showing part of her head. What does this say about our culture? What do we lose when the mermaid loses her body?

Not so long ago, the beautiful mermaid was an important icon for fighter pilots. In World War II, mermaids as well as pinups and movie actresses decorated their airplanes.

What are the distant origins of mermaid stories? The first known mermaid stories appeared in Assyria c. 1000 BCE in the form of Atargatis, the most important pre-monotheist divinity of the Levant and considered to be the first mermaid. Atargatis, whose followers eventually spread to Greece and Rome, was the half-human / half-fish Goddess of Earth, Fertility and Water. The Greeks called her Derketo and named Pisces, the constellation in the sky for her. Phoenician sailors brought Atargatis to Sicily. From there her followers spread northward to Rome, where she was known as *Dea Syria,* the Syrian Goddess. Her faith continued to grow and spread throughout the Roman Empire and toward the end of this era she reached the status of the Great Mother Goddess of the Empire.

According to Greek and Roman stories, mermaids sing to people or to the gods to enchant them, distracting them from their work and causing people to fall asleep, walk off a ship's deck or to run their ship aground. In Homer's *Odyssey*, Ulysses ties himself to the mast of his ship so that he can resist the sirens Scylla and Charbydis on his travels throughout the Mediterranean.

The Nereids are sea nymphs who can be friendly and helpful to sailors fighting perilous storms. They dwell with their father Poseidon in the depths of a silvery cave in the Aegean Sea. Sea trade was an important part of the Roman Empire and Nereids appeared everywhere in Roman mosaics.

When in 313 CE the Roman Empire became Christianized under the emperor Constantine, the stories attached to earlier mermaid images were recycled and used in telling the Christian story. The mermaids split their tails and became sirens, dangerous creatures who lured unsuspecting sailors to their death.

On the major European pilgrimage routes to the Holy Land during the Middle Ages, over two hundred cathedrals were built with stonemasons carving mermaids. Art and architecture were image books to teach the stories to the mostly illiterate populations of Europe. The seven deadly sins, carved in stone on many churches and cathedrals were a favorite. One of these seven sins was "unchastity," or lust, depicted as a split tailed mermaid, expressing fear of women's sexuality.

Medieval manuscripts depicted mermaids surrounding Noah's Ark and boats of faithful pilgrims. Hieronymous Bosch includes a mermaid in his Garden of Earthly Delights.

Cultures around the world tell of water creatures that are half-fish and half-human. Sometimes, they have odd details in common. Why do mermaids in Africa, Europe, and the Americas all carry combs and mirrors? These details were passed from Africa to Europe to the Americas as merchants and slaves spread mermaid stories and art around the world. And in many cases, water spirits that weren't originally mermaids took on that form only after outsiders introduced images of mermaids from other cultures.

One of the fascinating stories and image is *The Mermaid Chair* in Zennor, Cornwall. Sitting in the mermaid's chair was considered to be healing, bring about pregnancy and magic. (Sue Monk Kidd's book with the same title is a great read.)

In 2010, during the capture of Mohamar Gaddafi's palace in Tunisia, several rebels had their photos taken sitting in a Mermaid's Chair that was said to depict Kaddafi's only daughter.

Mermaids found their way to the Western Hemisphere early in the period of exploration. In the ocean near Haiti in 1493, Christopher Columbus—probably glimpsing a manatee—reported seeing three mermaids but said they were *"not as pretty as they are depicted, for somehow in the face they look like men."* And John Smith, famous for his legendary encounter with Pocahontas, claimed in 1614 that he saw a fish tailed mermaid with round eyes, a finely shaped nose, well-formed ears and long green hair. The creature, he said, was *"by no means unattractive."*

Today Mermaids are the civic symbols for Rothenburg, Germany and appear on the crest of Warsaw, Poland. Danish author and poet Hans Christian Andersen wrote about a mermaid who fell in love with a prince living on land and who came to shore everyday to see him. The statue of the Little Mermaid in Copenhagen is said to symbolize the fairy tale.

The Lorelei is a rock on the eastern bank of the Rhine which soars some 120 meters above the waterline. It marks the narrowest part of the river between Switzerland and the North Sea. A very strong current and rocks below the waterline have caused many boat accidents there. Myth describes the Lorelei who, sitting on the cliff above the Rhine and combing her golden hair, unwittingly distracts shipmen with her beauty and song, causing them to crash on the rocks. Scores of writers and composers have written about the Lorelei. Her power must still be strong as a tanker sank there in January 2011 backing up shipping for several weeks.

Part 2. Goddess Icon Spirit Banner Mermaids and Their Stories

Now let's look at some of my Goddess Icon Spirit Banner Mermaids and their stories.

Fish Goddess of Lepenski Vir

Lepenski Vir on the Danube is a 5,000 year old neolithic site whose stone fish images pre-date even Atargatis. The Fish Goddess of Lepenski

Vir (*Figure 82*) was placed on the altar at the end of a stone structure. She combines fish, woman and a bird of prey, all symbols of the Goddess of birth, death and regeneration. The large stone sculptures were found in triangular trapezoid shrines shaped like the mother mountain across the Danube river in the Iron Gate region. Similar images known as Sheela-na-gigs are found around the world. (*Source: Stone sculpture, Lepenski Vir, Serbia, 6500-5500 BCE Background: Stone architectual shape, Lepenski Vir*)

Fig. 82. Lydia Ruyle, *Fish Goddess of Lepenski Vir*, acrylic painting on nylon banner, 2004.

Fig. 83. Lydia Ruyle, *Kiev Medusa,* acrylic painting on nylon banner, 2002.

Kiev Medusa

A split tailed figure (*Figure 83*) from the Ukraine is surrounded by her serpents and dragons. She represents the transformative power of the goddess as does the vulva of birth and rebirth. She is a Russian Sheela-na-gig. Amulets worn with this image relieved pain and insured a healthy birth.

Other types of mermaid figures occur throughout Europe. Scottish Sheela-na-gig symbolizes the spiraling energies and winding pathways of transformation through the feminine. Her legs weave serpentine patterns which end in two mermaid's tails. A pattern of interlacing Celtic knots and colors create the background.

In Slavic mythology, a *rusalka* was a female ghost, water nymph, or mermaid-like demon that dwelled in a waterway. According to most traditions, the rusalki were fish-women, who lived at the bottom of rivers. In the middle of the night, they would walk out to the bank and dance in meadows. If they saw handsome men, they would fascinate them with songs and dancing, mesmerize them, then lead the man away to the river floor to his death. Lamia was used by mothers and nannies to induce good behavior among children.

A selkie is a creature from Scottish, Irish, and Icelandic folklore that lives a dual life. She lives part of her life in the sea as a seal, but can shed her skin and take human form to dwell on the land. In the stories, sometimes a selkie will steal the heart of a human being, and then break that person's heart when they return to the sea.

Fig. 84. Lydia Ruyle, *Melusine*, acrylic painting on nylon banner, 2011.

Melusine

Melusine (*Figure 84*) is the feminine spirit of fresh waters in sacred spring sand rivers. She is depicted as a serpent or fish from the waist down and occasionally with wings. There are many legends in Europe about Melusine including one where she and her triplet sisters grow up on the isle of Avalon. Melusine can turn into a dragon if her private space is invaded (*Source: Wikipedia internet image*)

Mermaids were noted in British folklore as unlucky omens – both foretelling disaster and provoking it. Some mermaids were described as monstrous in size, up to 2,000 feet. Several ballads depict a mermaid speaking to doomed ships; in some, she tells them they will never see land again, and in others, she claims they are near shore. They can also be a sign of rough weather. On occasion, mermaids could be more beneficent, teaching humans cures for disease.

Oshun

Oshun (*Figure 85*) is the African Yoruba Goddess of sweet waters depicted as a mermaid with long black hair in Latin America. Figureheads on European trading ships possibly influenced her image. In Brazilian Candomble, she is called Oxum. She is omnipresent and omnipotent. In Cuban Santeria, Oshun is an orisha spirit Goddess of love, maternity and marriage. Her color is yellow. Another imported mermaid hybrid is Yemaja. Festivals send boats of her out into the sea with offerings for good fortune and health for the coming year. (*Source: Sculpture. 1996. Casa Branca Terreiro. Salvador Bahia Brazil*)

Fig. 85. Lydia Ruyle, *Oshun*, acrylic painting on nylon banner, 2009.

Sedna

Sedna, the Ocean Goddess of the Arctic Inuit people (*Figure 86*), is both feared and loved. She is the guardian of all sea creatures and provides food for people. Prayers are sent to Sedna asking her protection in finding food and escaping the dangers of frozen waters. (*Source: Inuit stonecut print. 1961 Unknown artist*)

Fig. 86. Lydia Ruyle, *Sedna*, acrylic painting on nylon banner, 2008.

Fig. 87. Lydia Ruyle, *Nu Gua*, acrylic painting on nylon banner, 2003.

Nu Gua

Nu Gua (*Figure 87*) & Fu Xi of China lived as brother and sister in the Kunlun sacred mountains of the west. Once upon a time they sent up two clouds of smoke that united in the sky on the advice of the oracle who said it was a sign and their duty to marry. Nu Gua, who can repair and smelt things, holds a compass and Fu Xi holds a square measure signifying sound customs.

Nu Gua creates the world as a serpent Goddess. The tree of life grows from her and seven suns. Two of her animal spirits are the crow for death in the sun and the toad for rebirth in the moon. She created humans from clay that she baked in the oven. Some were overdone accounting for the black race and some were underdone accounting for the white race. Nu Gua invented the mouth organ and the flute. On the bottom is the Tao symbol of Yin Feminine and Yang Masculine.The Pa Kua Eight Diagrams, also known as the I Ching, is a Chinese system for accessing the intuitive energies of chi. (*Source: Funerary silk painting, Han dynasty tomb of Lady Dai, 2nd century, Mawangdui. Changdu)*

Island Mermaids

Mermaids appear throughout Asia and the Pacific with the Maori of New Zealand, in Bali and Japan. Nyai Loro Kidul is a legendary Indonesian spirit, known as the Queen of the Southern Java Sea, and consort of the Sultans continuing to the present day. The mythical creature is claimed to take the soul of anyone she wishes. Sirena is a Philippine mermaid who attracts fishermen and tourists. Sirenas are reportedly often seen ashore by fishermen, especially in the towns bordering the Pacific Ocean.

In Australia, the Aboriginal people speak of ancient spirits that made the land, trees and animals and that still live in sacred water holes. Some of these spirit beings, called Yawkyawks, look like mermaids: young women with fish tails and long hair resembling strings of seaweed or green algae. Some say they grow legs at night to walk on land, or even fly around in the form of a dragonfly. Yawkyawks have the power to give life—just going near a Yawkyawk's water hole can make a woman pregnant. They provide drinking water and rain so plants can grow, but if angry, they may bring storms. In other countries, water spirits took the form of mermaids only after that story arrived from Europe. But in Australia, the Yawkyawk already resembled a mermaid before Europeans arrived.

Mami Wata

In the 1500s, ships with statues of mermaids on their prows began arriving in Africa from Europe. Over time, the European mermaid legend blended with local stories, and Africans came to portray their water spirits as half-woman, half-fish.

The most powerful water spirit in over 20 African countries is known as Mami Wata. Most pictures of Mami Wata today are based on a version of an original German lithograph made in the 1880s of a Samoan snake charmer. My newest Goddess Banner of Mami Wata is making her debut here in San Francisco.

Mami Wata (*Figure 88*) is connected to the ancient African water spirit traditions regarded as female. In the last century, European traders brought a German lithograph image to Africa which influenced native images of Mami Wata. Her image figures prominently in the folk art of

Fig. 88. Lydia Ruyle, *Mami Wata*, acrylic painting on nylon banner, 2012.

Africa adorning walls of bars, living rooms, album covers, and other items. Mami Wata is a popular subject as well in the art, fiction, poetry, music, and film of the Caribbean. (*Source: Lithograph. ca. 1926 painted by German (Hamburg) artist Schleisinger, displayed in shrines as a popular image of Mami Wata in Africa and in the Diaspora.*)

Several years ago there was a fantastic exhibition titled "Mami Wata," which began at the UCLA Fowler Museum, then went to the University of Wisconsin in Madison, the Smithsonian and finished at Stanford where I saw it (Drewal, 2008).[2]

Mami Wata's name comes from the English "Mommy Water," and it is fitting that she has a foreign name, since followers believe she comes from the world of the sea. Mami Wata heals the sick and brings good luck to her followers. She also has a temper and will drown people who don't obey her, and she will cause confusion, sickness and visions in those she calls to serve her as mediums.

Mamba Mantu, another name for Mami Wata, shows a mermaid with clothing and hairstyle clearly influenced by cultures outside of Africa, perhaps pin-up calendars. Her appearance, wristwatch and jewelry represent foreign wealth. Paintings like these are often found in betting parlors as appeals for good luck.

The painting of La Sirene from the Congo shows a sassy mermaid artist amusing herself. The story of Lasirèn blends African and European mermaid stories with Caribbean culture. In Haiti, Lasirèn is part of the Vodou tradition, and her followers appeal to her for help in Vodou ceremonies, where the mermaid's spirit may enter the body of a female follower and bring good luck with work, health, money and love. Flags or banners with images of spirits are an important part of Vodou ceremonies. They are hung in temples or carried in processions to salute the spirits. A single banner may have more than 10,000 sequins. Altars and bundles use Barbie and other dolls in a creative example of recycling materials, images and stories.

Miscellaneous Mermaid Notes

- For centuries, artists have depicted mermaids including Peter Paul Rubens, Edvard Munch, Paul Delvaux and Marc Chagall.

- Katharine Skaggs (a friend from Ft. Collins) published a Goddess Tarot Deck that includes mermaids. It is also an iPhone / iPad APP.

- Mermaids are a favorite image for the tattoo crowd and Sailor Jerry's Spiced Rum with its Mermaid label celebrated its 100th birthday in 2011.

WHO would be
A mermaid fair,
Singing alone,
Combing her hair
Under the sea,
In a golden curl
With a comb of pearl,
On a throne?

~Alfred Lord Tennyson

Conclusion

Yes, mermaids are real in stories everywhere, and they have magical powers that can be both friendly and dangerous. May you encounter only friendly mermaids and please avoid the dangerous ones.

Bibliography and Related Works

Alexander, Sky. *Mermaids: The Myths, Legends and Lore*. Adams Media, 2012.

Anderson, Hans Christian. *The Little Mermaid "Den lille havfrue."* Denmark: C. A. Reitzel, 1837.

Antieau, Kim. *Church of the Old Mermaids*. Amazon Digital Services, Inc., 2008.

Berk, Ari. *The Secret History of Mermaids*. Candlewick, 2009.

Colbrun, Kerry. *Mermaids Sirens of the Sea*. Courage Books, 2003.

Cosentino, Donald J., Editor. *Sacred Arts of Haitian Vodou*. Los Angeles: Regents of the University of California & UCLA Fowler Museum, 1995.

Disney, Walt. "The Little Mermaid." Recorded November 17 1989. Walt Disney Feature Animation. 16MM

Drewal, Henry John. *Mami Wata. Arts for Water Spirits in Africa and Its Diasporas*. Los Angeles: Regents of the University of California & UCLA Fowler Museum, 2008.

Flandreau, Michelle. "Who is the Starbucks Siren: The Meaning Behind our Logo." December 23, 2016. https://1912pike.com/who-is-starbucks-siren/ (Accessed July 18, 2017).

Gifford, Elizabeth. *Secrets of the Sea House*. Australia: Atlantic, 2013.

Heiner, Heidi Anne. *Mermaid and Other Water Spirit Tales From Around the World*. Amazon Digital Services, Inc., 2011.

Kidd, Sue Monk. *The Mermaid Chair*. NYC: Viking Penguin, 2005.

McClure, Gillian. *Selkie*. Plaister Press, 2010.

Oleszkiewicz-Peralba, Malgorzata. *The Black Madonna in Latin America and Europe. Tradition and Transformation*. Albuquerque: University of New Mexico Press, 2002.

Rosen, Brenda. *The Mythical Creatures Bible: The Definitive Guide to Legendary Beings*. Sterling, 2009.

Skaggs, Katherine. *Mythical Goddess Tarot Deck*. Soul Sistas Creative Productions, 2009.

Shakespeare, William. *Comedy of Errors*. John Hemmings and Henry Condell First Folio, 1623.

Tennyson, Alfred Lord. The Works of Alfred Lord Tennyson. London: Macmillan And Co., 1893.

Ventura, Varla. *Among the Mermaids: Facts, Myths, and Enchantments from the Sirens of the Sea*. Weiser Books, 2013.

Wikipedia, "Atargatis." Accessed July 18, 2014. http://en.wikipedia.org/wiki/Atargati

Wikipedia, "Lorelei." Accessed July 18, 2014. http://en.wikipedia.org/wiki/Lorelei

---

Endnotes

1 Wikipedia *Mermaid* https://en.wikipedia.org/wiki/Mermaid

2 Drewal, Henry John. Mami Wata. *Arts for Water Spirits in Africa and Its Diasporas*. Los Angeles: Regents of the University of California & UCLA Fowler Museum, 2008.

SEEKING THE HOLY WIND:
ARTISTS AT WORK

Rae Atira-Soncea:

Fire Goddess and Water Goddesses, from *The Yurt*

Living and worshipping in the round fascinated Rae, and she was drawn to the Yurt concept even when she was working on the Tipi, an earlier project. The frame of Rae's Yurt was covered in black canvas. She hung "shards" of plexiglass mirrors from the underside of the rafters, to represent broken glass of the "stained glass ceiling" limiting women's roles in mainstream religion. The doorframe and door were decorated with symbols of women's spirituality.

Inside the darkened yurt, 5 individual fabric goddess figures were attached to the canvas. They included stuffed-work, embroidery, beadwork, shells, and felting. Each goddess had a mirror in place of her face, so that women moving around inside could see their own faces in the goddesses of Earth, Fire, Water, Buffalo and Spider.

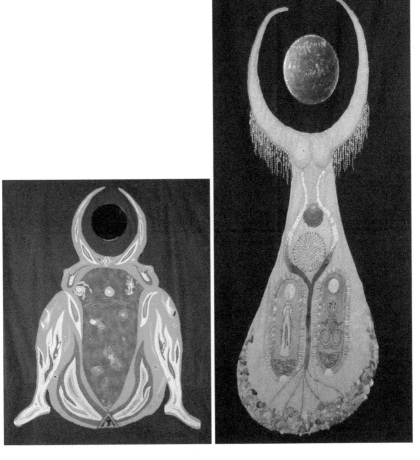

Fig. 89. Rae Atira-Soncea, *The Yurt: Fire Goddess and Water Goddess*,
fabric, mirrors and inclusions, 2005.

Denise Kester:

She Calls to the Soul Seeds Dancing at the Edge of the Universe

She calls to the Soul Seeds
dancing at the edge of the Universe
light sparking light – sparking life

Soul Seeds walking in God Mind
full of sensations and yearnings
full of desire and dreaming

She calls them home
and they come because they are in love
they follow her sacred voice

to the land of water
the holy land of water
where spirit and matter weave life

She calls to them – life time after life time, after life time
until they remember why they are here
until they remember where they come from

until they know who they really are and
they know her song by heart
the sound that resonates with all life –

The joy of being alive – here
in this precious sacred blue jewel of the Universe
the only one there is – called Earth

Fig. 90. Denise Kester, *She Calls to the Soul Seeds Dancing at the Edge of the Universe*, monotype/collage, 2003.

Helen Klebesadel: *Medusa Re-membered*

Our stories, myths and tales teach us what is expected of us. I am fascinated by how our myths and stories teach us who we are supposed to be, and how we are supposed to act and interact. I seek to understand the old myths and find the new ones as we create new social patterns to live by.

In my work, 'Facing Medusa' has become a metaphor for me of the acceptance and integration of those things in myself I have been taught to devalue or fear. In Greek mythology we are told that Medusa was a woman so powerful her glance could turn men to stone. Her head was cut off and used as a weapon. It was not her power, but who controlled it that was at issue.

To me facing Medusa means re-examining the definitions of our euro- and androcentric culture. It means facing those things in myself that have paralyzed me. In my art and my life I am attempting to re-member my Medusas. In so doing, I am taking back the power of self-definition, of action. In the act of facing, I am re-claiming, re-visioning, and re-membering myself as a whole person.

Fig. 91. Helen Klebesadel, *Medusa Re-membered*, watercolor diptych, 1989.

Louie Laskowski:
Praying Mantis & Butterfly Goddess

"Under the Wall Paper," is a series that explores layered areas of painted patterns. As owner of an 1858 home, I found myself peeling off wallpaper, one layer after another. This triggered a sense of wonder about the women who came before me, as I removed their personalities from my walls. I was inspired to recreate this sensation by filling space with painted patterns, just like time is filled with past memories.

In my garden, I observed praying mantises eating cabbage butterflies. Knowing that the mantis is named for how it holds its claws, I saw that the mantis could appear to be praying to the butterfly goddess. What would a butterfly goddess look like if she had a woman's face? A slender black Madonna clearly came to my mind. The painting is about the cycle of life and death, showing how one species sacrifices itself to give life to another.

The colors and textures in my work reveal cultural influences in Mexico, where my many travels have freed me to the joy of vibrant color and pattern. It expanded patriarchial limitations I had learned about good and bad art. I am grateful to have had my aesthetic values restructured and rearranged. Where I go, so goes my art; where my art goes, so do I.

Fig. 92. Louie Laskowski, *Praying Mantis & Butterfly Goddess*,
acrylic painting on canvas, 1995.

Lisa Levart:
Sherawali

Goddess on Earth, my ongoing project since 2009, uses socially engaged photography to illuminate ancient mythological stories and their contemporary significance. This manipulated photograph represents Sherawali, the warrior incarnation of the Hindu Goddess Durga, whose name means "invincible." Surrounded by marshes on Chappaquiddick Island, the activist horse breeder Francesca Kelly embodied this sacred myth, powerfully expressing the confidence to follow through with one's desires, and the willingness to battle for ideals. My passions are making visible the sacred, free of patriarchal construct and using artistic activism to catalyze gender equality, racial justice and inclusion. My art portrays archetypal myths embodied in women. It connects the past and present in subject matter, style and technique to evoke a deeper mindfulness of our collective memory.

Fig. 93. Lisa Levart, *Sherawali* (portrayed by Francesca Kelly),
digitally altered photograph, 2017.

Barb Lutz:

Honoring Lydia: A Double Goddess Altar

A phone call informed me that Lydia Rule had just died. This sad news was followed with a request to create an altar in her honor for the 2016 Matriarchal Studies Day. Without hesitating, I agreed. But, having said "Yes," I questioned how well I could deliver. What creation could elicit love and devotion to this beloved foremother? And how could the altar hold all our grief? Our gratitude? Our remembrance?

I walked into the woods, where Marija Gimbutas seemed to storm in front of me, projecting an image— of the double goddess figurine found in Vicki Noble's book, *The Double Goddess*. "Of course!" I thought.

I had created this image before, for Kim Duckett's Eleusinian Mysteries, where Persephone says farewell to Demeter. These words inspire us even as we part: "And it is time to say goodbye to the outer world …to Demeter… and we keep our eyes fixed on each other as the Wheel turns toward the darkness...toward the inner world...towards Hecate. Hold dear all that you two have shared and created together…So much I could not do without you," she says. " And I would not want to...Always remember this love, this devotion. Sweet dreams, daughter."

This altar lay on the floor. It was created with from dirt, beet juice powder, river sand, black sand and glitter. At the Matriarchal Studies Day, Vicki led us around the altar. We could see this goddess holding Lydia in her arms. At the end of the day, we tenderly gathered the body of dirt into our hands and carried it home with us.

Fig. 94. Barb Lutz, *Honoring Lydia: A Double Goddess Altar*
multimedia, 2016.

Lisa Noble:
Artemis Bee Labyrinth

My artwork is storytelling magic. Often, I illustrate my poems and stories; other times I'm inspired to create an image and a story is born and then sometimes my art illustrates me! It cries out: "Walk in the midnight woods by torchlight, wake up; the Goddess is sending a message: remember who you are!" The poem below is the translation of "Labyrinth Bee," which I created in honor of Artemis. The narrative within the labyrinth is written in runes. The Bee, one of Artemis' creatures, bears a monogram to honor her.

Artemis

Into the forest go I
A wild thing at night
I am a seed- a fireweed sprout
I am a she-bear; kindred spirit
Deep in the forest She waits
Shining in the torches- the candles- the stars
Eyes of Artemis
Twilight mirrors shining with truth
My home is in the wild forest
Cedar madrone sea-mist and bramble
My heart is wild in the tame day-to-day
My soul is free- tending the bees
Nootka rose and blackberry-wild honey and fern
Into the forest go I
Into the forest
Shining

Fig. 95. Lisa Noble, *Artemis Bee Labyrinth*,
pen and colored pencil, 2015.

Merry Grant Norris:
I AM CRONE

I painted this when I was in my early seventies and felt I was overdue to become a crone. My preconception of the meaning of "crone" was making it difficult for me to make the crucial spiritual step of owning that stage of my life. Far from being dried up and lacking in drive, my contemporaries are juicy, energized, and focused on fulfilling their life's purpose. My experience said that crones are vital, creative, connected to one another, and willing to inspire younger women by example rather than by maternal nurturing.

And so I decided to paint my vision.

I was inspired by Judy Chicago's "Dinner Party" to invoke crones by name in the triangular corners of the canvas and proclaim their qualities and emblems in shimmering silver around the borders. As the painting developed, sparks streaming from the central cauldron of soul energy spiraled into ribbons of flame, encircling the figures and soaring upward as a phoenix of rebirth. This affirmed my belief in the immortality of the soul. Expressing my belief visually allowed me to enthusiastically transition, and now I AM CRONE!

Fig. 96. Merry Grant Norris, *I AM CRONE*, acrylic painting on canvas
with Swarovski crystals, 2010.

Lauren Raine:

The "Masks of the Goddess" Project

I've always seen masks as "vessels for our stories." When I went to Bali to study sacred mask traditions, I was privileged to produce collaborative masks with Balinese mask makers. In 1999 I created 30 "Masks of the Goddess" as contemporary "Temple Masks" devoted to women and mythology. As I researched mythologies for the collection, I found myself in a grand conversation that grew as other women used the masks, bringing new meaning to a world-wide heritage. My masks have travelled for almost 20 years and continue to be offered to communities to explore these multi-cultural stories. What does the story of *Sedna*, ocean mother of the Inuit, have to teach us about ecology and reciprocity with the environment? What is the Gnostic "*Mirror of Sophia*"? How is the "*Descent of Inanna*" a potent story of psychological death and rebirth, the journey toward wholeness? How is *Spider Woman*, the ubiquitous great Weaver/Creatrix of the Americas, an important metaphor for our time? In 2013 I created "Numina: Masks for the Elemental Powers for a play by Anne Waters. It is my hope that these Masks will continue to travel, accumulating new meaning and "voice" as each community invents their story.

Fig. 97. Lauren Raine, *The Masks of the Goddess*, leather theatrical masks, 1998–2017.

Sid Reger:

Wisdom Harvest

Created in many spiritual traditions, mandalas offer the opportunity for spiritual reflection through repetition of imagery and symbolism. When I teach women's groups, I often invite them to create artworks to support their personal journeys. In one class, women worked together to decide on the best focal point for a mandala for their community. They chose the Willendorf goddess, one of the most familiar figures from prehistoric art, as a common ancestor for all women—past, present and future. Back in the studio, I created this Willendorf mandala. She stands in the center as the wise crone, taking stock of her own harvest of wisdom and experience.

Fig. 98. Sid Reger, *Wisdom Harvest*, pen and ink, paper collage, 2013.

Cristina Rose Smith:

la golondrina ibon

La golondrina ibon, the river swallow, speaks to me about my ancestors, and she teaches me to be *como pajaritas*, more like birds, flying and enjoying all that life has to offer. She is a hard worker too and builds her nests along the rivers, rivers that cross borders and cover the Earth. Putting her efforts into nepantla and babaylan endeavors, she is a mestiza creatrix whose erotic and empowered energy transform everything she touches. Indeed, all of the women in my family are like golondrinas. We have been flying from place to place, fleeing systematic violence and seeking a safe and nurturing space to call home on the Earth. This we do even though we have come from beautiful lands. My Abuela Priscilla is from Golondrinas, New Mexico: a sacred and rich land. My Lola Concepcion is from Cebu, in the Philippines: a place of waters with riches that one cannot even imagine. Though both of my grandmothers journeyed to Los Angeles to find new homes, I have journeyed and returned, in the past decade, to my grandmothers' homelands. I wanted to remember where I am from and find a home for myself. Thankfully, I have found a bit of home in the mountains of New Mexico, in Spain and on the islands around Cebu. And yet, in the process, I have also felt lost and divided. How can I have so many homes? And can there be homes in borderlands and in diaspora? Sadly, I have often felt so far from home while feeling a bit at home in my "motherlands." It is when I feel so far from home that I am reminded, by the golondrina ibons themselves, that my home is wherever I may be. Yes, I am drawn to the golondrina, because she is everywhere. We are everywhere.

Fig. 99. Cristina Rose Smith, *la golondrina ibon*, watercolor painting on paper, 2013.

Carmen R. Sonnes:

A GRANDMOTHER'S LOVE

(Media: Graphite and gesso on paper)

In this drawing I want to convey the utter joy of holding our new grand-child. It is timeless and it transcends borders, language, religion, and race. It is this unconditional and fierce love that bridges and binds the generations.

Fig. 100. Carmen R. Sonnes, *A GRANDMOTHER'S LOVE*, pencil on paper, n.d.

SECTION 5

HERSTORIES AND SOLIDARITIES

CALLING YOU-WHO!

I am calling you to me
You bakers and shakers
Calling you closer
Calling you to
Unbutton your tongue
Unclench your fist
Let your hands and hips sing!

I am calling you painters
You singers, you dancers
You dreamers and doers

I am calling you poets
You female artists, vital, fearless and free
You fire-breasted lions come to me!

You-who sculpt into being what is unborn

You-who draw inspiration from the dark well

You-who shape the key to my secret yearning

You-who shout
when the panther of rhythm
pounces on my bones
like a drumbeat

You are the ones who make *mater* matter
You feed my soul and make embodiment joy

As flour and water, I need you
As simple bread, I knead you

I am calling you to me now!
Let the great yeast rise!

~ *Ann Filemyr*

THE REPRESENTATION OF GODDESS IMAGERY IN FEMINIST ART

SIMONE CLUNIE

"we need a god who bleeds now a god whose wounds are not some
small male vengeance some pitiful concession to humility a desert
swept with dryin marrow in honor of the lord we need a god who bleeds
spreads her lunar vulva & showers us in shades of scarlet thick & warm
like the breath of her our mothers tearing to let us in this place breaks
open like our mothers bleeding the planet is heaving mourning our igno-
rance the moon tugs the seas to hold her/ to hold her embrace swelling
hills/ i am not wounded i am bleeding to life we need a god who bleeds
now whose wounds are not the end of anything."

~Ntozake Shange, *A Daughter's Geography*[1]

Introduction

I approach the writing of this project as an artist. One morning while listening to a radio station streamed from Jamaica, I was greeted by Helen
Reddy's "I am Woman" and a wish for the best for women on that day,
March 8th International Woman's Day, 2016. I remembered the fervor that
the song originally inspired in 1975 as an anthem to the first International
Year of the Woman. I experienced a feeling of immediate pride, a knowing and a satisfaction for acknowledgement by the song and in myself
of the strength of women over and above the overt and subtle expectations of femaleness during those times. I can still remember the feeling of
female camaraderie that enveloped my older women relatives when the
song played and the excitement it inspired. It is this pride, a continuous
discovering and creating of self that has drawn me to the mythology of the
Great Goddess, and by extension, her influence on me and my art practice. This paper is a reworking of a proposed catalogue for an imagined

exhibition focused on feminist art practice and how the Great Goddess's presence was resurrected in the contemporary imagination and art of so many female artists of the 60s, 70s and onward. In my own art practice, this inquiry is framed by the organic chaos of the sixties, when activism and intellectual thought, or what I refer to as simply thinking and writing, were not so diametrically opposed. This is a comment about a moment in time and how it has come to influence my ideas and my work as an artist. Feminist art has now gained some acceptance in academia and in the wider art world with such changes as the (final) acceptance of Judy Chicago's *Dinner Party* to the Elizabeth A. Sackler Center for Feminist Art at the Brooklyn Museum (Withers 2008, 426); the featuring of Feminist Art in prominent art publications and several anthologies of Feminist Art. There has also been a "nod" towards the goddess[2] such as Chicago's inclusion of the Fertile Goddess one of the place settings of *Dinner Party*.[3] Feminist art practice may now be seen less as a "contentious" form of female dis-content than at its inception.

> Every group that lives under the naming and image-making power of a dominant culture is at risk from…fragmentation (of identity) and needs an art which can resist it.
>
> ~ Adrienne Rich

In introduction to goddess imagery in feminist art, I call on Rich's words as a reminder of goddess (whether upper- or lowercase) as reflection of the female, represented as divine, particularly in a masculinist patriarchal culture. Since image making is a foundational part of culture, it can have transformational results. Growing up in Jamaica under the Presbyterian arm of Christianity, the power of spirituality or divinity rested within a male god; the female aspect was ignored or relegated to a secondary position. Via a meandering investigation and feminist consciousness raising, forays into Rastafarianism, and investigation of Yoruba spiritual tradition, exploration of the female as the seat of creativity seemed the more practical (fulfilling?) avenue for me. This continues as an in-progress investigation into creative power as being female. I agree with Rachel Pollack's statement:

> The modern Goddess religion is not trying to recreate con-ditions exactly as they were in the Stone Age, or in ancient

Crete, or any other time or place. Instead we seek to learn from those people as we allow the Goddess to come alive in a way that matches our own experience. (Pollack 1997, 2)

I am drawn to the idea that for women as a group an interest arose—even if it was only for a short-lived moment—through collective recognition that resulted in the widespread critique of all aspects of a woman's place in Western society and by extension in colonial and other societies. No longer content with a secondary power position, women considered their existence outside the expectations of males and patriarchy and began to inquire into the spiritual, focused on women as an initiator of creation. (Spretnak 1982, 147)

Historical Context

Feminism is an international movement: in each country or region of the world where women struggle, the movement is shaped by local socio-economic and ideological features. Beginning amid the social critique by women as a group in politics, the workplace, the home and marriage, feminist thought seeped into all aspects of the lives of women in the United States, United Kingdom, and Europe. The student rebellions, race riots and women's liberation movement were not exclusive to the United States but emerged almost simultaneously in nearly every urban center of Europe. Rejecting the ideological conservatism of the 1950s and seeking solace from the alienation produced by American capitalism, the sixties generation wanted an experience that felt like something. (Cottingham 2000, 122-23)

In conjunction with the sociological questioning of women's position, the female body came into question as Second Wave feminism challenged laws and social ideas about female bodies. Feminists in nation-states throughout the West challenged the laws and customs that control the female body, including, but not limited to: abortion and birth control prohibitions; marriage and child custody laws; lesbian rights; educational and employment discrimination against women; and rape and other forms of male sexualized violence against women. (Cottingham 2000, 126)[4]

The 1960s Women's Liberation Movement with its ongoing social agitation, confrontations and protests occurring "in the streets" was the catalyst for "…. feminist art [to] emerge as a response to a social movement ...and not from within the arts." (Kelly 1995, 224) Questioning the accepted rhetoric of the art world, which exhibited male artists as the epitome of artistic production, women in Great Britain and the United States set out, politically, to critique and protest their exclusion from "male dominated exhibitions and institutions" and their general lack of visibility in relation to men in the art world structure. Women artists' organizations[5] began with picketing the Whitney Museum of American Art's annual exhibition. The Whitney answered the protests by featuring four times as many female artists in the following year's annual exhibition. Feminist organizations on both coasts focused on documenting and questioning institutions concerning the lack of female representation.

Judy Chicago has been lauded as one of the "mothers" of feminist art practice in the United States.[6] As a professor, Chicago taught the first feminist art course in the United States at Fresno State College in 1969. In 1970, with fellow artist Miriam Shapiro, she founded the Feminist Art Program at the California Institute of the Arts. Out of this program came the norm-shattering installation project, *Womanhouse*, portions described by Cottingham:

> *Womanhouse* featured seventeen rooms including three bathrooms, (Robbin Schiff's *Nightmare Bathroom*, Camille Grey's *Lipstick Bathroom* and Chicago's *Menstruation Bathroom*): a pink kitchen where fried eggs sat on the stove while single breast forms climbed the wall (Vicki Hodgett's *Eggs to Breasts*); a Dining Room set for a meal of inedible food (Beth Bachenheimer, Sherry Brody, Karen LeCoq, Robin Mitchell, Miriam Schapiro and Faith Wilding); ...a female mannequin stuck between shelves of sheets (Sandy Orgel's *Linen Closet*); Related performances were given, some of which were featured in Johanna Demetrakas's 1973 *Womanhouse* film. [7]

In the call for collaborative work under the credo of "the personal is political" feminist artistic practice mirrored ongoing social activist practices. The subject matter for feminist art rested in the everyday experience of being a woman in a society that had specific gendered expectations despite the many political and educational gains for women in the early 20th century. Violence against women—domestic abuse, rape, incest and sexual harassment—became a significant focus for female performance artists engaging feminist concerns of women's every day experiences. Artists like Suzanne Lacy and Leslie Labowitz formed Ariadne: A Social Network in 1976. This performance group addressed the issue of violence against women through public performances such as *Three Weeks in May,* (1976), *Record Companies Drag Their Feet* (1976) and the 1977, *In Mourning and in Rage* which, respectively, dealt with rape awareness, sexism in the recording industry and the sensationalist media coverage of a Los Angeles serial murderer.

As part of the ongoing critique of male dominated art institutions women sought to form their own alternative spaces in which to meet and exhibit their own works. In 1973, the L.A. Women's Building opened housing galleries, a print workshop, performance spaces, its own school—The Feminist Studio Workshop and a bookstore. Other such venues opened thoughout the United States. Linda Nochlin published *Why Have There been No Great Women Artists,*[8] while researchers wrote about the lives and works of neglected female artists. Within the context of initiating dialogues in art criticism, Lucy Lippard discussed socially inspired and Conceptual Art.

Women who did not fall under the assumed categories of white, middle-class and heterosexual critiqued the lack of inclusion in feminist discourse. Black feminists in the United States critiqued the wider Women's Liberation Movement for the lack of voice concerning race and racism and challenged the univocal utterance of sisterhood by white feminists. One such group was the arts collective, "Where We At" Black Women's Artist Inc., in Harlem, New York. Coming out of the Black Arts Movement, artists Kay Brown, Dindga McCannon, Faith Ringgold, Carol Blank and others gathered in 1971 to plan an exhibition of black women artists to be hosted in Acts of Art Gallery in Greenwich Village.[9] The success of the exhibition led to the formation of the collective as an art making body and activist organization that focused on the black community as a whole. Other significant artists addressing the dual-oppression experience of black women include Betty Saar and Asungi, now AfraShe Asungi.[10]

Hispanic women made their own critique of both the wider Anglo-American feminist representations of sisterhood, in addition to critiquing the sexism within the Chicano movement. Forming coalitions and grass roots organizations Asian women, working class women, lesbians, and women with disabilities vocalized their specific challenge to the narrow constraints of white, middle class, heterosexual feminism proposing widening the concerns about women.

Feminist vocalization by women in the United Kingdom affected the visual arts there. [11] [12] [13] Feminist art questioned the sustaining power structures and the dismissal of women's art as merely decorative along with "representations in art of women as nature, identified exclusively with femininity and domesticity." Women artists formed support groups, produced magazines, and began to exhibit together.[14]

Black women organizing in the United Kingdom was mainly brought about by a lack of attention to women's issues in wider Black organizations and the underlying sexist behavior of Black men. Women who formed their own groups such as the Brixton Black Women's Group (1973) were more influenced by liberationist activity happening on continental Africa and the specifics of their place in British society than by the rhetoric of white feminists at the time. In the eighties Black women's art finally gained wider public exposure in the British art world, even though they had been exhibiting in their own communities much longer.[15] (Cottingham 2000, 173)

With the advent of female artists critiquing male images of divinity, women artists drew on their experiences of being female and having a female body as the impetus for the production of spiritually inspired images, which removed the denigrating connotations associated with femininity. Calling upon the archetype of the Great Goddess from traditions of goddess worship linked with ancient Mediterranean society, pre-Christian Europe, Native American traditions, Mesoamerica, Asia and Africa, various artist such as Monica Sjöö used the imagery of the goddess and goddess-worshipping religions as an affirmation of female power, the female body, the female will and women's connections and heritage.[16] In evoking what Orenstein calls an "earlier psychic state," where the sacred and divine were not separated from everyday living, the archetype of the goddess became a locus for transformation. Caputi calls this form of feminist mythmaking, "psychic activism" whether it is the resurrection through ancient mythology of the Great Goddess or the reclaiming of negative representations such as the Crone and Medusa as metaphors to raise women's power through women-identified mythmaking. Luisha Teish's observation is apt for counteracting the lack of female self-naming in the Western, patriarchal construct: "The veneration of our foremothers is essential to our self-respect." [17]

Marija Gimbutas's influence

Marija Gimbutas investigated goddess culture associated with the history of Old Europe.[18] Her *The Gods and Goddesses of Old Europe* is an examination of the way of life, religion and social structure of the peoples who inhabited Europe in Neolithic times. Formulating a theory of existence of these people prior to Indo-European invasion, Gimbutas proposed a peaceful society that was immersed in goddess worship, challenging the conventional archaeological framework for structuring culture. "Archaeologists and historians have assumed that civilization implies a hierarchical political and religious organization, warfare, class stratification and a complex division of labor." (Gimbutas 1982, viii) Tracing these societies from the Aegean area, the Balkans, east central Europe, down into the Mediterranean, Gimbutas structured her theory, taking an interdisciplinary approach. Combining fields such as archaeology, mythology, linguistics, and historical data, Gimbutas initiated the idea that the sacred and secular were interrelated in Neolithic times, with a Great Goddess as the central deity of worship. The primordial deity for our Paleolithic and Neolithic ancestors was female, reflecting the sovereignty of motherhood. Neolithic symbols and images cluster around a self-generating goddess and her basic functions as Giver of Life, Wielder of Death and as Regeneratrix. This symbolic system represents cyclical, non-linear, mythical time. (Gimbutas 1982, x)

Goddess imagery/symbols

In addition to representations of the Great Goddess, women artists resurrected mythological symbols associated with the feminine divine to signify the Great Goddess, including spirals, horns, moon symbols, chevrons, the earth, snakes, caves, bowls, cauldrons and other forms. Some were based on Gimbutas' cataloguing of archaeological sites and her interpretation of markings and female sculptural figures. In addition to ascribed symbols physical sites became identified with the Great Goddess archetype. According to Eleanor Gadon, "Catal Huyuk appears to be a city of shrines and may indeed have been the sacred center for other settlements on the surrounding Anatolian plain." (Gadon 1989, 28) Mellaart's suppositions of Catal Huyuk placed it as a developed society arranged along generally egalitarian lines: "data from Catal Huyuk and other Neolithic sites also indicate that in these societies, where women were priestesses and craftspeople, the female was not subordinate to the male."[19] Other physical or archaeological locations have been identified as sites for the Great Goddess such as Silbury Hill and structures in Malta,[20] indicated by female bodily shapes and their metaphoric equivalents, caves, tombs, and other natural formations.

Feminist Spiritual Movement

With the ongoing questioning of male dominated institutions like government and universities, religion was questioned by feminists for its rhetoric of female subordination and lack of strong positive female icono-graphic representation. The Virgin Mary, mother of Jesus Christ, was the only female role in Christianity and it called for submission, self-sacri-fice and a reification of motherhood. Wanting female representation of the creation principle, as opposed to the sole male as the progenitor of the Earth, feminist inquiry resurrected the image of the Great Goddess and an amalgamation of various pagan ritualistic practices. According to Wicca priestess Diane Stein, inspired by late 60s activism and publications like Helen Diner's *Mother's and Amazons*, Mary Daly's *The Church and the Second Sex*, and Elizabeth Gould Davis's, *The First Sex*, women began to look at witchcraft, feminist spirituality and the goddess as alternatives to institutional religion. Witchcraft practices of Wicca, also known as the Old Religion, engaged in chipping away constructions of "witch" (which originally meant "wise woman") and "witchcraft." Looking to nature and her potential, women performed rituals, spells, popularized the use of herbs, candles, incense and common iconography associated with witchcraft. The celebration of the solstices, the equinoxes and Sabbaths of the goddess were resurrected from Old Europe and became popular. Instead of celebrating faith-based holidays such as Easter or Christmas, themselves derived from Pagan celebrations, women began to form covens and spiritual communi-ties to celebrate the Wheel of the Year.

An explosion of published materials based in European pagan and witch-craft practices, Native American spirituality, African (West) spirituality, and its Caribbean interpretations occurred at the rise of feminist spirituality and inspired even more writers on the subjects. Authors Vicki Noble and Starhawk, regarded by many as at the forefront of this movement, became popular through their work in the United States. Noble's *Motherpeace* tarot deck, co-written with Karen Vogel, is a re-interpretation of the Tarot with female figures central to the imagery. [21]Starhawk's influential book, *The Spiral Dance: Rebirth of the Ancient Religion of the Great Goddess* was seen as required reading for an initial understanding of feminist spirituality. Hungarian born author and Wicca practitioner Zsuzsanna E. Budapest wrote the popular *The Holy Book of Women's Mysteries* published in 1989. African-American Osun priestess Luisah Teish published *Jambalaya: The Natural Woman's Book of Personal Charms and Practical Rituals*, which chronicles her development as a priestess and includes a history of Yoruba Orisha and their veneration in the African American community. [22] Barbara Walker compiled *The Woman's Dictionary*, documenting the Pagan origins of Christian traditions. Magazines, periodical and art journals such as *WomanSpirit* (1974), *Like Mind* (1983), *The Beltane Papers, Goddess Rising and Woman of Power* (1984) and *Sage Woman* (1986) were put out by women cooperatives, independent women's presses or through the fledgling Women's Studies departments at universities. (Stein 1992, 15-16)

Other authors engaged the Great Goddess archetype from the perspectives of religion and philosophy. Looking at the goddess archetype from a theological perspective, Merlin Stone had been researching her interest in a "feminine" principle with the onset of the wider Women's Liberation Movement. Starting in the late fifties, Stone had been collecting stories, myths and researching goddesses because of the lack representation in mainstream religious discourse concerning the female. Through the collection of prayers and legends associated with Isis, Ishtar, Demeter, Cybele, and Cerridwen, Stone was able to trace the changing expectations of a "feminine' power between ancient and contemporary women. Although references to the feminine were to be found in theories of psychology, philosophy and spirituality there had been no in-depth investigation. As Stone observed:

> For the last three millennia the mainstream religions of the world have stressed the masculine principle. Despite the many differences between Judaism, Christianity and Islam, each regards their highest or sole divinity as male. Buddhism, though not actually professing belief in a divinity, has placed the male figure of Buddha, Siddhartha Gautama, in the most exalted position of sanctity. Despite the power attributed to

Goddess figures such as Shakti or Devi, Hinduism is for the most part a religion of patriarchs and patriarchal attitudes. The holy figures in Mary in Christianity, Kwan Yin in Buddhism, and other sacred female images are paid honor today, but it is clear they are not regarded as primary powers in the universe. (Nicholson 1992, 5)

This observation led her and other women on a trajectory of investigating a female spirituality. Gaining information through anthropological records, translations of ancient texts, from travels to museums and excavation sites in the Near and Middle East, Stone gathered more than enough information to publish *When God Was a Woman* in 1975. As Stone states,[23] one of the main reasons for the reclamation of a feminine spirituality is the identification with a deity, which is close to the self in representation and in the ordinary, "...speak of the Goddess as being within all manifestations of life. And more and more women are relating to the idea of divinity not as an anthropomorphic image, or even a divine spark within ourselves, as much as it is the flowing energy in the very process of life and living." (Nicholson 1992, 19)

Eco-feminist influence

Historically, in many cultures the female body's reproductive and nurturing abilities have been seen as of the earth. When viewed as Mother Earth or Gaia, the ongoing destruction of the environment, due to industrialization and massive urbanization resulting in pollution of both air and water, was seen as parallel to patriarchal abuse of women. By broadening this new consciousness of the earth as the Great Goddess, this type of thinking initiated a conjunction of environmental concerns and feminism: ecofeminist theorizing.[24] Scholarly publications such as Susan Griffin's *Woman and Nature: the Roaring Inside Her*, 1978, and Carolyn Merchant's, *The Death of Nature: Woman, Ecology and the Scientific Revolution*, 1980, helped to spread feminist query of the connection between women and nature and the patriarchal structure of the contemporary world. Removing the mental hierarchy of humans as above animals and plant life, the recognition of the interconnectedness of people with nature initiated a self-awareness of the effects of abuse to the earth. Such abuse would in time, lead to harm of one's self. Ecofeminism spurred on artistic production as female artists identified their bodies, their consciousness and their spirituality with the earth. "The image of the Goddess connects all beings in the 'web of life.' Plants and animals and so-called beings are her 'children' or more exactly, part of 'her body'."[25]

Artists began producing work with the healing of Mother Earth in mind,[26] approached from performance and ritual. From the late seventies through late eighties, in a "movement called 'feminist matristic art'" artists produced work at the juncture of ecofeminism and feminist spirituality, drawing on research. Orenstein divides the juncture into six categories of the ways various artists produce work with the Great Goddess as a focus:

1. The journey to ancient prehistory and goddess-centered cultures,

2. The voyage inward into dream and psychic space,

3. The journey to sacred sites in nature and on the Earth,

4. A journey to the spirit world, a feminist matristic, shamanic voyage,

5. A visit with the Crone and a reclamation and celebration of the wisdom of Gaia,

6. A visit to the Outta-Sight, the Goddess in the City and the Clown.

Some of these works include Betsy Damon's performance, the *7,000-Year-old Woman* in 1977; Artist Cheri Gaulke's *This is my Body,* in 1982; Denise Yarftiz and Anne Gauldin's performances as *The Waitresses* troupe, a commentary on the waitress as the contemporary metaphor for the Great Goddess mother.[27]

I loosely call on both Orenstein's "list" along with my observations for what links the female artists I will be looking at: Monica Sjöö, Marybeth Edelson, Mayumi Oda, Yolanda Lopez, and Ana Mendieta. The first obser-vation central to the production of the images highlighted in this article is a uniform feminist "awakening to themselves" as female in a masculinist/patriarchal world, whether based on social, racial, ethnic, or political cata-lysts. For all, the social catalyst was recognizing their sexed body, and how being female put them in a subordinate position to males. At all levels of society this lesser positioning placed them at the receiving end of secondary treatment for wages, education, in intimate and social relationships. In their chosen field of art this subordination was more apparent in their treatment in art school(s) and in limited arenas for exposure in the "art scene." The potential of art critics writing about their work and avenues for selling their work were rare.[28] Racial and/or ethnic catalysts were more apparent for artists like Oda, Lopez, and Mendieta; theirs were "oppositional" histories to the European white identity that structured the societies of the United States and the United Kingdom. Oda was born and raised in Japan, married an Anglo-American and moved to the United States in the mid-60s. Lopez and Mendieta were associated with the histories of Latin America: Lopez was born to Mexican parents in the United States and Mendieta immigrated to the United States from Cuba as part of the Operation Peter Pan program.

A second observation is the use of the female body as a central image of these artists' practice. All the mentioned artists feature the female body as the principal focus of the works discussed here, whether expressly denoted or referenced by other means. Sjöö and Lopez primarily use a representational image of the female form in two dimensions on paper, wood and canvas. Edelson's medium is the altered photograph and Oda's is screen printing. Mendieta's imagery reemploys dimensional carving (into limestone) of an abstracted female form in a specific location. Sjöö s painting, *God Giving Birth*, the earliest piece, shows a central image, filling the length of the canvas, a sturdy looking female form in a semi-squatting position in the process of birth. Lopez's *Nuestra Madre* features a central floating figure which is a conjoined representation of female archetypal forms of the Virgin de Guadalupe and Coatlicue with their associated iconography. The figure bears the masked facial features attributed to Coatlicue in Aztec statuary: raised arms, clawed feet and the skirt of serpents. She is cloaked in a dark colored starred mantle and has a golden rayed aureole surrounding her. At her feet is the crescent moon, all associated with the Virgin de Guadalupe. Oda's serigraph, *Treasure Ship: Goddess of Earth* features a central floating female "leading" a boat overflowing with an abundance of produce over the ocean. In the background hangs a crescent moon. The figure wears only a delicate, billowy peach skirt and her breasts are bare. Mendieta's *Untitled (Guanaroca: First Woman)* is part of a larger collection of nine carved site-specific works, *Ruprestrian Sculptures/Esculturas Rupestres*, executed in the caves of Escaleras de Jaruco, Jaruco State Park in Havana, Cuba in 1981. Using an abstracted form associated with ceramic, stone, and bone prehistory female figures, her conceptual framework was to reference the female creation mythology of the Taino. This form features a representational slit where the vagina would be located on the female body

A third observation is an identification with the functions of the female body, natural cycles as strength and not as negative aspects of femaleness to be borne; such strengths include: female sexual desire; menstruation; the connection of the female body to nature and corresponding cycles such as the moon's-birth and death; the act of physically and mentally giving birth: all actions to be valorized. Sjöö, Edelson, and Oda have expressly stated in their own words that they identified a power to create after they gave birth. This is in opposition to widespread societal views of childbirth as a debilitating and negative (messy) experience for women. As part of reaching into the past to produce goddess imagery, Oda, Mendieta, and Lopez look to their genealogic histories outside of the western European roots and identifications of the societies in which they lived by calling on goddess imagery from varying mythological and spiritual traditions. Oda drew on the religion of her native country and childhood, Buddhism, and identified with the stories of female bodhisattvas, enlightened beings, in an effort to bring forth representations of female involvement and power in religious practice. Simultaneously, she was influenced by the rhetoric of the feminist movement and chose to interpret her responses to her investigations by identifying with an active-versus-passive female-based spirituality that co-mingles with nature. Orenstein writes of her work:

> Mayumi Oda's goddesses are often on wheeled vehicles for land transport, or on ships for journeys across the waters. Whether interpreted as psychic symbols or as political images, these are women in motion; their bodies are strong and free. They are sexually uninhibited, and they represent the sacred female force in the universe. In her world all the elements, air, fire, earth and water are represented as goddesses, so no longer will the nude body of woman be relegated to the shadows and silences of shame. (Orenstein 1990, 86)

Also influenced by the rhetoric of the feminist movement Mendieta in her series of carvings, *Ruprestrian Sculptures/Esculturas Rupestres* delves into Taino and Ciboney mythology where she found female spiritual representations of power within the creation stories of these prior inhabitants of Cuba. Lopez too, influenced by feminist rhetoric, applied a conceptual framework that combined the "everyday woman" of her female relatives (and herself) with the popularly respected religious iconography of the Virgin de Guadalupe for the *Guadalupe Series*. With these images, it was her intention to pay homage to "ordinary" Mexican American women by commingling their ordinariness with the sacredness of the Virgin to create affirmative representational identities. In *Nuestra Madre* she further expands the image of female spiritual power by combining the pre-Columbian Aztec imagery of Coatlicue, the creative/destructive goddess,[29] with that of the Virgin de Guadalupe, naming and merging the histories that produced the women around her and the strengths they bring to their lives.

The work of two of the artists can be considered as aspects of Orenstein's list. Edelson's photo collage, *Goddess Head*, a photograph of the artist, naked from the waist, with upraised arms, situated in nature is altered with china markers and oil paint. It can be said to reference "the journey to ancient prehistory and goddess-centered cultures." first on Orenstein's list. (Orenstein 1990, 112) Identifying with pre-historic imagery of Minoan "snake goddess" figures with raised arms showing reverence to the goddess, Edelson mirrors this practice in the central image of this work. Where her head should be Edelson has placed a spiraling shell, which also symbolizes the goddess. Mendieta's *Guanaroca* can be said to fall within the parameters of Orenstein's "the journey to sacred sites in nature and on the Earth." (Ibid) The artwork site is said to be associated with the pre-colonial inhabitants; Mendieta also incorporates the wider conceptual framework linking caves with goddess imagery, where images such as the "The Earth Mother of Laussel" [30] have been identified. In creating this image, along with eight others, she engages historical cave images along with a conceptual feminist framework.

Artists

Monica Sjöö (Sweden/Britain)
God Giving Birth 1968/69. Oil on canvas.

Born 1938, Harnosand, Sweden, Monica Sjöö states: "The Ancient Mother and Earth Spirit as a source of rejuvenating energy that has been denied by centuries of patriarchal culture but to which we humans have to return if we are to survive."[31] Mostly a self-taught artist, her work has revolved around goddess imagery and feminist politics, about which she published widely. She was active in the women's movement in Britain since the late sixties. Her 1968 *God Giving Birth* (*Figure 101*) was painted in response to the birth of her second son. According to Whitney Chadwick, "Sjöö's painting, monumental, simplified in form, iconic in its representation of woman as a force of nature, and has virtually no pictorial sources in western art." The central image of this painting is a female figure giving birth. Legs open in a semi-squatting position, the figure has the head of a

Fig. 101. Monica Sjöö, *God Giving Birth*, Oil painting on canvas, 1968/69.

child emerging from her vagina. Set against the backdrop of a blackened universe, housing planets and stars, this nude female figure implies an active yet grounded/solid presence. The face of the figure looks like a mixture of a mask and human face but with no significant identifiers to race or ethnicity. Between the figure's open legs, at the bottom of the canvas is a semi-circle that implies a globe or spherical shape. Above this sphere, "God Giving Birth" is stenciled. Regarding public reaction to the painting, Sjöö has stated:

> I would say that because "God" is seen as a non-white woman of great dignity, looking straight ahead unsmilingly, with a child coming out of her womb, between her legs...is disturbing. What I mean is that if it had been painted in bright colors, the "God" had had long blonde hair and been pleasantly smiling that would have probably been okay because she would have at least been seductive to men. Also, the image attacks the absurd myth that the creative force is male and phallic. (Parker and Pollack 1987, 189)

Fig. 102. Mary Beth Edelson,
Goddess Head, photograph, collage
and china markers, 1975.

Mary Beth Edelson (United States)
Goddess Head, Photograph, collage &
china markers, 1975

Born 1933, in East Chicago, Indiana, Mary Beth Edelson attended the Art Institute of Chicago, DePauw University where she received a BA in 1955. She received her MA from New York University in 1959. Edelson has worked as a painter, installation artist, and performance artist, as well as in photography to voice her concerns of women's place in historical and contemporary society. Like Sjöö, her focus on positive female imagery was inspired by her bodily changes in pregnancy, "I began to paint and draw images that spoke to women's power, and the power of our bodies, in 1961, when I was pregnant with my first child. … I experience what was happening to my body as holy, as sacred." (Spretnek 1982, 312) In *Goddess Head* (*Figure 102*), an altered photograph of her naked torso posed against nature/natural environment to reflect her connection to the goddess. Duford states of Edelson's work: "She has used her own body both as representation of the goddess and as a symbol for Everywoman, evolving rituals around the idea of the body as the house of wisdom." (Duford 1989, 91) With upraised arms associated with praise/reverence, she also mirrors gestures found in Minoan female figures. The spiral shell, another symbol equated with the great goddess serves as her head, my interpretation of where her "head is at"; a central identification with an ultimate female divine Creatrix. Additionally, she has been succinct about the theoretical roots of her work explained in a letter response to American art critic, Thomas McEvilley:

> In using my body as a sacred being, I broke the stereotype
> that the male gender is the only gender that can identify
> in a firsthand way with the body and, by extension, the

mind and spirit of a scared being. Furthermore, these ritual images were connected directly to Goddess as an expanded image of woman as a universal being and not limited to the stereotype of woman as "other."[32]

Mayumi Oda (Japan/United States)
Treasure Ship: Goddess of the Earth, Serigraph, 1976

Born 1941, in Tokyo, to a middle-class religious family, Mayumi Oda graduated in 1966 from the Tokyo University of Fine Arts and moved to New York that year with her husband. Oda has lived in the United States for the past 30 years working with various goddess-inspired imagery. She started this process when she turned to art after the birth of her children, "...the experience of giving birth of raising children and being an artist at the same time made me realize my own strength and the potential power of all women. Deep inside me a voice was saying "We are strong: we must realize our own strength." (Oda 1981, 49-50) It was later when she started to re-investigate her Japanese heritage that she started to look at and identify with the female bodhisattvas in the Buddhist tradition. Oda's image, *Treasure Ship: Goddess of Earth (Figure 103)* is taken from a catalogue of 31 woodblock printed images, simply titled *Goddesses*, published first in 1981. Throughout the catalogue she recreates female deities as central to creativity and uses this imagery as her "talisman" to produce buoyant, colorful images of goddesses riding bicycles, sailing boats, feeding infants and communing with nature. Using the medium of printmaking, she calls on traditional and invented mythological figures from Buddhism, Taoism, Shinto, Christianity

Fig. 103. Mayumi Oda, *Treasure Ship: Goddess of the Earth*, serigraph, 1976.

and ancient Greek religion. In *Treasure Ship: Goddess of the Earth* the centralized female figure floats, foregrounded atop waves of the ocean leading a boat form loaded and almost overflowing with fruit and vegetables, an implication of the bounty of the earth and sea bringing sustenance for all. As Oda, says, "…to me, the image of the creator has to be female. Chinese Tao is the Mother of the universe who embraces us all."

Fig. 104. Yolanda Lopez, *Nuestra Madre Coatlicue* [*Our Mother Coatlicue*], oil and acrylic painting on Masonite, 1981–88.

Yolanda Lopez (United States)
Nuestra Madre Coatlicue. Oil and acrylic on Masonite, 1981-88

Born 1942, in San Diego, California, of Mexican heritage, Yolanda Lopez was raised by her mother and maternal grandparents. Lopez earned her BA in Drawing and Painting from San Diego State University in 1975 and her MFA in visual arts from the University of California in San Diego, in 1978. She has worked in a variety of media: installation, painting, and print making. Lopez's work focuses on issues of identity specific to the Mexican American experience. In reference to her role as an artist, Lopez "…. has viewed her work as an artist as a tool for political and social change and sees herself as an artistic provocateur."[33] Lopez works to promote her Chicana identity and an understanding of issues affecting the Chicana/Chicano community. Using the popular Catholic iconography of the Virgen de Guadalupe, Lopez re-interprets aspects of the stationary, self-sacrificing representation of motherhood in her popularly known **Guadalupe Series** (*Figure 104*). Of transforming the usual serene passivity of the Guadalupe image she states:

> Because I feel living, breathing women also deserve the respect and love lavished on Guadalupe, I have chosen to transform the image. Taking symbols and her power and virtue, I have transformed them to women I know. My

hope in creating these alternative role models is to work with the viewer in a reconsideration of how we Chicanas portray ourselves. It is questioning the stereotypes we as women are assumed to attempt to emulate.[34]

In her series of three images, Lopez represents herself, her mother and grandmother in the guise of the Virgin. All three are representations of contemporary urban Mexican-American woman. Taking the same ideas, Lopez cross-fertilizes the pre-Columbian image of the Aztec goddess, Coatlicue, with that of the attributes associated with la Virgen de Guadalupe as a goddess, incorporated into these family portraits. Centralizing the image as one of reverence, and also referencing her family of women, Lopez is juxtaposing the divine and the mundane, the qualities of all as a cue for women to remember their strength and greatness. They straddle all those attributes not just those set forth in patriarchal society's binary "oppositions."

Ana Mendieta (Cuba/United States)
Untitled (Guanaroca: First Woman). Carving in limestone cave.
(Ruprestrian Sculptures/Esculturas Rupestres, 1981 Photo etching & Chine colle on Arches cover paper.

Ana Mendieta was born, 1948, in Havana, Cuba and moved to the United States at the age of twelve due of the political climate in Cuba and her family's political affiliations. As an art student attending the University of Iowa she produced conceptual work based on women's issues from a feminist perspective using her experience as fodder. Over the course of her career Mendieta produced the long-term series until her passing in 1985 where she continually represents herself as merging with nature by outlining her body onto the earth as a way to form a connection with Mother earth—a way to reconcile her feelings of exile. In places like Iowa City, Oaxaca and mostly wherever she went, Mendieta drew on a variation of materials such as gunpowder, stones, blood, flowers, ice, mud and fabric to mark her body in and with the natural environment to con-join her silhouette and by extension a symbolic female silhouette with and on Mother Earth. In some of the Mendieta's works and pieces from the series, the arms are raised like those associated with the Minoan Snake Goddess/priestess images, and other female forms constructed near riverbanks, the ocean., This image (*Figure 105*) is part of a project, *The Rupestrian Sculptures/Esculturas Rupestres*, which is a collection of nine

255

low relief carvings of variously shaped female forms based on her studies of the Taino and Ciboney, who were the indigenous peoples of Cuba before Spanish colonization.[35] Mendieta created her carvings in the limestone caves of Jaruca National Park just outside of Havana when she returned to Cuba in 1981. Mirroring petroglyphs of other known prehistoric sites, Mendieta paid homage to a female divinity based on Taino creation stories she researched before her visit. Naming each "earth work after Amerindian goddesses of the moon, wind, menstruation and waters"[36] Mendieta documented them through photographs and film, with the intention of later creating a book. In her own words, Mendieta has said of the: "[it was] an intimate act of communion with the earth, a loving return to the maternal breasts."[37]

Fig. 105. Ana Mendieta, *Untitled (Guanaroca: First Woman)*, carving in limestone cave, part of a collection of nine site-specific carved works, *Esculturas Rupestres [Ruprestrian Sculptures]*, executed in 1981 in the caves of Jaruco State Park in Havana, Cuba. © Estate of Ana Mendieta Collection, LLC, Courtesy of Galerie Lelong & Co. Photograph etching and chine colle on Arches Cover paper, 1981.

Conclusion

As stated in the introduction, this is a look at a small group of female artists who were influenced, directly or indirectly, by the framework and thinking of the concepts and images of the Great Goddess, initiated by the feminist inquiry of the sixties and seventies. Interest in the symbol of the Great Goddess continues in various ways but on a more subdued level and not as much in institutional art settings. Crafts based on goddess iconography still abound in small businesses and web sites. Pagan rituals and covens exist on a quieter note, holding private and public Sabbat celebrations and ceremonies. The publishing explosion has since waned but feminist cooperatives like We-moon continue to publish material that focuses on goddess and feminist spirituality. Destinations like Catal Huyuk or the temples on the Maltese Islands, as sacred to the Great Goddess, have initiated a specific type of goddess-focused tourism. Despite analyses now available, through hindsight, as to the practicality (and/or naivety) of this frame of thought, given the passing of the years and dismissals in parts of academia, Merlin Stone still encapsulates some of the fervor of the time and the unabashed openness with which the Great Goddess archetype was embraced.

The goddess has been waking up and so have we. Our discussions of the meaning of the feminine principle may include certain controversies or disagreements about specific details, but these discussions only serve to enrich and expand our contemplations and perceptions. The way of the goddess appears to be that of inclusion and adaptability, rather than exclusion and rigidity. We have no need to set up theories that become so rigid we might be tempted to ignore additional ideas and information just to protect the theory. The theory itself is not sacred. It is our ongoing process of building the theory that becomes a sacred act. And perhaps the very fact that we enter into this process together, with compassion, cooperation, nurturance, intuition, respect for intuition, sympathy and empathy capable of sensing process and flow, and with love for each other, each of us a part of the unity of the goddess, will say more about the feminine principle than any specific article or book. (Nicholson 1992, 22)

References

Austen, Hallie Iglehart. *The Heart of the Goddess: Art, Myth and Meditations of the World's Sacred Feminine.* Berkeley, CA: Wingbow, 1990.

Brooklyn Museum, "Fertile Goddess." Accessed October 13, 2017. www.brooklynmuseum.org/eascfa/dinner_party/place_settings/fertile_goddess.

Brown, Kay. "The Emergence of Black Women Artists: The 1970s, New York." *International Review of African American Art* 15, no. 1 (1998): 45–51, 54–57.

Butler, Cornelia, and Lisa Gabrielle Mark, eds. *WACK! Art and the Feminist Revolution.* Cambridge, MA: MIT Press, 2007. Published in conjunction with the exhibition of the same name, shown at the Museum of Contemporary Art in Los Angeles, CA, the National Museum of Women in the Arts in Washington, D.C., PS.1 Contemporary Art Center in Long Island City, NY, and Vancouver Art Gallery.

Caldecott, Léonie, and Stephanie Leland, eds. *Reclaim the Earth: Women Speak Out for Life on Earth.* London: Women's Press, 1983.

Caputi, Jane. "On Psychic Activism: Feminist Mythmaking." In *The Feminist Companion to Mythology,* edited by Carolyne Larrington, 425–40. London: Pandora, 1992.

Chadwick, Whitney. *Women, Art, and Society*. 4th ed. London: Thames & Hudson, 2007.

Childe, V. Gordon, *How Labour Governs: A Study of Workers' Representation in Australia*. 2nd ed. Melbourne: Melbourne University Press, 1964.

Christ, Carol P. "Rebirth of the Religion of the Goddess." In *Encyclopedia of Women and Religion in North America*, edited by Rosemary Skinner Keller, Rosemary Radford Ruether, and Marie Cantlon, 1200–07. Bloomington, IN: Indiana University Press, 2006.

Christian, Barbara. "The Race for Theory." *Cultural Critique* 6 (1987): 51–63.

Cisneros, Sandra. "Guadalupe the Sex Goddess." *Ms. Magazine*, July/August 1996, 43–46.

Cottingham, Laura. *Seeing Through the Seventies: Essays on Feminism and Art*. Amsterdam: G+B Arts International, 2000.

Dames, Michael. *The Silbury Treasure: The Great Goddess Rediscovered*. London: Thames & Hudson, 1976.

Diamond, Irene, and Gloria Feman Orenstein. *Reweaving the World: The Emergence of Ecofeminism*. San Francisco: Sierra Club Books, 1990.

Dunford, Penny. *A Biographical Dictionary of Women Artists in Europe and America Since 1850*. Philadelphia: University of Pennsylvania Press, 1989.

Friedan, Betty. *The Feminine Mystique*. New York: W. W. Norton, 1963.

Gadon, Elinor W. *The Once and Future Goddess: A Symbol for Our Time*. New York: Harper & Row, 1989.

Gaze, Delia, ed. *Dictionary of Women Artists*. 2 vols. London: Fitzroy Dearborn Publishers, 1997.

Gimbutas, Marija. *The Goddesses and Gods of Old Europe, 7000–3500 BC: Myths, Legends, and Cult Images*. Berkeley and Los Angeles: University of California Press, 1982. First published in 1974 as *The Gods and Goddesses of Old Europe, 7000–3500 BC: Myths, Legends, and Cult Images*. Page references are to the 1982 edition.

———. "Pre–Indo-European Goddesses in Baltic Mythology." *Mankind Quarterly* 26 (1985): 19–25.

Gimbutas, Marija, Miriam Robbins Dexter, and Edgar C. Polomé. *Varia on the Indo-European Past: Papers in Memory of Marija Gimbutas*. Journal of Indo-European Studies: Monograph, issue 16. Washington, D.C.: Institute for the Study of Man, 1997.

Göttner-Abendroth, Heide. *The Dancing Goddess: Principles of a Matriarchal Aesthetic.* Translated by Maureen T. Krause. Boston: Beacon, 1991.

Kelley, Jeff. "The Body Politics of Suzanne Lacy." In *But Is It Art? The Spirit of Art as Activism,* edited by Nina Felshin, 221–49. Seattle: Bay, 1995.

Lippard, Lucy. *The Pink Glass Swan: Selected Essays on Feminist Art.* New York: New Press, 1995.

Lorde, Audre. *Sister Outsider: Essays and Speeches.* Trumansburg, NY: Crossing, 1984.

Mendieta, Ana, and Bonnie Clearwater. *Ana Mendieta: A Book of Works.* Edited by Bonnie Clearwater. Miami Beach, FL: Grassfield, 1993.

Nicholson, Shirley. *The Goddess Re-Awakening: The Feminine Principle Today.* Wheaton, IL: Theosophical Publishing House, 1989.

Nochlin, Linda. *Women, Art, and Power and Other Essays.* 1988. Icon Editions reprint. New York: Harper & Row, 1989.

Oda, Mayumi. *Goddesses.* Volcano, CA: Volcano/Kazan, 1988.

Olson, Carl. *The Book of the Goddess Past and Present: An Introduction to Her Religion.* New York: Crossroad, 1994.

Oransky, Howard, Laura Wertheim Joseph, Lynn Lukkas, Raquel Cecilia Mendieta, John Perreault, Michael Rush, and Rachel Weiss. *Covered in Time and History: The Films of Ana Mendieta.* Edited by Howard Oransky. Berkeley, CA: University of California Press, 2015.

Orenstein, Gloria Feman. "Review Essay: Art History." *Signs* 1, no. 2 (1975): 505–25.

———. *The Reflowering of the Goddess.* New York: Pergamon, 1990.

Parker, Rozsika, and Griselda Pollock, eds. *Framing Feminism: Art and the Women's Movement,* 1970–85. London: Pandora, 1987.

Pollack, Rachel. *The Body of the Goddess: Sacred Wisdom in Myth, Landscape, and Culture.* Shaftesbury, UK: Element, 1997.

Raven, Arlene, Cassandra L. Langer, and Joanna Frueh. *Feminist Art Criticism: An Anthology.* Ann Arbor, MI: UMI Research Press, 1988.

Reilly, Maura, and Linda Nochlin, eds. *Global Feminisms: New Directions in Contemporary Art.* London: Merrell, 2007.

Rich, Adrienne. *Blood, Bread, and Poetry: Selected Prose 1979–1985.* New York: W. W. Norton, 1986.

Rizvi, Uzma Z., and Murtaza Vali. "The Fertile Goddess at the Brooklyn Museum of Art: Excavating the Western Feminist Art Movement and Recontextualizing New Heritages." *Near Eastern Archaeology* 72, no. 3 (2009): 143–45.

Robinson, Hilary, ed. *Feminism–Art–Theory: An Anthology 1968–2014*. 2nd ed. West Sussex, UK: John Wiley & Sons, 2015.

Roth-Johnson, Danielle. "Back to the Future: Françoise d'Eaubonne, Ecofeminism and Ecological Crisis." *International Journal of Literary Humanities* 10, no. 3 (2013): 51–61.

Shange, Ntozake. "We Need a God Who Bleeds Now." In *A Daughter's Geography*. Electronic edition. Alexandria, VA: Alexander Street Press, 2011. First published 1983 by St. Martin's Press.

Sirmans, M. Franklin, and Mora J. Beauchamp-Byrd. *Transforming the Crown: African, Asian, and Caribbean Artists in Britain, 1966–1996*. New York: Franklin H. Williams Caribbean Cultural Center/African Diaspora Institute, 1997.

Smith, Valerie. "Abundant Evidence: Black Women Artists of the 1960s and 1970s." In *Entering the Picture: Judy Chicago, the Fresno Feminist Art Program, and the Collective Visions of Women Artists*, edited by Jill Fields, 119–31. New York: Routledge, 2012.

Spretnak, Charlene, ed. *The Politics of Women's Spirituality: Essays on the Rise of Spiritual Power Within the Feminist Movement*. Garden City, NY: Anchor, 1982.

Stein, Diane. *The Women's Spirituality Book*. St. Paul, MN: Llewellyn, 1986.

Stone, Merlin, Carol P. Christ, Luisah Teish, Starhawk, Charlene Spretnak, Jean Shinoda Bolen, Susan Griffin, et al. *Women and Spirituality: The Goddess Trilogy*. DVD. New York: Alive Mind Media, 2007.

Turner, Jane. *The Dictionary of Art*. Vol. 2. London: Macmillan, 1996.

Viso, Olga M. Unseen Mendieta: *The Unpublished Works of Ana Mendieta*. Munich: Prestel, 2008.

Williams, Annette Lyn, Karen Nelson Villanueva, and Lucia Chiavola Birnbaum. *She Is Everywhere! An Anthology of Writings in Womanist/Feminist Spirituality*. Vol. 2. Bloomington, IN: iUniverse, 2008.

Withers, Josephine. "All Representation Is Political: Feminist Art Past and Present." *Feminist Studies* 34, no. 3 (2008): 456–75.

Endnotes

1 Shange, Ntozake, 1948-, *A Daughter's Geography* Electronic Edition by Alexander Street Press, L.L.C., 2011. © Ntozake Shange, 1982.

2 Rizvi, Uzma Z., and Vali Murtaza. "The Fertile Goddess at the Brooklyn Museum of Art: Excavating the Western Feminist Art Movement and Recontextualizing New Heritages."

3 "Fertile Goddess" https://www.brooklynmuseum.org/eascfa/dinner_party/place_settings/fertile_goddess

4 The advent of political advocacy for abortion rights, the availability of contraceptives, and equal pay for equal work, gave way to women publicly voicing their concerns on about issues like such as rape, spousal abuse, and incest in a public arena. Books publications such as Betty Friedan's 1963, *The Feminine Mystique* (1963) belabored the drudgery and isolation of the suburban housewife and its isolation, and critiqued the ongoing socialization of American women into 'full-time housewifery. #'. Other authors published books based on female acculturation and sexist educational practices. Books like such as Simone de Beauvoir's, The Second Sex, Shulamith Firestone's, *The Dialectic of Sex: The Case for Feminist Revolution*, Kate Millet's *Sexual Politics*, and Robin Morgan's anthology, *Sisterhood is Powerful: An Anthology of Writings from the Women's Liberation Movement*, edited by Robin Morgan, were major critiques of a male male-dominated society. Political organizations like such as the National Organization for Women (NOW), which formed was founded in 1966, helped to initiate other local and national women's organizations.

5 In New York, the women from the male-dominated Art Worker's Workers' Coalition (AWC) formed Women Artists in Revolution (WAR) in 1969; the Ad Hoc Women's Group, and in 1970 another women's group, was formed called the Ad Hoc Women's Group in 1970.

6 Whitney Chadwick. *Women Art and Society* (London: Thames & Hudson. 2007), 357.

7 I include this lengthy description to acknowledge and emphasize the collaborative nature of the project. As an art student, the controversy of Chicago's 'authoritarianism' was repeatedly emphasized because of a lack of inclusion of the other artists in earlier written materials, in reference to the *Dinner Party*. I would be remiss in not including what I have come across for the participants of this project.

8 Linda Nochlin. *Women, art and power*. (New York: Harper & Row/Icon Editions. 1988), 145-178.

9 Brown, Kay. "The emergence of black women artists: the 1970s, New York." *International Review of African American Art* 15, no. 1: 45. *Art Source*. 1998, 20.

10 Visual artists like Betty Saar critiqued the status and stereotypical images of African American women. in her 1972 mixed media assemblage, *The Liberation of Aunt Jemima.*, a black mammy, in quintessential head tie and holding a gun in one hand and a broom in the other, a "black mammy" in quintessential head tie, is positioned behind the 1960s Black Power movement's symbolic raised fist. In her *Weeping Witches*, Faith Ringgold constructed masks of mourning, drawing on with the knowledge of the double oppression of being 'black and female' in the United States. Inspired by the ritual masks from of Africa, that were used in a woman's initiation ceremony, to get in touch with the "'powers of the spirit,'", Ringgold voiced a different reality different to than the dominant feminist discourse.# Also influenced by African ties, artist Asungi, now AfraShe Asungi, produced a series of images of Amazons to honor honor black women resulting from her "'need to see strong self-contained and focused black women.'"# She depicted images of black women's bodies in a positive light as a way to make affirmative associations for and about black women's sexuality given the harsh history of treatment they have received in the United States.

11 The Women's Liberation Art Group, was formed in London in 1970, mounting and mounted its first exhibition, the following year with artists, Monica Sjöö, Valerie Charlton, Sally Frazer, Margaret Harrison, Ann Colsell, Allison Fell, Sheila Oliver and Liz Moore, at the Woodstock Gallery in London the following year.

12 Chadwick, 355.

13 A protest of the Hayward Gallery organized organized by the 1975 members of the Women's Workshop of the Artists' Union. Pressure of from the organization and supporting agitation led to five artists, —Tess Jaray, Liliane Lijn, Kim Lim, Rita Donagh and Gillian Wise Ciobotaru—being invited to select the contributors to the second *Hayward Annual Exhibition*, in 1978. The London included Women's Art Alliance, formed "'to challenge, in different ways, the dominant notions of the artist and the definition of art.'" (Parker and Pollack 1987, 157) # Monica Sjöö, Liz Moore, Beverley Skinner and Ann Berg organized the exhibition *Womanpower*, that which garnered complaints of indecency and accusations of pornography.

14 In By 1976, the amount number of women contributing to this exchange grew had grown, and they held exhibitions in Manchester, Birmingham, Edinburgh, Liverpool and Coventry's Women's Aid Centre. *Portrait of a Housewife*, which opened in June 1977 at London's Institute for Contemporary Art (ICA), and featured an installation by the artists "'which transformed the impersonal empty

spaces of the ICA into a more domestic environment, emphasizing that they were inserting works from the private sphere into a professional, public setting.'" (Parker and Pollack 1987, 23) #

15 One such exhibition was organized by Lubaina Himid as part of the 'Black Woman Time Now Ffestival' held at the Battersea Arts Centre. Some of which is documented in the Selected Chronology of the catalogue, *Transforming the Crown: African, Asian & Caribbean Artists in Britain 1966-1996.*

16 Chadwick, 371.

17 Jane Caputi. "On Psychic Activism: Feminist Mythmaking." In Larrington, Carolyne. *The feminist companion to mythology.* (London: Pandora. 1992) 425-440. Caputi quoting Teish, 429

18 Kees Bolle. The great goddess. In Marija Gimbutas, Miriam Robbins Dexter, and Edgar C. Polomé. *Varia on the Indo-European past: papers in memory of Marija Gimbutas.* (Washington, DC: Institute for the Study of Man.1997), 83-102

19 Quoted in Nicholson p 30, who is quoting Eisler quoting Mellaart (1975), Gimbutas (1977, 1982) and Childe (1964).

20 Michael Dames. *The Silbury treassure: the great goddess rediscovered.* (London: Thames and Hudson. 1976), 83.

21 Using symbols equated with the Great Goddess archetype, Noble and Vogel's intent was to open up the female consciousness to the self as a sacred place. Other books by Noble include, *Motherpeace, A Way to the Goddess Through Myth, Art, and Tarot, The Motherpeace Tarot Playbook: Astrology and the Motherpeace Cards, Shakti Woman: Feeling Our Fire, Healing the World—The New Female Shamanism, down is Up for Aaron Eagle: A Mother's Spiritual Journey with Down Syndrome;* and *Making Ritual with Motherpeace Cards: Multicultural, Woman-Centered Practices for Spiritual Growth.*

22 Teish has also published, *Carnival of the Spirit: Seasonal Celebrations and Rites of Passage* and *Jump Up: Good times Throughout the Seasons with Celebrations from around the World.*

23 in her introduction to Shirley Nicholson's *The Goddess Re-Awakening: The Feminine Principle Today*

24 Influenced by the writings of French feminist and philosopher, Françoise d'Eaubonne, and her 1974 book *Féminisme ou la Mort* (Feminism or Death), American feminist academics incorporated into their own writings the term *eco-féminisme* by d'Eaubonne. D. Roth-Johnson. "Back to the future: Françoise d'Eaubonne, ecofeminism and ecological crisis." (*International Journal of Literary Humanities.* 10 (3) 2013), 51-61.

25 Carol Christ. "Rebirth of the religions of the Goddess." Rosemary Skinner Keller, Rosemary Radford Ruether, and Marie Cantlon. *Encyclopedia of Women and Religion in North America*. (Bloomington: Indiana University Press, 2006), 1200-1207. 1206

26 As Gloria Feman Orenstein lists in her book, *The Re-Flowering of the Goddess*.

27 Edith Altman, another performance artist whose intention was to "'exorcise patriarchal religious oppression and use feminist matristic symbols in transformative ways'" initiated the 1987 piece, *Rebuilding the Temple: We are Given a Gold Tent and All of Life is the Folding and Unfolding of the Tent; .#* Israeli artist, Miriam Sharon worked with Bedouin culture and the desert that she saw as a goddess space, defining '*holy*' as descriptive of a place without "'shrines or temples, holy in its being alone; .'" Donna Henes's created the environmental sculpture *Spider Woman* and as well as her solstice and equinox rituals whose aim it was to remind people of the interconnectedness of everything; Architect Mimi Lobell's built Goddess Temple built in Colorado in the 1970s, Suzanne Benton's constructed a throne for the *Sun Queen* in the early seventies in the New York State Art Park in the early 1970s; Ann McCoy's work, such as *The Temple of Isis*, was inspired by her dreams and visions.

28 Laura Cottingham. *Seeing through the Seventies essays on feminism and art*.

29 Cisneros, S. 1996. Guadalupe: The sex goddess. Ms, no. 7. Page 43.

30 Elinor Gadon. *The Once and Future Goddess The once and future goddess: a symbol for our time*. (New York: Harper & Row. 1989), 230.

31 See Turner, volume 2.

32 Edelson's response to a lecture given by Thomas McEvilley. *Male Grazing: An Open Letter to Thomas McEvilley*. (1989). This letter reproduced in Hilary Robinson's Feminist Art Theory. Pages 54-59.

33 http://cemaweb.library.ucsb.edu/lopezbio.html The initial website where this quote was referenced no longer exists based on the most recent search performed-6/5/2016.

34 Arlene Raven, Christine L. Langer, Joanna Frueh, *Feminist art criticism: an anthology*. (Ann Arbor, Mich: UMI Research Press. 1988), 199

35 Olga Viso and Ana Mendieta. *Unseen Mendieta: the unpublished works of Ana Mendieta*. (Munich: Prestel. 229-232. 2008), 230.

36 Ibid.

37 Rachel Weiss's 'Difficult Times: watching Ana Mendieta's films'. In *Covered in History and Time*, 2015), 55

STORYTELLING AND GODDESS SCHOLARSHIP*

NANCY VEDDER-SHULTS

Since the advent of email, Facebook, and Twitter, I have noticed that the people in my life tend to separate into two groups—telephone callers and users of email or the internet. Personally, I much prefer using the telephone. Letters on the screen may convey content efficiently, but when I talk on the telephone I listen to the other person's tone of voice, intensity or calm, and nuances of phrasing, all of which give me a better understanding of the emotional totality of what I'm hearing. Of course, the best conversations happen face-to-face, where the appearance and movements of the other person express thoughts as well.

Most storytelling and scholarship belong on the two ends of the same spectrum—from the embodied tale on one side to the abstract scholarly article on the other. Since I am both a storyteller and a scholar, it was only a matter of time before I began to notice the connection between storytelling and scholarship. What I've discovered is that my storytelling has an effect on how I experience the various myths I analyze and interpret. It creates a deeper connection to the tale, a more embodied understanding of what the ancients might have been transmitting and, as a result, a greater resonance with the story. All of this helps my goddess scholarship.

The first time I realized the significance of storytelling and how it affected my scholarship was about twenty years ago, when I spent several weeks studying the myths of Kali for an article I was writing. As the goddess of life, death and rebirth, Kali is usually depicted as a dark-faced,

---

* Editors' Note: We are excited to include this piece, featuring the vibrant voice of a practitioner and touching on the power of narrative in studies of women and mythology. This essay contributes fresh perspectives that can infuse insight into academic and scholarly discourses on these topics.

voracious hag dancing in the cremation grounds while holding in her four hands a sword, a severed head, a bowl of blood and a noose. But one of her myths describes Kali as a graceful, pregnant woman emerging from the waters of the Ganges.[1] When she reaches the shore, she gives birth to a beautiful baby, whom she suckles until it is content. Then she takes on her more familiar appearance as a frightening old woman. In that ferocious aspect, she then lifts the infant to her mouth, crushes it between her teeth and swallows it whole. Without a backward glance, Kali then returns to the waters from which she emerged, disappearing from view.

She's not a pretty picture. But in focusing solely on her bloodthirsty side, we in the West tend to misrepresent and misunderstand this goddess. For she is also the goddess who gives birth to the entire universe, something we can see in her myths as well. She is Shakti, the inherent energy in the universe, the force that activates what is potential and creates the world.

Studying Kali's myths, I first became intrigued, and then confused and finally ecstatic—something I didn't realize could happen to me as a scholar. What changed my understanding of this goddess was finally catching a glimpse of her unbounded nature, utterly beyond the constraints of human imagination. Like the tale I have just summarized, her stories depict Kali as a *coincidentia oppositorum* or "coincidence of opposites." She is life giver and destroyer, light and dark, order and chaos, goddess and demon, everything and the void. What I learned from her myths is that the bright and dark sides of the sacred are just human divisions of one holy reality and that when we participate in that divine reality we too are wild, unbound and free.

Hindus depict this divine freedom as *lila*, the sacred play of the gods and goddesses. Kali's *lila* involves her ecstatic dance that both creates and destroys the world. What I felt in my body after reading and rereading Kali's myths was that I, too, and everything in the universe shares in this divine reality. My understanding was not just intellectual. I walked around for days with a little smile on my face, in love with life. I felt vibrant, joyful and sensuous, suffused with Kali's *lila*. In this blissful, awake state, my inclinations often moved me beyond the reflective or contemplative. Living in the moment, I wanted to twirl or skip, to dance or run, to sing right out loud, however strange it might appear to others. So what if the neighbors thought I was crazy or if people couldn't deal with my exuberance? Flowing with life's pulse, in Kali's mad dance, I celebrated instant by instant. Her ancient hymn to life and death opened me to spontaneity and freed me from fear. I felt that I could plunge into life, awake, alive, in awe, with my heart open, finally taking those exciting risks I had been putting off for far too long.

This is exactly what Kali's devotees are said to experience. Her worshippers feel freed to join in the dance of life, to act spontaneously, to let go, to sing, dance or shout. Kali grants the boon of freedom to her followers, enabling them to revel in life.

I guess, in retrospect, I shouldn't have been surprised that Kali's myths affected me. Story is an embodied art. We use our voices, facial expressions, gestures and larger physical movements, as well as our words, to tell a tale. In addition, storytelling involves empathy, interaction and participation. When we hear or tell a story, we vicariously live through it.[2] In my research, I had felt into Kali's myth, discovering a deep resonance with her. In some mysterious way, I had assimilated her myth into my sensual awareness without experiencing it out loud. Perhaps this occurred because I subvocalized as I read her stories. As a singer, I tend to be an extremely auditory person.

Burrowing into her myths brought Kali's reality much closer to the surface for me and enabled me to realize that the seeming paradoxes of her stories—like a Zen *koan*—provide a profound opening into sacred reality. Kali's tales invited me to join the divine dance of the Hindu gods and goddesses and move with the sap and blood of life's pulse. In the West, we often speak of beauty or use aesthetic metaphors to describe our experiences of the sacred. But Kali's *lila* propelled me beyond these passive images— images that separate us from the divine by representing it as *other*[3]—to active participation in Kali's and life's dance.

The only word that does justice to the change in my experience after engaging with Kali's myths was that I *grokked* her story,[4] understanding what her myths had to tell with my entire body-mind. Symbols evoke emotional and sensual responses, so a powerful symbol such as Kali's was bound to affect my life. I opened myself to her story—both physically and intuitively—and some of her ecstasy entered my body. In order to make this emotion intelligible—as I hope I've done in this article—I had to tell my own personal story of how Kali changed my life, evoking her effect on me rather than analyzing it.

Telling the tale of Demeter and Persephone led me to other types of realizations. When I first began to study goddess myths, I was uninterested in the Demeter/Persephone story. My initial investigations of Greek mythology in the 1970s suggested that Demeter was a patriarchally diminished goddess, limited to the surface of the Earth, unlike her mythological ancestor Gaia, who represented the entire planet. Even as my private life forced me to recognize that Demeter was one of my personal goddesses—my sixteen-year-old daughter was *incommunicado* and living thousands of miles away, just as Persephone was lost to her mother, Demeter—I hesitated to fully embrace her until I understood her feminist potential. After working with her myth for years, I finally grasped the fact that only within a patriarchal culture could I find a feminist goddess, one who gives direction for countering patriarchy in daily life. This insight would have been impossible without my storytelling.

When I first told the tale of Demeter and Persephone, I based it on Charlene Spretnak's germinal work *Lost Goddesses of Early Greece: A Collection of Pre-Hellenic Myths.*[5] Spretnak reconstructed this myth as the pre-Hellenic tale of a child growing up and leaving home, a story intertwined with nature's changing seasons. As Spretnak tells the tale, Demeter's grief at her daughter's departure initiates the first winter, since sorrow halts the flow of her energy to the plants in forest and field. And Demeter's joy when Persephone returns brings the first spring.

The love of a mother for her daughter, which I was experiencing in a particularly poignant way, brought this story alive for me. The parallelism of my experience with Demeter's enabled me to realize in greater detail what this myth conveys, namely the turbulent emotions that we encounter when we experience grief: fear, denial, anger, sadness and depression. These emotions were the very same ones that I was feeling while parted from my daughter. Unfortunately, in my personal life I focused on Demeter's grief rather than her joyful reunion with her daughter. I needed to remember that, as I stated in my rendition of the story, "spring will surely come."

In Spretnak's version of the tale, Demeter and Persephone are two sides of the same goddess, one ruling over the underworld and the other over the upper world. Their lives exemplify the entire cycle of growth, death and rebirth in plant life. In researching pre-Hellenic Greece, I discovered that, as Spretnak had intuited, this myth reflected the religious life of the time. At the center of society was the living plant. As agriculturalists, the prehistoric inhabitants of Greece depended on plant life, especially grains, for their survival. As a result, pre-Hellenic Greeks celebrated the cycles of the grain's growth and death, mourning its loss in the winter and celebrating its return in the spring.

Many artifacts from this period picture a sun or plant goddess—possibly an early incarnation of Persephone—leaving in a boat loaded with vegetation. She raises her hand in a gesture of mourning, indicating that she is departing for the winter.[6] With the arrival of winter and with their lives much closer to nature (and to starvation) than our own, prehistoric Greeks must have felt emotions very similar to our modern experience of grief: fear for the future, depression in the face of this barren time of year, and anger and sadness at being separated from the vibrancy of life.

In contrast, the *Homeric Hymn to Demeter*—the earliest written example of this story[7]—reflects a time after the patriarchal Hellenes had arrived in the Greek archipelago. During that era, life for women was in the process of changing from matrifocal to patriarchal mores. We can see this in the myth. On the one hand, Demeter has a child but no husband. Her freedom reflects the greater power of the goddesses—and of women—in prepatriarchal culture. On the other hand, Persephone is abducted and raped. From one mythological generation to the next, bride theft— a man kidnapping the woman he desires and raping her—was introduced as an acceptable form of marriage.[8]

In this form of the story, Demeter openly confronts this violence done to her daughter. She protests her brother Hades's attack on Persephone and her brother Zeus's collusion in it. The *Homeric Hymn to Demeter* couches this protest in emotional terms: Demeter is "grief-stricken," "oppressed" and "angry." But in telling this story, I focus on Demeter's actions instead of her emotions. I believe that her actions give us information about how a woman can confront the control of patriarchal dominance.

In my modern retelling, I describe Demeter's steps as forms of passive nonviolence, a terminological updating of her actions. Her first move is to leave Olympus. In doing so, she boycotts the power structure that oppresses and exploits both her and her child. Next, she goes on a hunger strike. She withdraws her life-giving energy from the world, forcing all—including herself—to go hungry. The people starve and, as a result, the gods receive no sacrifices.

The hunger strike and its aftermath force Zeus to deal with Demeter. At first, he tries to bribe her, sending other gods and goddesses to offer her a variety of gifts and honors if she ceases her strike. But Demeter stands fast. She compels the king of the gods to negotiate.

Because Persephone has eaten while in the underworld, Demeter, too, must compromise in order to secure her daughter's return for two-thirds of each year. To do otherwise, Demeter would have to impose her will on the other gods, exactly the kind of high-handedness that she has been protesting. Her actions show that compromise—although a dirty word in today's political culture—can be a constructive tool in resolving conflict.

Translating the *Homeric Hymn of Demeter* into my own storytelling, rather than studying and analyzing it, prompted me to discover a variety of strategies for using our power as women to make our voices heard: We can boycott, participate in hunger strikes or other forms of civil disobedience, refuse bribes offered by patriarchy, persevere, negotiate, and perhaps even compromise in order to improve women's lives.

With all of these tales, storytelling helped me uncover new understandings. I didn't set out to become ecstatic when encountering Kali's stories. I didn't go looking for an emotional understanding of barrenness in the winters of our lives. And I had no idea that I would encounter Demeter as a feminist activist. All I did in each case was to *feel* into the story—with Kali, in my mind, and with the Demeter myths, by finding the gestures, tonal inflections, facial expressions, movements and words that would bring the myth alive. I looked for everyday words and idioms, not the abstractions I would use if I were writing an academic article. Instead, I brought the story into my body-mind, and what emerged was a new, deeper experience of the tale. By using storytelling, I was able to tap into my tacit knowledge about these tales, knowledge that can't be expressed directly in words but rather is simply understood in the body.

If I had used analytical tools to approach these tales, I would have been limited by the categories, the conceptualizations and the logic of the academy. Abstract analysis has its uses. It is good at dissecting things, categorizing them and then examining the components for the cohesiveness of their supposed logic. But this type of abstract reasoning detaches us from our feelings, intuition and physical sensations. It separates us from our bodies and, as a result, reinforces the cultural dualism of body and mind. It isn't good at discerning holistic patterns. What it leaves out is the fullness of life as a sensual experience—the sights and sounds and tastes and smells of daily life.

To a large degree, our culture approaches not just scholarship but reality itself as something that can be logically parsed. Cause and effect are major players in this understanding, as are objectivity and the reduction of reality to laws and rational truths. In relying on logic, we strip reality down to its bare bones, down to the abstract concepts that supposedly undergird it, or at least to a stable system of categorization that we have come to see as the foundation of existence in the West.

Unfortunately, our reliance on reason at the expense of other ways of knowing makes us dependent on received information, long-term assumptions about reality and expertise of those who build on this foundation with new layers of knowledge. Thus, our reliance on reason makes it more difficult for us to discover our own truths, since they have to be buttressed by arguments that are either logical (i.e. reliably inferred from what is already accepted as real) or supported by testimony from experts in the field, who until very recently were mostly men. We need to acknowledge that rational understanding is only one of many ways of knowing, including methods that are more subjective and intuitive, methods that help us to rely on our own understandings of the world.

If we want to create new feminist frameworks for scholarship—ones unconstrained by the history and weight of patriarchal scholarship—a useful place to begin is storytelling. Storytelling enables us to directly challenge the intellectual assumptions of patriarchy by creating new perspectives that emanate from our own stories and our own bodies. In addition, storytelling can become a powerful tool in research, because it connects us to a deeper understanding of reality that taps into the sensual and emotional aspects of our lives. It conveys truths in a participatory, lived way rather than a conventional, rote way. And it evolves over time, while logical understandings remain fixed.

Once upon a time, storytelling was the only method for preserving cultural knowledge. In oral societies—including all of our ancestral cultures—human events accrued meaning only to the extent that they formed a part of a "storied universe," according to David Abram in *The Spell of the Sensuous: Perception and Language in a More-Than-Human World*.[9] In a sense, storytelling was and continues to be the most important form of indigenous learning. All of us goddess scholars use imagination to explore the myths we interpret—whether by envisioning the interactions between mythic characters or by intuiting the responses of the people who heard these myths. Let's take the next step and, like our ancestors, deepen our scholarship by using the fully embodied technique of storytelling.

Fig. 106. Linnea Vedder, *Dancing*, ink and gouache on board, 2017.*

---

* Artist Linnea Vedder has shown her work at Jackie Klempay Gallery, Hal Bromm Gallery, The Brucennial, and Exit Art in NYC. Her work has been published by *Revolve-R* magazine in London and *Perfect Wave* Magazine in New York. She also illustrated the recent book, *The World is Your Oracle: Divinatory Practices for Tapping Your Inner Wisdom and Getting the Answers You Need*, by Nancy-Vedder-Shults, her mother. "Dance" was a painting in that series of illustrations.

References

Abram, David. *The Spell of the Sensuous: Perception and Language in a More-Than-Human World.* New York: Vintage Books, 1996.

Goodison, Lucy. *Moving Heaven and Earth: Sexuality, Spirituality and Social Change.* London: Pandora Press, 1992.

Gowin, Joshua. "Why Sharing Stories Brings People Together." *You, Illuminated* (blog), *Psychology Today* (website). June 5, 2011. http://www.psychologytoday. com/blog/you-illuminated/201106/why-sharing-stories-brings-people-together.

Gupta, Mahendranath. *The Gospel of Sri Ramakrishna.* Translated by Swami Nikhilananda. New York: Ramakrishna-Vivekananda Center, 1942.

Heinlein, Robert. *Stranger in a Strange Land.* New York: G. P. Putnam's Sons, 1961.

Hesiod, *Theogony.*

Lincoln, Bruce. "The Rape of Persephone." In *The Long Journey Home: Revisioning the Myth of Demeter and Persephone for Our Time,* edited by Christine Downing. Boston: Shambhala, 1994.

Spretnak, Charlene. *Lost Goddesses of Early Greece: A Collection of Pre-Hellenic Myths.* Boston: Beacon Press, 1978.

Endnotes

1 Many of the myths about Kali depict her as young, sexual and sensual. In fact, one of her best-known representations shows her straddling the god Shiva, transforming him from a corpse into a lover ready with an erect phallus to satisfy Kali's unbridled desire. It is Kali who brings Shiva back from the dead and gives him life, because she is his Shakti. The myth that I have recounted in this article specifically shows Kali giving birth. It is from Mahendranath Gupta, *The Gospel of Sri Ramakrishna,* trans. Swami Nikhilananda (New York: Ramakrishna-Vivekananda Center, 1942), 21–22.

2 Scientific studies have demonstrated that when we hear a tale, the same parts of our brains are activated as those of the teller. Uri Hasson and a team of scientists at Princeton University recently showed that you can almost literally transfer experiences from one brain to another by telling a story. Using MRI, they demonstrated that when the various parts of a storyteller's brain lit up, so did the same parts of the brains of the listeners. See Joshua Gowin, "Why Sharing Stories Brings People Together," *You, Illuminated* (blog), *Psychology*

Today (website), June 5, 2011, http://www.psychologytoday.com/blog/
you-illuminated/201106/why-sharing-stories-brings-people-together.

3 The process involved in these aesthetic metaphors is usually one of hyposta-
tizing, which, according to *Webster's New World Dictionary*, 4th ed., means, "to
make into, or consider as, a distinct substance or reality."

4 Robert Heinlein coined the word *grok* in his novel *Stranger in a Strange Land*
(New York: G. P. Putnam's Sons, 1961). According to the novel, to grok "means
to understand so thoroughly that the observer becomes a part of the observed—
to merge, blend, intermarry, lose identity in [an] experience." It can also be
understood as intimately sharing someone else's reality. The *Oxford English
Dictionary*, 2nd ed., defines grok as "to understand (something) intuitively or by
empathy; establish a rapport."

5 Charlene Spretnak, *Lost Goddesses of Early Greece: A Collection of Pre-
Hellenic Myths* (Boston: Beacon Press, 1978), 103–18.

6 Lucy Goodison, *Moving Heaven and Earth: Sexuality, Spirituality and Social
Change* (London: Pandora Press, 1992), 332–3. The parallels between the story
of this earlier goddess and the story of Persephone are rife, suggesting that
Persephone's myth grew out of these earlier traditions. However, there are two
important changes in the myth that we have inherited: a chariot, the preeminent
symbol of Hellenic warfare, has replaced the boat, and Persephone doesn't leave
of her own volition but rather is kidnapped.

7 Scholars have dated this epic poem to the 8th century BCE as the product of
oral tradition and to the 7th century BCE in written form. There is at least one
earlier reference to this myth in Hesiod's *Theogony*, but that reference merely
mentions the abduction.

8 See Bruce Lincoln, "The Rape of Persephone," in *The Long Journey Home:
Revisioning the Myth of Demeter and Persephone for Our Time*, ed. Christine
Downing (Boston: Shambhala, 1994), 171.

9 David Abram, *The Spell of the Sensuous: Perception and Language in a More-
Than-Human World* (New York: Vintage Books, 1996), 187.

STORIES OF MULTICULTURAL INTEGRATIVE SOLIDARITY:
A Mestiza (Xicana, Filipina, and Euroamerican) Approach to Creative Texts

CRISTINA ROSE SMITH

> By creating a new mythos—that is, a change in the way we perceive reality, the way we see ourselves, and the ways we behave—*la mestiza* creates a new consciousness.—Gloria E. Anzaldúa[1]

> Our culture is rich in myths and legends. They are an invaluable resource for recalling our collective memory, for myths and legends are said to be faithful mirrors of the existing conditions of the society that produced them. . . . Despite the long years of colonization, in several mountain communities, indigenous religious sects still honor women's leadership and continue the *babaylan* tradition.—EATWOT *Women in the Philippines and Asia*[2]

*L*a mestiza embodies a multiplicity of ancestral locations, ethnicities and cultures. On the borders and in diaspora, she often is internally divided within a socially constructed white masculinist framework and a pervasive white masculinist mentality that would have her locate herself as being from one homeland and identify as either woman of color or white. This dominant framework is interconnected with colonial and patriarchal epistemologies. In this study, I explore how it, often invisibly, encourages racism within the mestiza's psyche and in multicultural women's spiritual communities.

In this study, I seek to heal traumas of racism by employing a transdisciplinary mestiza approach—using feminist and indigenous, or decolonized, lenses—to engage with the nuances in between white and color, where the mestiza is situated. This study steps into mestiza-situated space to hear stories of recovering indigeneity by recognizing, grieving and deconstructing "whiteness," in particular, those stories of mestizas nurtured in colonial mentality and able to contextually pass or cover as white. Within these stories—particularly the Xicana and Filipina—are evidence of the old myths and legends passed on to us in word and in body by our *abuelas* or *lolas*, in our families, and by the *nepantleras*, transformers and *babaylans*, the culture bearers of our communities. These stories are faithful mirrors of indigenous practices that celebrated and continue to celebrate women's leadership.

Also within these stories is evidence of spiritual *mestizaje,* the "sacred renewal"[3] or transformation of mestiza selves toward what I call multicultural integrative solidarity. By multicultural integrative solidarity, I mean an integration of borderlands and diasporic consciousness within the mestiza and within multicultural women's communities. It is a uniting of multiple ancestral locations, ethnicities and cultures through the necessary actions of conscious social activism to decolonize and deconstruct racism in all of our relationships. This focus on integrative solidarity adds to the discussion of AnaLouise Keating, a scholar of Gloria Anzaldúa, who has highlighted the work of transformational multiculturalism in our communities.[4] My work on integrative solidarity takes the discourse from this intermediate level, the community, to the micro level, mestizas and their relationships within themselves.

Organized around the literary element of character that is employed in the several creative texts, this study explores the story of a mestiza, me, for integrative solidarity. Drawing upon ethno-autobiographical and literary criticism methodologies, I have searched within creative texts that I, a Xicana-Filipina-Euroamerican, have written and also analyzed other authors' creative texts that have influenced my journey: (Xicana) Ana Castillo's *So Far From God*, (Filipinas) Jessica Hagedorn's *Dogeaters* and Merlinda Bobis's *Flight is Song on Four Winds*, and (Euroamerican) Starhawk's (Miriam Simos) *The Fifth Sacred Thing*. Ultimately, I offer two theoretical insights from this research on characters of integrative solidarity within this new mestiza mythology or, as I call it, literary mestizaje. We are 1) challenged by indigenous healers to decolonize and embrace our ancestral roots and 2) encouraged to grieve.

Mestiza Ethnoautobiographical Methodologies and Personal Creative Texts

To begin the body of my work, I offer my creative text titled "I ask my younger sister." This poem delves into my desire to include characters in my creative texts who look like me—that is, who embody the multiplicity of ancestry, with Xicana, Filipina and Euroamerican attributes—and inspire me to do the same.

I ask my younger sister

I ask my younger sister,
"Do you think people see you as a woman of color?"

"No," she says, "it's like this:-
I've only ever had two traffic tickets.
The white policeman marked me down as 'Hispanic' on the ticket;
The Hispanic policeman marked me down as 'white.'"

"And we're really not even woman of color," she says.
"We're half or less. Remember our last name is Smith
And Grammie's family is from Spain.
That's white."

I look at her Anglo nose and know it looks much like mine. I note her brown shoulders. I consider our pear-shaped bodies. I see:

Our full lips,
Our wide feet, and
Our almond eyes.

I try to tell her about the name for women like us—*mestiza.*
I try to talk about our family's unspoken shame at being made fun of as kids
Because they weren't white-skinned,

how that shame passed on to us—
the shame of being people of color—
how they wanted us to be all-American—
shave that upper lip, go to school, speak English, don't be like those
Mexicans—

how I feel whitewashed.
Don't you feel the same, sister?

But she can't hear me.

I don't tell her about the altar for our ancestors I have set up in my
apartment.
I tell her, "It's not like I'm going to start wearing traditional Mexican
clothes like Frida Kahlo or name my children Filipina names, whatever
those are."
I don't tell her I *want* to dress like Frida Kahlo.

But all along, what I don't tell her is that
I really just
want
to
cry.

It is the physical attributes in my poem that I find worthy of note as
I approach my creative text seeking character role models through this
feminist and indigenous lens. For it is with almond eyes and pear-shaped
body that I describe myself. Moreover, I admit in my internal conversation,
with my sister in mind, my longing for connection with both my Mexican
heritage, in Frida Kahlo, and my Filipino heritage, with a Filipino name.
My overall desire has been to embody these characteristics. Moreover, my
goal is to find or tell a story in which there is a place, as my sister cannot in
her exchanges with law enforcement, between white and Hispanic as well
as to transcend those labels.

In Xicana scholarship, this place is called "the in-between place
of *nepantla*," and Anzaldúa wrote that it is our "home" as mestizas.[5]
When mestizas are agents of nepantla, when they embrace the bridge of

borderlands and diasporic sense of self as home, they are nepantleras, trans-formers who, through their creativity, bring healing to their communities. In contrast, the members of my Xicana family—with its roots in New Mexico, Mexico and Europe—have consciously or unconsciously chosen to subscribe to a whiteness framework in their reading or writing of their mestiza stories;[6] my work at uncovering these stories is, in part, what I see happening in my poem, when the narrator speaks, albeit apologetically, of her desire to dress like Frida Kahlo. Frida is perhaps one of the most famous mestizas. Born of an indigenous mother and a German father, she was known for integrating her indigenous sense of self into her artwork. What dressing like Frida means to me, as the narrator in the poem, is the desire to know and understand the cultural practices that were suppressed by colonization. I see this desire manifested now, in my research on mes-tizas such as Anzaldúa, Cherríe Moraga, *la Virgen*, and Ana Castillo, whose work I have studied in depth.

In Filipina scholarship, the space where multiplicities come together in integrative solidarity is *kapwa*. Kapwa, indigenous Filipina scholar Elenita Fe Luna Mendoza-Strobel wrote, is rooted in the goodness of the universe and in a "relationship to Land," ancestors, and community.[7] She asserted that those who take it upon themselves to pass on kapwa traditions, take on the spirit of the indigenous Filipina healers—Earth-grounded—and culture bearers, the babaylans. In my poem, I briefly mention my Filipina heritage, endeavoring to explain to my sister my hesitant desire to know and understand the Filipina culture of our grand-mother. There is, in that creative text, an opportunity to return to the names, particularly the names of important female figures, from my grandmother's region of the Philippines. The indigenous honoring of *diwatas*, a word that the English word goddess only begins to describe, such as Mebuyan, is like the honoring of *la Virgen*, a symbol of strength and abundance, a symbol of resistance to the white masculinist framework and endurance of the indigenous presence. I integrate my understanding of the diwata Mebuyan and the babaylans into my spirituality, which honors *Mahal na Ina* (Sacred Mother),[8] my own sacred mother being my father's Cebuana mother (from the island of Cebu).

Like my Xicana family, my Filipina ancestors also have stories that have been colonized or whitewashed. My grandmother listed herself as Filipina on the marriage certificate for her and my (Missouri-born soldier) grandfather. Oddly enough, she listed both of her parents as Spanish. When she came to the United States after World War II, she left behind her languages and most of her ethnic and cultural traditions. She assimilated to U.S. culture and, specifically, to Missourian culture in the 1950s, when antimiscegenation laws were still in place. Again, I see her assimilation as evidence of her pursuit of white privilege, but I do not judge her. I cannot even imagine her life in Missouri as perhaps the only Filipina. Only recently have I learned that my lola saw visions and had premonitions. Her shamanistic spirituality may have been colonized by Catholicism and my grandfather's violence, but her indigenous gifts endured. My own relationship with her drew me to remember indigenous healers, called babaylans.

Indeed, in working to be deliberate about integrative solidarity, I cannot forget all of the Euroamerican ancestry in my family and the Euroamerican role models who have worked toward transformation in women's spirituality communities. Exploring my Spanish and other European ancestry can be challenging, as I have mentioned. Like the encounters with policemen from my poem, whom my sister identified as white and Hispanic, parts of our ethnicity are often invisible. I have encountered friends who completely dismiss my Spanish roots. In their eyes, the Spanish in me is not a part of my ancestry, because the Spaniards were the colonizers. As I attempt to explain to my sister in my poem, I often feel so whitewashed already, having been raised in the way that we were—as if we were white—but I want integrative solidarity, a sense of integrity that advocates for the Xicana and Filipina in me while embracing and compassionately challenging the Euroamerican in me. I seek Euroamerican female role models within an indigenous, or decolonized, paradigm. In my poem, I speak about the altar I have in my apartment; in particular, Euroamerican role models have a place on the altar. These role models include the dark madonnas of Spain.

Exploring the treasures of my ancestors is both challenging and enjoyable, and I see myself as part of the next generation of nepantlera and babaylan-inspired healing and transforming role models who will, perhaps, be main characters in the new mythology of a younger mestiza's life.

Mestiza Literary Criticism Methodologies and *So Far from God, Dogeaters, Flight Is Song on Four Winds* and *The Fifth Sacred Thing*

I have been encouraged in this new mythmaking by Ana Castillo's *So Far from God* and, particularly, her character Caridad. Caridad's rough start, as a disfigured survivor of assault, and final disappearance when she jumps off the cliff in Sky City, may seem to make her a poor role model, but her enduring passion encourages creative transformation in her readers. It is, perhaps, through a multi-ethnic feminist and indigenous, or decolonized, lens that her strength as a role model becomes apparent. Indeed, she, among the daughters of Sofi, exhibits Euroamerican features. She also is the one labeled a whore. Finally, she is the one who becomes the symbol of la Virgen to the people of Tome. Her story begins tragically but becomes miraculous: She returns home one day after having been assaulted, but she is healed by her sister La Loca, is trained by Dona Felicia, the town medicine woman, and becomes a healer. This personal transformation, catalyzed by Dona Felicia, leaves Caridad in a state where she can receive love. She goes into a cave in the Sangre de Cristo Mountains, to pray, and she does not return until a year later. The Christian faithful of Tome see in her as a virgin with a halo; however, she is simply a woman healer. Caridad, as Castillo's character, is a whole woman who is a survivor and healer in nepantla space. In love and in danger, Caridad simply disappears one day, jumping off a mountain when she hears the indigenous mother calling her.

I assert that, from the perspective of mestiza literary criticism, Caridad's character and her role modeling of personal growth are a playground of intermixed ethnic cultural practices and stories. Her disappearance in the cave can be interpreted as having Euroamerican roots, similar to the cave imagery of Plato's cave; in contrast, her emergence as a medium and then as a bird called by the indigenous mother of humanity has Native significance. In addition to the indigenous lens, a feminist approach to literature provides another interpretation. Caridad's year in the cave can be thought of as a nurturing of her feminist role model attributes that bring her into greater leadership as a healer in her community. Finally, Caridad's symbolic rebirth to the indigenous mother enlivens a feminist hope in an afterlife which, unlike the white masculinist one of Tome, nurtures and mothers women.

In conclusion, Caridad is a role model who embodies and creates transformative and healing space, because she is both believable and unbelievable. Her story, like my own, involves emancipation from the dominant Western ways of knowing and being; her story is perhaps the story of many women (and men). Yet, there is much magical realism in Castillo's recounting of Caridad's personal history, and for that reason, Caridad as a character exists as both real and unreal, allowing readers to embrace the limitless possibilities and rebirths available to them as they heal and transform their own lives.

Within Filipina literature, I also have been encouraged to recast stories with transformative, empowered and empathetic characters. Both Hagedorn and Bobis offered mother figures in their works *Dogeaters* and *Flight Is Song on Four Winds*.

Hagedorn's Our Mother role model stands in the transformative space, like a culture bearer, bearing fruit of the Philippines that reaches the United States. Even as Hagedorn points to the horrors and grief of sexism and racism—external and internal—throughout her novel, she has Our Mother bring a conclusion to the story, albeit a painful one. Hagedorn's readers—many in diaspora—can read the prayer and love song and fully resonate with the grief of her characters as well as with the narrator. Additionally, the narrator questions the oppressions portrayed in the novel, which are displayed on the body of Our Mother. There is, Hagedorn emphasizes throughout *Dogeaters*, much to grieve: the raping of Filipinas by Christian colonizers as well as the need to "invent [their] own history" sometimes altogether.[9] Hagedorn's narrator in the final chapter of *Dogeaters*, "Kundiman," expresses rage and directs these emotions toward Our Mother, who is also called by many other names, including "Our Blessed Virgin Mary of Most Precious Blood, menstrual, ephemeral, carnal, eternal."[10] The narrators describe a mother figure who is a real, embodied, blood-filled woman with both temporary and infinite significance.

As an intermixture of the many bloods, this mother figure becomes a role model to Filipinas, women who cannot be codified and are, instead, open wounds.[11] Hagedorn's mother figure represents "overlapping and flexible centers,"[12] being profoundly multiple. "Rose Mystica, Black Virgin of Rhinestone and Velvet Mystery," this mother figure is an intermixture whose name is "Madonna of Volcanoes and Violence."[13] Looking back at the names, both sacred and profane, given to Our Mother, the narrator also is able to recognize the fruits of this multiple, integrated role model—a very transformational multi-ethnic position. Hagedorn dismantles the potential for selective memory, by including the painful names—the names used against her as a feminine intermixture with indigenous roots. Our Mother is the one who inhabits the multiple and liminal; hence, Hagedorn creates a new mythology with an Our Mother who looks like us and calls us to question and transform the culture we bear.

And the fruits Hagedorn offers of this woman—"Blessed . . . among women"—are of the Earth particular to the homeland. "Kundiman" concludes with a celebration of these fruits of the Earth: "Blessed are the fruits of thy womb: guavas, mangos, santol, mangosteen, durian. Now and forever, world without end. Now and forever."[14] Although the fruits come from the Philippines, and the celebration ends with the finality of "now and forever," the typical "amen" is missing. Although this ending leaves open the potential for continued transformation, Hagedorn's use of the Eurocentric Catholic words suggest that she is able to remove from her literature the white man but not the white framework. Retelling the old story, Hagedorn uses the voice of an empowered writer and critic to critique the Catholic, colonized system that disempowered the Philippines. Interestingly enough, this same system then empowered her to write, albeit from a position of assumed white masculine power. Her work connects deeply with mestiza literary criticism that aims to complicate the Filipina mestiza mother role model figure and make visible whiteness and masculinism as forming the normalized framework. Our Mother may not be a babaylan or able to fully step into her indigenous power; however, I argue that she has that potential if she were given more time. Altogether, Hagedorn's prayer is a sacred remix of the Lord's Prayer, to Our Mother instead of Our Father. Moreover, Hagedorn's role model expands the characteristics of integrative solidarity to include the reality of Filipinas and Filipino Americans as individuals and as a community.

Bobis, as well, explores a mother figure as a main character and role model with life-giving properties. It is perhaps no mistake that Bobis also alludes to Christianity's influence in the Philippines. She, like Hagedorn, includes a prayer, and yet, instead of a prayer to Our Mother, she writes a letter to the woman whose name is most associated with Spanish speaking Christianity, Maria. In the poem "For Maria," she writes about a character who is in her "bamboo forest" when she is "filled with the child by air" because of her "love for the lost." The narrator speaks of the "lost strange wind" that came into the "all-year-round feast" of Maria's "green body" and was "welcomed . . . with jasmine." Maria, perhaps as the Earth herself, then births the narrator. In the now of the poem, the narrator is "birthing poetry and life."[15] In this poem, Bobis highlights this character's nurturance with suggestions of the Earth's nurturance as well. With a profound love for the lost, Maria's womb carries in it the poet herself. Sensually greeted with floral scents and music, she is held in the womb until she is able to birth her own creations. Bobis's narrator connects with her roots, which are entrenched in motherly, earthen signifiers. The writing too moves forward into discovery while the narrator also looks to her ancestry to manifest her ethnic roots. Because Bobis appears to be the narrator-poet in "For Maria," the poem may be considered a semiautobiographical creative text. In this perhaps ethno-autobiographical text, whether Bobis herself experienced silence when she wanted to know about her ethnic and cultural differences is anyone's guess. Still, Bobis has survived to find this Maria role model to rebirth her into the darkness often associated with deathlessness. In the mother's earthen body, Bobis seems to have found what she needed—motherly nurturance from a role model and character that had an earthen body. The narrator poet in Bobis's poem, too, becomes a Maria who can nurture newness. This woman can transform, as she herself has been transformed in the Earth-like womb of her role model. This female figure has, above all, created a space for growth. Moreover, Bobis creatively intermixes dark and light as well as death and rebirth—in the Maria-mother that the poet herself becomes, through combined ethnic, feminist and tribal perspectives. She creates an empowered mestiza role model who, like nepantleras and babaylans, ushers women into "poetry [creative expression] and life."[16]

Finally, this mythology of multicultural integrative solidarity is within Euroamerican literature as well. Starhawk developed this in her mestiza character Madrone in *The Fifth Sacred Thing*. Madrone is the adopted mestiza healer granddaughter of the town's Jewish elder, Maya. These two women have a relationship similar to that of Dona Felicia and Caridad. Madrone is able to come into her own power when Maya gives up some of her power to ask for healing from Madrone. Moreover, Madrone claims her personal power and lets go of being a savior of her community by calling on the Aztecs' serpent-skirted Mother of the Gods to hide and save her.[17] Madrone's connection with the serpent is intimately tied to the Xicana mestiza association with serpents. Madrone, as a character, is a transethnic feminist, tribal leader and healer. Her ethnicity is multiple, she is empowered, and she, particularly when associated with the Mother of the Gods, is the embodied tribal elder rooted in indigenous ways of being. In sum, I read *The Fifth Sacred Thing* as a story of integrative solidarity between Madrone and Euroamerican Maya, who recognizes, deconstructs and then passes on her power to Madrone, as well as between Madrone and herself as she comes into her indigenous gifts. Through these two steps of integrative solidarity, Madrone is transformed into a nepantlera-inspired healer.

Altogether, these characters—Caridad, Our Mother, Maria and Madrone—challenge readers to stand in solidarity with their painful experiences and to transform them. They give readers examples of holistic, integrated, empowered social activist healers.

Conclusion: Two Insights

In conclusion, I offer two brief insights. The first is that mestiza and women's spirituality communities must, in their growth toward integrative solidarity, embrace the process of knowing their indigenous roots. Of course, women's spirituality facilitates a growing awareness of the mother line; however, what this study has revealed is that the process of recovering indigenous roots cannot begin without the work of decolonization and, similarly, without the aid of transformational multiculturalism. Both decolonization and transformational multiculturalism include shared understandings, but no works that I have researched in this study speak to all three perspectives including women's spirituality. In this study, I have brought forth my world view of the trinity of indigenization, decolonization and transformational multiculturalism.

Only with this trinity have I found a way in which mestizas can acknowledge their privilege, deconstruct the hierarchical dualisms that are created from racism and return to their indigenous heritage. I found the work of embracing indigenous roots to bring equitable unification within mestiza and women's communities in Castillo's description of Caridad's mestiza body and in her acceptance of the call of the indigenous mother;[18] in Hagedorn's depiction of the Black Virgin of Rhinestone and Velvet Mystery, whose womb gives the native fruits of "guavas, mangos, santol, mangosteen, durian. Now and forever, world without end";[19] in Bobis's portrayal of Maria's body in the "bamboo forest" and her love for the lost";[20]

and, finally, in Starhawk's picture of Madrone's "bronze skin" and healing skills that she gained from the Aztecs' Mother of the Gods.[21]

My second insight is that grieving is required as we come into integrative solidarity. This study has been one of fumbling, trusting and letting go as I (re)learn how to speak to myself in ways that affirm all ancestral parts of myself. I decolonize to move through racism and embrace my darkness. I speak to the need to simply cry in conversations with my sister about my mestiza sense of self. In truth, I have been drawn to these particular characters because of how they model this fumbling yet emancipatory process. Moreover, like these characters, I have been navigating my growth while in relationships with my family and my community. Learning from the stories of colonization told by my abuelas and lolas and letting go of old visions and languages for the future, as do the characters of Castillo, Hagedorn, Bobis and Starhawk, I have come into integrative solidarity with profound vulnerability. I am challenged to express my rage like Hagedorn's narrator, find solace in Maria like Bobis's narrator, and let go of needing to be a savior, as Madrone did. At this point in my personal mythology, my literary mestizaje, my search for a mestiza approach to my spirituality, I have come through much grief to celebrate my location on the borderlands and in diaspora, both within my psyche and within women's communities.

References

Anzaldúa, Gloria. *Borderlands/La Frontera: The New Mestiza.* San Francisco: Aunt Lute Books, 1987.

———. "now let us shift . . . the path of conocimiento . . . inner work, public acts." In *this bridge we call home: radical visions for transformation.* Edited by Gloria E. Anzaldúa and AnaLouise Keating. 540–78. New York: Routledge, 2001.

Bobis, Merlinda C. *Ang Lipad ay Awit Sa Apat na Hangin* (*Flight Is Song on Four Winds*). Manila: Babaylan Publishing Women's Collective, St. Scholastica's College, 1990.

Castillo, Ana. *So Far from God.* New York: Plume, 1995.

Delgadillo, Theresa. *Spiritual Mestizaje: Religion, Gender, Race, and Nation in Contemporary Chicana Narrative.* Durham, NC: Duke University Press, 2011.

EATWOT Women in the Philippines and Asia. *Toward an Asian Principle of*

Interpretation: A Filipino Women's Experience. Patriarchy in Asia and Asian Women's Hermeneutical Principle. Theology/Spirituality of Struggle Series. Manila: Forum for Interdisciplinary Endeavors and Studies, Institute of Women Studies, EATWOT, 1991.

Hagedorn, Jessica. *Dogeaters.* New York: Penguin, 1990.

Keating, AnaLouise. *Teaching Transformation: Transcultural Classroom Dialogues.* New York: Palgrave Macmillan, 2007.

Mananzan, Sister Mary John, OSB. *Woman, Religion, and Spirituality in Asia.* Manila: Anvil and the Institute of Women's Studies, 2004.

Mendoza-Strobel, Elenita Fe Luna. *A Book of Her Own: Words and Images to Honor the Babaylan.* San Francisco: T'Boli, 2005.

Rustomji-Kerns, Roshni, with Raini SriKanth and Elenita Fe Luna Mendoza-Strobel. Introduction to *Encounters: People of Asian Descent in the Americas.* Edited by Roshni Rustomji-Kerns, Raini SriKanth, and Elenita Fe Luna Mendoza-Strobel. Lanham, MD: Rowman and Littlefield, 1999.

Starhawk (Miriam Simos). *The Fifth Sacred Thing.* New York: Bantam, 1993.

Endnotes

1 Gloria E. Anzaldúa, *Borderlands/La Frontera: The New Mestiza* (San Francisco: Aunt Lute Books, 1987), 80.

2 EATWOT Women in the Philippines and Asia, *Toward an Asian Principle of Interpretation: A Filipino Women's Experience. Patriarchy in Asia and Asian Women's Hermeneutical Principle,* Theology/Spirituality of Struggle Series (Manila: Forum for Interdisciplinary Endeavors and Studies, Institute of Women Studies, EATWOT, 1991), 14.

3 Theresa Delgadillo, *Spiritual Mestizaje: Religion, Gender, Race, and Nation in Contemporary Chicana Narrative* (Durham, NC: Duke University Press, 2011), 1.

4 AnaLouise Keating, *Teaching Transformation: Transcultural Classroom Dialogues* (New York: Palgrave Macmillan, 2007), 9–11.

5 Gloria E. Anzaldúa, "now let us shift . . . the path of conocimiento . . . inner work, public acts," in *this bridge we call home: radical visions for transformation,* eds. Gloria E. Anzaldúa and AnaLouise Keating (New York: Routledge, 2001), 574.

6 Keating, *Teaching Transformation,* 85

7 Elenita Fe Luna Mendoza-Strobel, *A Book of Her Own: Words and Images to Honor the*

Babaylan (San Francisco: T'Boli, 2005), 165, 176.

8 Sister Mary John Mananzan, OSB, *Woman, Religion, and Spirituality in Asia* (Manila: Anvil and the Institute of Women's Studies, 2004), 230.

9 Jessica Hagedorn, *Dogeaters* (New York: Penguin, 1990), 239.

10 Hagedorn, *Dogeaters*, 250.

11 Roshni Rustomji-Kerns with Raini SriKanth and Elenita Fe Luna Mendoza-Strobel, introduction to *Encounters: People of Asian Descent in the Americas*, eds. Roshni Rustomji-Kerns, Raini SriKanth, and Elenita Fe Luna Mendoza-Strobel (Lanham, MD: Rowman and Littlefield, 1999), 3.

12 Rustomji-Kerns, introduction to *Encounters*, 7.

13 Hagedorn, *Dogeaters*, 250.

14 Hagedorn, *Dogeaters*, 250.

15 Merlinda C. Bobis, *Ang Lipad ay Awit Sa Apat na Hangin* (*Flight Is Song on Four Winds*) (Manila: Babaylan Publishing Women's Collective, St. Scholastica's College, 1990), 68.

16 Bobis, *Flight Is Song on Four Winds*, 68.

17 Bobis, *Flight Is Song on Four Winds*, 79.

18

19 Hagedorn, *Dogeaters*, 251.

20 Bobis, *Flight Is Song on Four Winds*, 68.

21 Starhawk (Miriam Simos), *The Fifth Sacred Thing* (New York: Bantam, 1994), 8–10.

RESPECTFUL ENGAGEMENT WITH LIVING TRADITIONS

KATHRYN HENDERSON

G oddess spirituality is eclectic in that we practitioners pursue scholarly research about female deities from traditions spanning time, culture and space and creatively use that information in our spiritual practices. We draw on many sources, ranging from scholarly research generated from the study of ancient surviving images and texts to oral tradition mythologies to our own intuitional or psychic connection to sacred energies. We also draw on contemporary spiritual traditions—our own and others— from texts and direct experience. However, engagement of deities and religious practices of living traditions outside our own raises the thorny issue of balance between attempts at cultural inclusiveness and cultural appropriation.[1] I approach this topic wearing my multilayered academic and spiritual identities: sociologist, ordained priestess of goddess spirituality in the Wiccan tradition and apprentice teacher of the 21 Praises of Tara dance in the Tibetan Buddhist tradition. This article began as part of my final work for ordination.

Yemaja from Yoruba tradition, Erzulie from Vodou tradition, Kali from Hindu tradition, Selu from Native American tradition, Quan Yin from Buddhist tradition and Tara from Tibetan Buddhist tradition, among others, are invoked as goddesses by a variety of practitioners of goddess spirituality. Some practitioners call or invite them into circles, while others may feel that doing so is inappropriate. On the one hand, awareness of the need for cultural inclusiveness has dawned throughout our spiritual and educational communities, spawned by concern about the health of our planet and witness of increasing global communication, trade, and exploitation of the earth. For myself and, I suspect, for others, this awareness raises a consciousness of discomfort when Sabbat after Sabbat and season after season see only Anglo-featured, Western-origin goddesses invited into our rituals. Just as we want to foster diversity in our Pagan congregations, circles and groves, we also seek diversity in our pantheons. Hence, including deities from living traditions in our rites has a strong appeal.

On the other hand, most of us are well aware of colonialism's heritage and the outcry by indigenous peoples condemning the acts of dominator cultures. These colonial powers robbed them of their natural resources, destroyed, desecrated or seized their sacred lands, enslaved their people or killed them outright with weapons or by exposure to European diseases to which they had no immunity. Then, as a final killing blow, the colonizers forcibly removed their children to schools where punishment for speaking their native tongues or maintaining their sacred traditions was the main curriculum. The ultimate insult, then, is the commandeering of sacred practices, artifacts and deities by the descendants of those very colonialists, we children who find our inherited culture bereft of reverence for the earth and all of her creatures. Hence, our dilemma: How do we find the balance point between honoring living traditions and fostering inclusiveness without reaching the tipping point and falling into cultural appropriation?[2]

To foster a dialogue about how such balance may be achieved (or at least approached) and how we may build bridges between practitioners of goddess spirituality and practitioners of living traditions, I asked five women in leadership roles in their traditions--Tibetan Buddhism, New Orleans Vodou, Hinduism, Yoruba spirituality and Lakota spirituality--for their input.[3] These interviews were open-ended and interactive. Although the interviews started with a series of questions used in all of the interviews, participants were encouraged to raise additional issues and to question me as fully as I questioned them, in an interactive format. Before I discuss these interactions, I want to ground this discussion by locating myself in the traditions in which I partake and by providing some background regarding how I have thus far attempted to avoid cultural appropriation.

I practice two Wiccan traditions and a Tibetan Buddhist tradition. I have practiced Wicca for approximately twenty years with the Re-formed Congregation of the Goddess, International, a woman-only practice in which I am ordained as a priestess of goddess spirituality. Over the years, I have attended numerous goddess-oriented workshops, camps and rituals led by diverse teachers who incorporate diverse approaches to goddess spirituality. I have even led some. I also have practiced within the co-ed Reclaiming community, as a member of a local teaching cell and of a national Permaculture Intentional Community planning group. I am also an apprentice teacher with Prema Dasara, creator of the 21 Praises of Tara dance in the Tibetan Buddhist tradition, and I continue to lead these meditational dance practices monthly and by invitation. I am a tenured professor of sociology and women's studies at a research university. My academic training and methodological orientation is qualitative research that views participant observation, in-depth, open-ended interviews and interactive conversations as the best means for empowering research participants to convey their own meanings and for researchers to give voice to multiple meanings.

Why Are We Attracted to Living Traditions?

Practitioners of goddess spirituality have been in the process of re-inventing Earth-reverent goddess religion for more than fifty years now in the United States. We acknowledge that we make up much of what we do as we go along. At the same time, observation of living tradition practice has provided us a richness and depth of information not available to us concerning ancient Western goddess worship. Our knowledge of ancient Western traditions is dependent on scanty data and too often filtered through the lenses of antagonistic or patriarchal cultures and biased writers and publishers from the theology of conquering Greeks to the ethnocentrism of own era. Recognizing their neglect of women's needs, women's leadership and women's power, we have turned our backs on the biased worldviews of our upbringing and looked elsewhere for spiritual models.

And what we have found in living tradition is layer upon layer of interlocking spiritual meanings that incorporate movement, sound, art, poetry, number, rhythm, style and culture, woven together in ways that focus energy and are simultaneously understandable at both simple and complex levels. Many of us draw on the eclecticism of Santeria and Vodou folk altars as we gather disparate items that make sense to us for our personal worship space. We are also drawn to communal chanting, dancing, drumming and other elements from living traditions to use in our own ritual practice, because they raise powerful energy.

My intent here is to enter into a deeper dialogue about how we draw on deity and practice from living traditions. Currently there is a strain in our communities between the view that everything belongs to us and we can take whatever we want, without acknowledgment of its source, and the view that anything from living traditions should be considered hands-off. I am proposing another way, a stance intended to be more responsible, by developing guidelines for more grounded practice based on consultation with those in living traditions about our use of elements from their spiritual practices. Not only does consultation with practitioners of living traditions provide us with more information, the very act of consulting them and letting them know that we are interested in their spiritual practices begins building bridges between our groups and theirs. This is no small thing, for many reasons that I will discuss shortly. To build such bridges, we need to make clear that we are undertaking our endeavors with respect for both the tradition at hand and its practitioners. This is especially important if the practitioners come from cultures that have experienced unkindness, insensitivity, exploitation and worse from our Western cultures.

Equally important is the significance of practice itself. R. J. Stewart, Victor Anderson, and the Dali Lama, among others, have stressed that, no matter what we choose as our daily spiritual practice, it is the consistency of the practice that brings us what we seek, whether we call it enlightenment, personal growth, connection to the sacred or something else. So, if we are going to engage energy from a living tradition, it makes infinite sense to consult those who have been engaged in practice with that energy for some time about how to begin and how to proceed. That said, such an undertaking is not necessarily simple. One must become very familiar with the tradition and practices around the particular deity or concept chosen. One must find practitioners of the tradition under consideration and find a way to approach them if no previous close connections with them exist. One may encounter both resistance and avoidance on the part of fellow eclectic practitioners and on the part of practitioners of living traditions. Not surprisingly, in the past we have often avoided reaching out or made other, easier choices; that is all the more reason we should endeavor to proceed differently in the future.

Some Older Models

The topic of cultural borrowing versus cultural appropriation is not new. But the time is overdue to build bridges between our "resurrected" practice and living goddess practice by opening and continuing dialogue. Though not all, many living traditions that have been closed to outsiders in the past are seeking connection now. The door is opening. We have the choice to walk through it. But first we should take a look back.

The two Wiccan traditions that I practice, Dianic Wicca and the Reclaiming Tradition, in the past have attempted to walk the blade's edge between inclusiveness and cultural appropriation by careful language choice and/or cultural specificity. One practice in Dianic Wicca has been to call the goddess by her attributes instead of choosing a specific name for her: "She who __" (fill in the blank). This is an attempt to be inclusive and yet avoid cultural naming, the intent being that no goddess with the specified attributes is left out but that cultural appropriation is avoided. For instance, "She who is the Queen of Heaven and Earth, Our Nurturing Mother, and Creator of the World" or "She who rules the waters of the world, nurtures the plants and creatures of the land and sea" may be used as invocations and include many culturally specific notions of the goddess.

While this approach to language is fine as an occasional choice, depending on the intent of the work, I find it problematic in the same way that the 19th century notion of the "melting pot" is problematic for our multicultural understandings and growing global awareness. The erasure of cultural specificity implied in the term *melting pot* was used in 19th century education to minimize differences along with the commercial incitement to become American by filling one's house and closet with items from the Sears catalog. Such practices erased cultural identity and cultural pride. To permanently blend the rich depth and beauty of culturally specific spiritual practice into bland language does the same kind of disservice. A lovely example is Ursula Le Guin's novel *The Lathe of Heaven,* in which a well-intentioned psychologist makes a magical attempt to erase ethnic strife by turning everyone gray.[4] Not only is skin color made homogenous, culture too is reduced to the lowest common denominator of homogeneity, and the spice of ethnic diversity is lost to humanity.

Another approach to avoid cultural appropriation in the United States has been for practitioners to engage only pantheons that are assumed to be from "our own" cultural heritage: Celtic deities representing Anglo-American cultural and ethnic roots. Starhawk, rethinking the underlying assumptions of re-created Celtic-only practice, has addressed the problems of such exclusivity by pointing out that our heritage in the United States is much more far-flung and that our descendants are much more ethnically diverse, This suggests to her that we could become more inclusive in our choice of pantheon(s) in a way that reflects our multi-cultural nation and world. The *Reclaiming Quarterly*, the magazine of the Reclaiming community (the feminist witchcraft tradition founded by Starhawk) addressed the theme of diversity in traditions in 2002. Pamela Harris and Culebra De Robertis, both women of color, discussed the distinctions in the way each honors deity in Santeria within her home culture and individual practice in distinction to within Reclaiming's group practice. I am proposing some next steps, along this line of thinking, as a way of promoting more dialogue among ourselves and between feminist pagans and practitioners of living traditions.[5]

Below are the introductory statement and questions that I used in my interviews of five practitioners of living traditions. Most of the interviewees preferred that their names be used; one did not. Some of them followed the structure of my initial questions in their answers; others did not. Everyone had much more to say on the topic than the question structure facilitated. While I have edited the answers for succinctness, the included quotations are verbatim. I have included additional statements worthy of note from my participants in a separate section at the end of this article.

Interview Introductory Statement and Questions

Dianic Wicca, also sometimes called goddess spirituality, is eclectic in that we pursue scholarly research about female deity from worldwide traditions and use that information in our spiritual practice, drawing on historic and contemporary traditions. Some who avoided invoking goddesses from living cultures in the past have rethought this and are suggesting that Wiccans and Pagans become more inclusive in our pantheon in a way that reflects our multicultural world. For me, this raises the question osf how can we be inclusive in our practice but also be respectful and avoid cultural appropriation. So I am consulting a number of leaders in living traditions for their input. These are my questions:

1. How can those within the goddess spirituality perspective, who want to honor and praise Tara, [Hindu, Yoruba, Vodou and Native American goddesses] go about it in a respectful manner?

2. Is "goddess" the correct term for naming the female deity in your tradition?

3. Are there things that would be seen as normal and respectful in a Wiccan perspective that could be seen as disrespectful in your tradition? Examples might include putting her statue or image on an altar that contains items dedicated to other deities, the directions or Wiccan tools such as a wand, chalice or sacred blade.

4. Is it is acceptable to invoke Tara [Hindu, Yoruba, Vodou and Native American goddesses] in a Wiccan circle? If so, what would be a respectful way to do this?

5. Are norms different for public and private worship?

6. How might Wiccans and practitioners from your tradition join together in worship? Would it be permissible to conduct a ritual with elements from both traditions so that we build bonds across our traditions?

7. Is there anything dangerous in the practice of contacting female deity in your tradition, for those not initiated?

8. Is there anything I have not thought to ask that you want to tell me about this topic?

Interview with Prema Dasara, Creator and teacher of Tara Dance Meditations in the Tibetan Buddhist tradition

(answers follow the numbered sequence of the questions)

1. Tara . . . said, "Call my name." We know she is available to anyone. All you need to do is call her name and she will respond to need if you have a connection to her. Now, in the Dance, because it came through the Tibetan tradition, I try to preserve a certain amount of protocol just because I'm using their view . . . For example, the texts that I hand out, because they come from traditional sources, should not be placed on the floor or shown any disrespect. If you want to divest yourself of it, do it in an appropriate way, by burning or burying. Burying is Earth-purifying. Mostly it's a matter of consciousness. Flawed Xeroxes can be recycled.

2. Diva or Devi is a being who appears and evolves themselves into in a light body, who has certain qualities, *Diva* or *Devi*, depending

on the translation—"Hla" in Tibetan. Tara is a Bodhisattva. What distinguishes a Bodhisattva from a Buddha is that a Bodhisattva is one that achieves enlightenment and turns back to help humankind. Tara is referred to as the first female Buddha. (She chose, against tradition, to come to enlightenment in a female body instead of a male body.) It has nothing to do with gender.

3. The key is benefit of others. Using Tara practice solely for our own purpose is not appropriate, not in the spirit of what Tara is trying to help us achieve. But if it is for the benefit of all beings, it is fine.

4. Tara doesn't really belong to the Tibetans. She is much greater than one tradition. Many traditions appeal to her and access her. Many women will want to do this dance and are not Buddhists. Because the dance and text are in lineage tradition, we need to follow it— not just anyone can teach it. But the Mantra Dance of Universal Peace, anyone can teach. It's a matter of showing respect. In the dance we are using methods of personal transformation. Tara is not an external being. The practice has the potential to create enlightened mind in the individual. When we manifest as Tara, we do not channel. We use the outside to stimulate the inside. Tara is present when we dance; we dance AS Tara.

5. Everyone has the right to integrate what they have learned for themselves, but it's tricky if they present to others. I take a couple of lines from this prayer or that, but it needs care, not to present it publicly without permission. If you want to use this in any public context, please ask permission.

6. There is no reason why we cannot have something together. What I often do is coin a prayer where I have the elements of:

   • Motivation—We are here to manifest the wisdom, compassion and power within us.

   • Refuge—The broadest motivation is some sources of refuge—not for ourselves but for the sake of all beings. Always seal with "May all beings be happy, May all beings be free."

7. A light being has no emotional response like worldly gods such as the Greek gods.

8. The basic thing is to inspire each other, [to] hold a place of respect for the work we are engaged in. Any exchange is not superficial. Depth can happen at any moment.

Interview with Renu (pseudonym), Hindu Scholar and Teacher

(answers follow the numbered sequence of the questions)

1. In the Hindu tradition, we approach the goddess for her grace, much like young children approach their mothers. . . . She is the living matrix from which the universe springs. Hinduism in general is a very tolerant religion, and there is nothing that prohibits mixing traditions.

2. In my view, there should be no need for separate altars for Hindu deities and Wiccan tools, *et cetera*. These are simply energies of different attributes of god consciousness that have been named and given a form so humans can find it easier to approach them.

3. Usually, if you're going to chant mantras they should be chanted correctly and with some expertise. Otherwise, they can be harmful. There are some things that are considered unrespectful by the Hindus, such as letting your shoes touch the altar area or even sitting with your legs pointing towards the altar. In general, however, if you follow acceptable rules of respect there should not be a problem.

4. Understanding the attributes of the specific goddess would be the first place to start. There are many hymns and mantras for each of the goddesses you wish to invoke, which can be used. Mantras are very powerful and should generally be used with more caution, but hymns can be used by anyone. Or, if you have understood the main attributes of a particular goddess, you can make up your own hymn to describe her.

5. I think anything that connects you with the particular deity and invokes deep devotion and love for the goddess will be transformative and help you to reach the grace of the deity.

6. Most traditional Hindus, unless terribly orthodox, would not have a problem with attending a Wiccan ritual. Deity, after all, for the

Hindus is all-pervading and encompassing. However, I think most Hindus would not be comfortable with rituals combining elements from the Wiccan and Hindu tradition. Hinduism is a complete system of worship with elaborate rules and rituals and ceremonies. Therefore, most Hindus would not be excited about the idea of building bonds across traditions. They, however, would have no problem with others borrowing from their traditions.

7. The deities can either be honored on their own or with their consorts. There are no hard fast rules. It just depends on what deity appeals to you and what you are trying to accomplish.

8. In the tradition that I have studied, we do recommend that certain goddesses be approached with caution, especially for example, Goddess Kali, who is a powerful force to be reckoned with as her job is to annihilate the ego, which means invoking her without being prepared for it could increase suffering in life, which we may not like.

9. There is remarkable religious tolerance in the Hindus, allowing everyone to experience the divine in a way that suits them best at a particular time. The Hindus believe that God will come to you in any form that you find him or her in—even if you choose to simply worship a stone. If your prayer and devotion are sincere, then you can realize the divine through that. Hindus also allow a path by worshiping God as a formless consciousness/energy—this is considered the most difficult path to spiritual growth and not recommended for everyone. Human beings find it much easier to work with God when they can describe him or her in a form they can relate to.

Interview with Priestess Miriam, Vodou Priestess, New Orleans

(answers do not strictly follow the numbered sequence of the questions)

People tend to relate to separate things (an individual goddess or orisha) more than they are able to see the relation of all things to one another. Word formation created deity. The concept of "Venus" evolved from the reproduction system of humans. Venus is the overall picture of the reproductive system, which invigorates male and female to reproduce. When we reduce such systems to a one-person tradition, how do we retain the inspiration of mind that belongs to it and the energy too?

We need to be more open in how we define traditions, not conceiving of them as opposed to one another. The way the universe speaks to humans is the way to see energy forces. If we have an open mind to different concepts of tradition, we are better able to meet the need to establish emotional stability. Something well beyond ourselves is hosting us, and it takes thought form.

Deity is the caller and we are the hearer. We must have clear vision. Just because we hear, does not mean we are to act. We need to sit and let it be made clearer. Then we can become more certain of how to apply the thought. It may take another twenty to forty years of life to achieve clarity. Why does it take so long to become spiritual? Things must become better understood. Tradition locks us in.

I went to Russia to bring Vodou. The young people invited me. They see Vodou as exciting. The group who invited me had been working with archaeologists and studying religion. They introduced me to Russian history. The Volga River runs like a messenger. We did the blessing at the Caspian Sea in the fall of 2000. It was not about individual concepts of religion. There were Mongolians, people from the Steppes and many others in clothes from the past. There was a female Matron. They had a white old man of the crossroads, just like Legba, the old man [in Vodou tradition], to set guidelines. They had a burning bowl. They put salt in while it was burning. The whole city was there. It was a universal sacred place like Stonehenge. There was a priestess under the Tibetan tradition, now exiled, who had met the Dalai Lama. She is restoring her living now; [she] does healing and takes care of the community.

We did a spiritual circle. I had no idea what they were saying, but I responded to the energy. We did head washing and anointing with water. A rainbow swept across the inner circle. The energy of spirit swept in. The priestess poured rum on the altar and did a Buddhist prayer: One in Unity. Spirit prayer and sharing of food: a beautiful communion. Questions were asked: What would we like to see? What is our service? How can we let spirit serve us? I saw a castor oil bush there in Russia, but they did not know it was for healing. . . . I made healing teas from the castor oil leaves. Participating with them taught me a lot.

Unless asked to do otherwise, sit and observe. Never go and project. Never state what you are (with pride); people can formulate any thought about you. When you are firmly set in your work, you don't have to step out to defend yourself. Spirit has everything dressed up how to be served. We must be with our own character.

If I say I have invited Oshun, then people make assumptions. We must question more deeply: What is the purpose? Hold the vision. It is OK to call Erzulie if calling the heart chakra or Kundalini energy. If the blood is called up, it will be integrated. However, it is dangerous to just toss up any old thing—like a doctor who prescribes a powerful medicine, not through understanding, but just to try it. There could be other physical conditions not considered. We need experience and we have to work together. Anyone who puts keeping their own tradition before consideration of the good of all others you cannot trust.

All things are a condition of mind. There are those who see sharing their deities like "I don't want to share my lover." Treasuring the intimate part is respect. One can still keep the beautiful part even as we share. The Lover has to go make some bread. . . .

Speaking about reading about Vodou traditions, when we only read we can become more confused. If it is the right, open time, the gate opens up. However, many people sensationalize or do not integrate their work or work to open the gate. We must come out of the shadow.

Interview with the late Yoruba Chief Aina Olomo, Author and Lecturer

(answers do not strictly follow the numbered sequence of the questions)

The easiest way to honor goddesses or orishas such as Yemaja is not to worship them. When you move to worship, there will be things in the tradition that you do not know. This can result in bringing negative, not positive, energy. It is acceptable to make an altar to her, honor her image or sing songs to her. Actually calling an orisha could be dangerous for those not initiated into the practice, as they might offend the deity by not using the appropriate practice. Practices have lineages in themselves—not only African [ones] but also regional ones and family ones. You cannot read them in books. Without having been initiated into these, you will not know them. We build a relationship with our primary deities. Mine is Shango. Because I have a log-time relationship with him, he is more patient with me.

Joint rituals with Wiccans or others are fine. We do them all the time. But it would be disrespectful, for instance, if Oshun was called in a collective ritual by a Wiccan when there was an Oshun priestess present who knows the deity best. I suggest that, when calling deities of African Yoruba tradition, that, before you start calling, you ask their permission and acknowledge your unfamiliarity to them.

Yemaja is the sea. Sometimes people just want to adore her. They forget that the sea and rivers are dangerous places. So are the rivers of our body—the circulation system. When not approached the correct way, they could respond in an unkind way. Lots of traditions have loving deities. Ours is not that way. What you read in a paragraph does not describe our deities. It has taken me an entire lifetime to get a clue.

At the same time, this is a period in which spiritual leaders are reaching out. It doesn't matter what spiritual tradition. We have to change the way we think and do things. This is especially important in Earth-based religions, to seek unity among us. . . . We want to join hands and go beyond [old boundaries]. We have to find language to share among our communities. I want to share the word of Oshun, [to] take the transcendent leap. I would like to do a workshop on female orishas and who they are so people can ask questions and so get skills: "When you go to the river, this is what you do to honor Oshun." We might as well empower each other. It's not about telling people NO. For us, those are divinations, and one has to know how to read them. We hear that Mother Earth is dying. Rather, we believe that she is just getting old. We need to read the cycles. What does that particular thing mean? We all do ritual, but what does that mean in terms of incorporating with one another? It demonstrates that we have respect for the realm that we occupy. Spiritual leadership is important.

Interview with Shari Valentine, Hoyokoh-Lakota Spiritual Leader

(answers do not strictly follow the numbered sequence of the questions)

The medicine will police itself. Nothing is spiritually different with the Dine, Ojibwa or Wiccan practitioners from Lakota, outside of ethnocentricity. Wiccans use the elements and are nature-based too.

Our tradition is not deity oriented. . . . Rather, we have spirit entities—streams of energy. The prominence of animals and elements are not gendered. Spider Calling Song has no gender; Buffalo Nation, no gender. Not all traditions think of Spider as female; it depends on the nation. The Hopi/Dine are more likely to personify. Inviting spirits is like inviting the governor to your wedding. He or she may not come. You are not in charge; they do whatever. It is trouble to call what you are not familiar with. Does the woman with lightning bolts on her skirt really want to call that? What would you do if Thunderbird really showed up? Like the [Celtic] Morrígan, don't mess around with her without good reason.

The medicine will police itself: Herbs, pipe [and] artifacts used to make medicine will decide "who wants to play with whom today." Some practitioners will not mix Crow and Eagle or Eagle and Hawk. Yet use is more fluid in practice, more like the Wiccan concept of a kitchen witch [who creates energy from whatever is at hand]. One high-profile practitioner built a healing fire with tires when no wood was available. Like a chocolate cake can be made with different chocolates.

Unless you're doing ceremony on the reservation, you have already crossed over. . . . Native spiritual leaders have been in ceremonies to pray for peace in Jerusalem; Sun Dance Ceremony flexibility allows pan-Indian participation. . . .

Wiccans use the elements and are nature-based too. By sincerely making an effort to know as much as we can—being sensitive to ways we are different—we can show respect.

What is tricky for integrating is women's blood. Pipes and women on their moon are not supposed to mix. This is not prejudice. It is about women's power. Moon time is the breaking down of an altar for creation, which is counter to setting one up. It is like the waxing and waning moon—one energy moving down to the earth [and] the other moving up and out. When I experienced these combined, it felt like being ripped apart. Making a cedar circle around women on their moon is the answer.

Serendipitous Sharings of Wisdom

This is a period in which spiritual leaders are reaching out, . It doesn't matter what spiritual tradition. . . . We have to find language to share among our communities.

—Aina Olomo

God will come to you in any form that you find him or her in—even if you choose to simply worship a stone. If your prayer and devotion are sincere, then you can realize the divine.

—Renu (pseudonym)

Unless you're doing ceremony on the reservation, you have already crossed over. . . . Wiccans use the elements and are nature-based too. By sincerely making an effort to know as much as we can—being sensitive to ways we are different—we can show respect.

—Shari Valentine

If we have an open mind to different concepts of tradition, we are better able to meet the need to establish emotional stability. Something well beyond ourselves is hosting us, and it takes thought form.

—Priestess Miriam

The basic thing is to inspire each other, hold a place of respect for the work we are engaged in. Any exhange is not superficial. Depth can happen at any moment.

—Prema Dasara

Discussion

The purpose of this article is to begin a dialogue between practitioners of contemporary Earth-based belief systems and practitioners adhering to traditional cultural systems. As the reader can see, my interview questions elicited very different perspectives and very different forms of answers, along with infinite wisdom beyond the scope of my questions. In this set of interviews each spiritual leader responded based on her own rich experience. In respect for these intelligent, wise voices, I feel it inappropriate for me to try to offer any sort of summary.

However, I do feel called to offer some general guidelines for those of us who would like to practice with honor in relation to living traditions, and would like to reach out to practitioners of living traditions. These are given below. I hope readers will consider these issues in shaping their own practice and research, and will contribute to our ongoing conversation across traditions.

1. A. Start with honor and respect for living spiritual practice: the deity, her practitioners and their traditions.

   B. Do your homework by researching the deity and her tradition.

   - Find out whether there are local practitioners of that tradition, and consult with them about how to proceed with respect.

   - Be aware of symbolism in artifacts, jewelry, etc. In some traditions, only those who have been initiated to certain levels of practice have the right to use certain things—including words, practices and objects. For you to use those things could be perceived as disrespectful.

2. If your ritual is public, do your best to find out whether a practitioner of that tradition will be present. If one will be, ask whether and how he or she would like to participate.

3. Do not touch or fondle jewelry, beads or artifacts belonging to practitioners of living traditions unless the practitioners have given permission.

4. Ask permission of deities in living traditions to invite them into your ritual. Do not command. Invite.

5. Do not assume that all practitioners of a given living tradition will give you the same answer to a question or agree with one another on all details.

6. Do not assume that you are an expert just because you have read one or more books, attended a workshop or heard a speaker.

Epilogue

The first draft of this article was written just prior to my ordination in 2008 and then was presented at the first ASWM symposium, in 2008 in Madison, Wisconsin. Since that time, I have continued my Wiccan and Buddhist practices and have had more opportunities—challenging growth experiences—to put my own guidelines into practice. Doing that is not always an easy task. I share some of these challenges in the hope that others will find them useful for dialogue. Our Tara dance practice has grown, and I have been blessed that younger teachers have emerged to share in the work. This has meant closer affiliation with the local Buddhist temple; we do one of our two monthly practices there. Consequently, I am called not only to be mindful of lineage tradition, as I am while dancing with goddess women, when I set up the altar and when I begin to dance, but to be fully aware of and conduct or share in the appropriate prayers that must precede the dance. I am fortunate that my two younger teachers are from the Tibetan Buddhist tradition and joyfully guide me and answer my questions. On their advice, I asked the temple lama to fill the hollow base of my Tara statue with blessings, because that was a requirement for it to be on the temple altar when we dance there. That Tara statue, which was a gift from a friend, is now doubly blessed and comes to all of our dance practices.

A recent challenge came last year, when we hosted a workshop and Tara empowerment given by the resident lama, both at the temple. A suggestion was made that at the beginning of the event, as the three teachers hosting the workshop with Prema Dasara, we three make full-body, on-the-floor traditional prostrations in front of the twenty-foot-tall, gold, male Buddha statue (the temple is also full of a multitude of Thanka images, including several images of Tara). As an ordained priestess in Dianic Wicca, who had taken an ordination vow to serve women, I found this prostration a challenge. I discussed the dilemma with my Buddhist co-teachers and my Wiccan co-priestesses. I was reminded that we—including the lama who would give the empowerment—each become Tara when we do our practice. I called on my sociological perspective as a postmodern social constructionist, acknowledging that all acts are given different meanings by different persons. I looked for a compromise. I finally settled on one that I found rather unsatisfactory— to invoke my sixty-plus years and bad knees to make a slighter bow.

The day of the workshop and Tara empowerment came. In the flow of the complicated happenings—the overcrowded small space, a long, complex schedule, multiple organizers and, I suspect, something else—the occasion for the prostrations never occurred. Reflecting on that now, I find that the value of my deliberation was in the dialogues that took place, the sharing of thought and the closer connections with my communities that I built through discussion.

Jean Shinoda Bolen, in *Moving Toward the Millionth Circle* (2013),[6] wrote about the gift of synchronicity: "If I am involved in something that has meaning for me, synchronicities happen: they provide feedback, commentary, help in the form of the people who come into my life then, stories that inspire or fit what I am doing."[7] The dialogue around my non-event indeed felt like a synchronicity. Bolen further wrote about the synchronicity in her life in her meetings with the Dalai Lama and about hearing his statement that the "world will be saved by the western woman."[8] In the face of the current climate of political pandering to disempower women, now, more than ever, our attention to building bridges through respectful engagement with living traditions holds propitious potential.

References

Andreas, Judy. "Wicca, World Deities, and Me." *Reclaiming Quarterly* 87 (Summer 2002): 17–18.

Barrett, Ruth. *Women's Rites, Women's Mysteries: Creating Ritual in the Dianic Wiccan Tradition*. Bloomington, IN: Authorhouse, 2004.

Bolen, Jean Shinoda. *Moving Toward the Millionth Circle: Energizing the Global Women's Movement*. San Francisco: Conari Press, 2013.

Franklin, George. "Working in Diverse Traditions." *Reclaiming Quarterly* 87 (Summer 2002): 16–21.

Harris, Pamela, and Culebra De Robertis. "Santeria and Reclaiming: Walking Two Paths, An Interview with Pamela Harris and Culebra De Robertis." *Reclaiming Quarterly* 87 (Summer 2002): 19–21.

Le Guin, Ursula. *The Lathe of Heaven*. New York: Avon Books, 1971.

Teish, Luisah. *Jambalaya: The Natural Woman's Book of Personal Charms and Practical Rituals*. San Francisco: Harper Collins, 1988.

Endnotes

1 In this article, I address only these issues around female-gendered deities. Although the same issues apply to male-gendered deities, the feminist interest

in female deities in living traditions has tended to be more intense, because of the manner in which goddess spirituality is often interpreted as corrective to the male-centered character of dominant Western religions.

2 Others also have addressed these issues. For example, see Luisah Teish, *Jambalaya: The Natural Woman's Book of Personal Charms and Practical Rituals* (San Francisco: Harper Collins, 1988); Ruth Barrett, *Women's Rites, Women's Mysteries: Creating Ritual in the Dianic Wiccan Tradition* (Bloomington, IN: Authorhouse, 2004); George Franklin, "Working in Diverse Traditions," *Reclaiming Quarterly* 87 (Summer 2002): 16–21.

3 This was a convenience sample. It also is merely the beginning of what I hope will become a more extensive dialogue. Certainly, input from many other traditions is needed, and I regret the limits and exclusions of perspectives from a wider range of traditions.

4 Ursula Le Guin, *The Lathe of Heaven* (New York: Avon Books, 1971).

5 See Franklin, "Working in Diverse Traditions, 16; Judy Andreas, "Wicca, World Deities, and Me," *Reclaiming Quarterly* 87 (Summer 2002): 17–18; Pamela Harris and Culebra De Robertis, "Santeria and Reclaiming: Walking Two Paths, An Interview with Pamela Harris and Culebra De Robertis," *Reclaiming Quarterly* 87 (Summer 2002): 19–21.

6 Jean Shinoda Bolen, *Moving Toward the Millionth Circle: Energizing the Global Women's Movement* (San Francisco: Conari Press, 2013).

7 Bolen, *Moving Toward the Millionth Circle*, 95.

8 Bolen, *Moving Toward the Millionth Circle*, 96.

O GREAT MOTHER OF CREATION:
A PRAYER FOR SHEALING THE MATRILINEAL LINE

I take a deep bow to the foremothers.

I take flight with the foremothers
Who have been born aloft by the spirit winds of vision for liberation—
the foremothers, all the womyn who ever paused, wind in their hair,
listening to bird song, clarifying freedom.

I rise in conflagration's journey in search to stars:
I crouch at fire's verge with the foremothers who have been burnt
in pyres of desolation,

And wind-whip-whinny, air-alight, with all the womyn who have ever
gazed at bright flame and changeling coals of circle-fire, and circled,
and sang.

I stoop and drink the water my foremothers drank
she-they who have floated in the shealing waters, with flower petals
and sacred herbs, and been restored,
Weeping and strengthened with the moon's wild gyres.

I step onto this Earth where my foremothers danced
Made from my foremothers' dust
—the foremothers who knew the cycle of return, who grew garden
from seed to fruit and flower.

I inhabit the same womon's body of wisdom and sinew and vim
My foremothers crafted.

I take a deep bow to myself
And smile the deepest smile of delight and crafty knowing.

I hear the sacred blessing from the foremothers forward
My deepest heart sparkles with their radiant blessing.

~ Marna Hauk

AFTERWORD

CRISTINA BIAGGI

This notable and variegated anthology contains scholarly as well as hands-on writings, art and poetry about diverse aspects of goddess scholarship and spirituality.

These essays, poems and works of art offer a new vision for our lives, centered on the sacred feminine and forging a new path forward in a world that has become increasingly militarized, in which predator capitalism is on the upswing, in which the disparity between the haves and the have-nots has hit its highest point yet, and in which there is a total lack of concern for women's issues and for the health of the Earth. At the same time that the current administration in the United States has hit an all-time low in its myopic, pessimistic, grasping vision of our world, one in which naked greed is paramount, we are also witnessing an awakening across the globe. That awakening—set against such a narrow, damaging, chaotic reality—is inspired by the feminine and the need to preserve our beautiful Mother Earth and all of her plant and animal inhabitants.

The works in this volume attest to this new positive vision inspired by the sacred feminine divine that nourishes, clothes and encourages us rather than stripping us of our rights, our power and our beauty as stewards of the Earth in all her majesty and beauty.

In conclusion, this amazing gem of an anthology—full of wisdom, new ways of seeing and inspiration—is a welcome addition to the growing library of goddess scholarship, which serves to nourish us, inspire us and beckon us toward a new world filled with hope and light.

ACKNOWLEDGMENTS

We acknowledge the labor of love of so many to generate this volume.

In particular, we thank those who read articles and lent scholarly expertise, including (alphabetically by first name) Drs. Joan M. Cichon, Kathryn Henderson, Michelle Sandhoff.

All praises to Dr. Anne Key whose brilliance, insight, and service all along the way made this volume possible.

In support of our "Honoring Our Artist-Scholar Foremothers" section, we want to especially thank the families and friends of our featured foremothers, including Bob Ruyle and Katie Hoffner (for preserving Lydia Ruyle's legacy), and Patricia Alles (for cataloging all of Lydia's Goddess Icon banners). Additionally, we thank Sr. Susannah Miriam Kelly, Mary B. Kelly's daughter, and Ann Berger Frutkin, her sister, and Professor Keith Millman, New Media Program at Tompkins Cortland Community College (for providing images, information, and archival materials on Mary's life and art).

We are grateful for the contributions of editor Paula Bauman and copyeditor Louann Pope.

APPENDIX
PUBLICATIONS BY MARY B. KELLY

BOOKS

1989. *Goddess Embroideries of Eastern Europe.* Winona, MN: Northland Press of Winona.

1992. *Embroidering the Goddesses of Russia.* Denver, CO: Counted Thread Press.

1992. *Goddess Images in Czechoslovakia, Postcards from Bulgaria.* Denver, CO: Counted Thread Press.

1995. *A Visit to the Changeless Carpathians.* Children's exhibition catalogue. New York: Ukrainian Museum.

1995. *Embroidering the Goddesses of Slovakia.* Denver, CO: Counted Thread Press.

1997. *Embroidering the Goddesses of Ukraine.* Denver, CO: Counted Thread Press.

1997. *Embroidering the Goddesses of the Greek Islands.* Denver, CO: Counted Thread Press.

1999. *Goddess Embroideries of the Balkan Lands and the Greek Islands.* McLean, NY: Studiobooks.

2004. *Making and Using Ritual Cloths.* McLean, NY: Studiobooks.

2007. *Goddess Embroideries of the Northlands.* Hilton Head, SC: Studiobooks.

2008. *Embroidering the Goddesses of Old Norway.* Hilton Head, SC: Studiobooks.

2010. *Kaspaikka Muistiliina* (Memory Cloth). Leena Sappi, ed. Helsinki: Maahenki Press.

2010. *For the Love of Strangers,* by Jacqueline Horsfall. Illustrations and cover art by Mary B. Kelly. Powell, WY: Leap Books.

2011. *Goddess, Women, Cloth: A Worldwide Tradition of Making and Using Ritual Textiles.* Hilton Head, SC: Studiobooks.

ARTICLES

1986. "First Time Computer Graphics." *Computers and Graphics* 10 (spring).

1986. "Ritual and Ritual Fabrics." *Esprit* (spring).

1986. "Classroom Computer Graphics." *Computer Graphics Forum* 3 (spring). Norwich, England: University of East Anglia.

1987. "Fabrics for the Goddess." *Threads* (spring).

1988. "The Artist Learns Computer Graphics." *Colleague.* State University of New York.

1989. "Eastern European Motifs in the Work of Three Women Folk Artists." *New York Folklore* XV, 1-2.

1990. "Russian Batik Artists." *Threads* (October 1990).

1991. "In Search of the Goddess." *Slovakia* 5, 2: 4-5 (summer).

1992. "Embroidery for the Goddess." In *Stitchery and Needlelace* from *Threads Magazine.* Newton, Conn.: Tauton Press.

1992. "Goddess Embroideries of Eastern Europe." In *Gender, Culture, and the Arts.* R. Dotterer, ed., 28-31. Susquehanna University Studies. Cranbury, NJ: Associated University Presses.

1992. "Natalya Muradova: Dream Paintings on Textiles." *Fiberarts* (September/October).

1995. "A Visit to the Changeless Carpathians." In *The Changeless Carpathians - Living Traditions of the Hutzul People.* Exhibition catalogue. New York: Ukrainian Museum.

1996. "The Ritual Fabrics of Russian Village Women." In *Russia, Women, Culture.* Helena Goscillo and Beth Holmgren, eds., 152-176. Bloomington: Indiana University Press.

1997. "The Shrine of the Black Virgin Series." Art Showcase. *The Beltane Papers* 13.

2000. "Living Textile Traditions of the Carpathians." In *Folk Dress in Europe and Anatolia" Beliefs about Protection and Fertility.* Linda Welters, ed. Oxford: Berg Press.

2001. "An Eyeglass Case to Applique and Embroider." *Piecework* (March/April): 46-47.

2002. "Vlach Women: Cultural Continuity, Cultural Exchange." *Anuarul Muzeului Ethnografic al Bucovinei Suceava,* n. 2: 69-80. Suceava, Romania: Ministry of Culture.

2003. "A Tour to Textile Traditions of Old Europe." *ETN Textil Forum* 2 (June): 37-38. Hannover, Germany.

2003. "Chuvash Pointed Helmets." *Chuvash Art: Theoretical Questions and History* 5. Cheboksary: State Institute of Humanitarian Sciences.

2006. "Seasons and Cycles of Life: Traditional Motifs in Czech and Slovak Textiles." *Slovo* 7, 1. Cedar Rapids, IA: National Czech and Slovak Museum.

2008. "Motifs in Migration." *The Beltane Papers* 40.

2009. "Sacred Symbols on Ceremonial Cloth." *Needle Arts* 40, 1 (March-August): 16-21.

2009. "Exquisite Embroidered Symbolism; Norwegian Ceremonial Cloths." *Piecework* 17, 4: 16-24.

2009. "Sacred Symbols on Ceremonial Cloth." *Vesterheim Magazine* 7, 1: 5-10. Decorah, IsA: Vesterheim Norwegian American Museum.

2009. "A Collection of Ceremonial Textiles." *Bunad* 4 (December): 34-40.

2010. "A Walk with Berehinia." In *Goddesses in World Culture,* v. 2. Patricia Monaghan, ed. New York: Praeger.

2011. "Preserving Embroidery Traditions." *Needle Arts* (December).

2013. "Nordic Wasit Purses: Practical and Beautiful." *Piecework* (September).

2014. "Red the Universal Color." *Piecework* (April).

ABOUT THE CONTRIBUTORS

Rae Atira-Soncea was a featured panelist at ASWM's first symposium, in 2008. She received her MFA from the University of Wisconsin-Madison (1994), her MS in environment, textiles and design from the University of Wisconsin-Madison (1991), and her BA in art and design from Iowa State University in Ames, Iowa (1985). Sadly, Rae died on Sunday, March 1, 2009, silencing her strong voice for justice. Rae was an artist, activist, educator, organizer, priestess and interfaith ambassador. She worked at the Overture Center for the Arts in Madison, Wisconsin, where she was the coordinator of education, community engagement and accessibility. hedgecroft.net/blogs

Virginia (Gina) Subia Belton is a thanatologist, educator and, arising out of her mestizaje lineage, an emerging indigenous scholar. Gina is passionate about social justice, community, liberation and ecopsychology, particularly where they concern Native American mental health and the promotion of wellness for all in our end-of-life relationships. Her research and private practice explore the lineages of depth and humanistic existential psychology in approaching aging, life-limiting illness, death, grief and loss. redwoodpalliativepsychology.com

Cristina Biaggi, artist, activist and scholar, has achieved international recognition as a sculptor of bronze and wood and a creator of large outdoor installations and collages in two and three dimensions. Her work has been exhibited throughout the United States, Europe and Australia. She is a respected authority on the Great Goddess, Neolithic and Paleolithic prehistory, and the origin and effect of patriarchy on contemporary life. Her fourth book, *Activism in Art*, with a foreword by Gloria Steinem, is about how the global feminist movement of the 1960s through the 1980s motivated her activism, which in turn inspired her artwork. cristinabiaggi.com

Yuria Celidwen is a mystic, mythologist and cultural psychologist from Chiapas, Mexico. She is a doctoral candidate in mythology and depth psychology at Pacifica Graduate Institute and a graduate in contemplative sciences and contemplative psychotherapy from the Nalanda Institute for Contemplative Sciences. Her research focuses on ethics and compassion within world mythologies and mystical traditions from an interdisciplinary approach that bridges reason and emotion, scientific inquiry and contemplative practices. She writes about the sense of identity, ecstatic and religious phenomena, neuroplasticity for individual transformation, and social and environmental justice.

Joan M. Cichon, a retired history professor and reference librarian, has a PhD in women's spirituality from the California Institute of Integral Studies. Her dissertation, "Matriarchy in Minoan Crete: A Perspective from Archaeomythology and Modern Matriarchal Studies," reflects her interest in Bronze Age Crete, archaeomythology and modern matriarchal studies. Joan has published an article tracing the origins of the Eleusinian Mysteries to ancient Crete, and another elucidating how archaeomythology enables us to understand the spiritual life of ancient and modern societies in *Myths Shattered and Restored*.

Simone Clunie is an artist who lives in Florida. When she moved to the United States from Jamaica in the mid-1980s, she discovered that she had an affinity for clay. She earned a BFA in visual arts from Florida International University in Miami. A feminist conceptual framework is the impetus for her work and research, primarily using the female body as a metaphoric container for/of magic and women's mythology.

Miriam Robbins Dexter holds a PhD in ancient Indo-European languages, archaeology and comparative mythology. In *Whence the Goddesses: A Source Book* (1990), she translated texts from thirteen languages. She completed and supplemented Marija Gimbutas's final book, *The Living Goddesses* (1999). Her book, co-authored with Victor Mair, *Sacred Display: Divine and Magical Female Figures of Eurasia*, won ASWM's Sarasvati Award in 2012. The author of many articles on ancient female figures, she also has edited and co-edited sixteen scholarly volumes, including (with Vicki Noble) *Foremothers of the Women's Spirituality Movement:*

Elders and Visionaries (2015), which won the Susan Koppelman Award for best edited feminist anthology in 2016.

Ann Filemyr is a poet, teacher and mentor who currently serves as vice president of academic affairs and dean at Southwestern College (SWC), a consciousness-based graduate school in Santa Fe, New Mexico. Ann is also director of the certificate in transformational ecopsychology at SWC's New Earth Institute. She served as one of the principal *oshkibewis* (helpers) of the late Keewaydinoquay Peschel, and she continues to provide ceremonial leadership and spiritual mentoring for that lineage. Her poetry books include *Love Enough* and *The Healer's Diary*. She is a regular contributor to the We'Moon calendar. annfilemyr.com

Annie Finch is a poet, writer, speaker and performer. Her eighteen books include *Eve, Calendars, A Poet's Craft: A Comprehensive Guide to Making and Sharing Your Poetry, Spells: New and Selected Poems* and *Among the Goddesses: An Epic Libretto in Seven Dreams*, which received ASWM's Sarasvati Award in 2010. A graduate of Yale with a PhD from Stanford, Annie currently teaches for the low-residency MFA program in creative writing at St. Francis College in Brooklyn, New York, and offers inspirational talks, rituals and workshops about language and spirit. She has recently completed a new book, *The Witch in You*. anniefinch.com

Laura Fragua-Cota, MA, is an art therapist at a public school near her Jemez Pueblo village. She teaches introduction to art therapy at the Institute of American Indian Arts (IAIA), and she is an IAIA alumna. Her inspiration comes from the many aspects of her life as a woman, an artist and a Native American. Her expressions of creativity can be seen in various two-dimensional and three dimensional art mediums. Laura was the recipient of the New Mexico Governor's Award for Excellence in the Arts: the Allan Houser Memorial Award. She continues to express herself and display her work in art shows exhibiting nationally and internationally. www.southwestart.com/native-american-arts/laura_fragua_cota_artist

Judy Grahn has published thirteen books, including two book-length poems, several collections of poetry, a reader, an ecotopian novel and five nonfiction books. Her mythic history, *Another Mother Tongue: Gay Words, Gay Worlds*, was vital to the gay rights movement during the 1980s and

1990s. Her *Blood, Bread, and Roses: How Menstruation Created the World* remains influential to scholars examining ideas about human origins. Judy has received more than 20 awards for literature and activism. She holds a PhD from the California Institute of Integral Studies. Her dissertation research in Kerala, India, compared goddess rituals with menarche rituals. judygrahn.org

Marna Hauk directs the Institute for Earth Regenerative Studies in Portland, Oregon, innovating programs at the convergence of creativity, ecorestoration and living-wisdom traditions. A postdoctoral scholar teaching ecofeminism, sustainability education and climate change education at Prescott College, Marna is a Community Climate Change Fellow at the North American Association for Environmental Education (NAAEE). With more than ninety peer-reviewed presentations and publications, she serves on the board of the *Journal of Sustainability Education* and co-edited the book *Community Climate Change Education: A Mosaic of Approaches* (2017). She cultivates transdisciplinary Gaian methods and frameworks for regenerative creativity across personal, collaborative and wisdom-school contexts. earthregenerative.org

Kathryn Henderson, associate professor emerita of sociology and women's studies at Texas A&M University, is also ordained clergy of the Re-formed Congregation of the Goddess, International. Her research explores visual knowledge from design engineering to mental maps and human–animal networks of disaster survivors. Her spiritual research includes pancultural mythic connections between women and deer, viewed from a post-humanist perspective. Her "The Deer Mother: Earth's Nurturing Epicenter of Life and Death" appeared in volume 2 of *Goddesses in World Culture*. She is currently exploring connections between Cretan octopus representations on funerary pottery, spirituality and new research on octopus consciousness and communication.

Mary B. Kelly (1936–2016), artist, author and teacher, conducted groundbreaking research into prehistoric and folk arts throughout Europe for more than forty years. She explored the history and symbolism of embroidery and textile art, providing insight into a hidden heritage of goddess imagery in traditional ritual cloths. Mary was also an accomplished artist whose goddess paintings used motifs that she found in her research. She served on ASWM's advisory board from 2009 until her death.

Denise Kester is a nationally known artist. She has been a full-time studio artist for 35 years. She is the owner and distributor of Drawing on the Dream, a business that creates art prints and note cards, established in 1992. She studied art and education at the University of Georgia and printmaking at Southern Oregon University in Ashland, Oregon. She specializes in monoprint and monotype viscosity printing as well as multimedia, drawing and painting. She teaches a variety of workshops on the creative process, including printmaking, bookmaking, surface design, collage and block printing. Her studio is located in Ashland, Oregon. drawingonthedream.com

Helen Klebesadel maintains her art studio in Madison, Wisconsin. She has exhibited her richly detailed watercolors nationally and internationally for three decades. She was a featured panelist at ASWM's first symposium, in 2008. Her paintings are in many private and public collections. Helen's paintings address woman-centered and environmental themes. She starts with detailed drawings and then develops the images with layer upon layer of color washes and dry-brush technique mixed with occasional areas of wet-into-wet spontaneity. She regularly offers workshops on art and creativity. klebesadel.com

Louie Laskowski is an artist, ritualist, and organizer. She was recently ordained in the Re-formed Congregation of the Goddess, International. She taught high school art for 34 years in West Lafayette, Indiana. She is now retired from public school teaching but in full renewal for the rest of her life as a crone and artist. She presented her artworks at the 2011 ASWM symposium in Madison, Wisconsin. louielaskowski.com

Lisa Levart is a visual artist and photographer. She creates large scale, immersive multimedia installations of women embodying goddess archetypes. She is the author of *Goddess on Earth: Portraits of the Divine Feminine*, which won the GOLD Nautilus Book Award in 2012. Lisa's work has been featured in exhibitions worldwide, including the Kiek in de Kök Museum in Tallin, Estonia; Gallery Verita in Tokyo, Japan; and The

Alternative Museum, the Carter Burden Gallery, Soho Photo Gallery, and Art in General, all in New York City. goddessonearth.com

Barb Lutz. In 2002, Barb entered Kim Duckett's Year and a Day Sacred Mystery School for Women in Asheville, North Carolina. Soon thereafter, Barb began to serve that community by creating unique nature-based art altars, shamanic rituals and sacred spaces. Later she cocreated and cofacilitated the Wheel of the Year as a Spiritual Psychology for Women (WOTY) program. Barb's work in creating altars and artworks of natural materials has been featured at gatherings of the Re-formed Congregation of the Goddess, International; ASWM conferences; ordinations and women's rites of passage, including handfastings, weddings and ceremonies for the dying.

Joan Marler is the executive director of the Institute of Archaeomythology, author (with Harald Haarmann) of *Introducing the Mythological Crescent* (2008) and editor of *The Civilization of the Goddess* by Marija Gimbutas (1991), *From the Realm of the Ancestors: An Anthology in Honor of Marija Gimbutas* (1997), *The Journal of Archaeomythology* (2005–present), *The Danube Script* (2008), and other publications. She is completing her doctorate in philosophy and religion with an emphasis in women's spirituality at the California Institute of Integral Studies, where she taught as an adjunct professor for a number of years. archaeomythology.org

Patricia Monaghan (1946–2012), poet, writer and activist, was a tireless advocate for goddess scholarship. She wrote more than twenty books on such topics as Earth spirituality, Celtic mythology, the landscape of Ireland and meditation. In 1979, she published the first encyclopedia of goddesses, which in 2009 was republished as the two-volume set titled *The Encyclopedia of Goddesses and Heroines*. She was founder and senior fellow at the Black Earth Institute, an organization dedicated to inspiring artists to work toward inclusive spirituality, social justice and protection of the earth. With Sid Reger, she founded ASWM. patricia-monaghan.com

Aprina Murwanti is a researcher, curator, textile artist and lecturer. Aprina holds a PhD in visual art practice from the University of Wollongong Australia. A lecturer in the visual arts education program study at Universitas Negeri Jakarta Indonesia, she has given guest lectures and research presentations in Australia and Europe. Besides lecturing and practicing visual art, Aprina supports various ministries and international cultural institutes' projects in Indonesia. One of her past projects is the *Slow Fashion Lab* exhibition at the Goethe Institute (2017). Her interests include practice-led research, art and ritual, politics, feminism, installations and textile arts, and art business continuity. aprinamurwanti.tumblr.com

Lisa Noble is an exhibiting artist, poet, novelist and illustrator. A contributor to We'Moon Publications as well as Sage Woman, 4Culture's Poetry on Buses program and other media, Lisa was honored to be a member of the We'Moon Artists' panel at the 2015 ASWM symposium in Portland Oregon. She is the creator of the Char Man Chronicles and the Halfway to Babylon series, and she has recently illustrated *Tony and Jules* by Burien, Washington, author Virginia Wright. She has self-published two illustrated chapbooks: *Into the Light* and *Longing for Bohemia*. lisasstoriesblog.wordpress.com

Merry Gant Norris is an artist, teacher and creativity mentor who worked for 35 years to develop community resources for women in recovery from addiction. A painter of both goddesses and mandalas, Merry has been honored with five solo shows. In 2000, she opened Merry Nova Studio as a safe place for women to explore their spirituality through art. Merry gives mandala workshops. She also founded Goddess and Angel, a joyful program that helps women to discover their sacred wholeness. She discussed her paintings and her inspiring workshops at the 2011 ASWM symposium in Philadelphia. goddessandangel.com

Lauren Raine is an artist whose *Masks of the Goddess* are based on worldwide female mythologies. For 20 years, the masks have traveled to diverse communities, enabling storytellers, theaters and ritualists to give new meaning to the universal legacy of the Divine Feminine. She also has found inspiration in the Native American Creatrix myth of *Spider Woman* and has produced two community art projects, called *Spider Woman's Hands*, exploring interdependency. laurenraine.com

Arisika Razak, RN, MPH, is a professor emerita and former chair of the women's spirituality program at the California Institute of Integral Studies. A former president of the American Academy of Religion, Western Region, she co-chaired its Womanist-Pan African section for five years. Arisika is a regular contributor to books and journals; her film credits include *Fire Eyes*, the first full-length feature film by an African woman about female genital cutting and *Alice Walker: Beauty in Truth*.

Sid Reger is an artist and independent scholar whose passions are prehistoric art and symbols, mandalas, archaeology and matrifocal cultures. A daughter of the Appalachian Mountains, she draws on the wisdom of the natural world for artistic inspiration. Her doctorate in adult education has been put to use in a long and varied career in teaching and arts administration. She is ordained clergy in the Re-formed Congregation of the Goddess, International, and on the faculty of the Women's Thealogical Institute. She is cofounder and president of ASWM.

Lydia Ruyle (1935–2016) was an artist, author and scholar emerita of the visual arts faculty of the University of Northern Colorado (UNC) in Greeley, Colorado, where the Lydia Ruyle Room for Women's Art was dedicated in 2010. She held an MA from UNC and studied with Syracuse University in Italy, France and Spain and with the Art Institute of Chicago in Indonesia. For twenty years, she led workshops and women's pilgrimage journeys to sacred places. Lydia created and exhibited her art throughout the United States and internationally. Her Goddess Icon Spirit Banners, which made their debut in 1995 at the Library of Celsus in Ephesus, Turkey, have flown at countless conferences and gatherings in 36 countries.

Mei-Mei Sanford, the Iyalode Osun of Iragbiji (an Osun priestly title), teaches in the Africana studies program at the College of William and Mary. Mei-Mei is the co-editor of *Osun Across the Waters: A Yoruba Goddess in Africa and the Americas* and the author of many articles and conference papers about Yoruba and Yoruba diaspora religions and arts. She received *smicha* (ordination) from Kohenet Hebrew Priestess Institute.

Cristina Rose Smith, granddaughter of Priscilla of New Mexico and Concepcion of Cebu, was born in Los Angeles, California. She earned a PhD from the California Institute of Integral Studies. As a mother, artist, writer and professor of gender and ethnic studies at California State University, Dominguez Hills, she engages with women-affirming and indigenous-rooted communities based in Long Beach. cristinagolondrina.com.

Carmen R. Sonnes is a Mexican-American artist who divides her time between the lush greenness of the Pacific Northwest and the arid deserts and canyons of the Southwest. Her work, which has appeared in We'Moon Publications, was selected for ASWM's 2015 symposium in Portland, Oregon. Her work is both intensely personal and immensely universal, but always it is the expression of one woman's gentle, passionate voice. carmenrsonnes.com

Toni Truesdale, artist, educator, writer and illustrator, celebrates women, the natural environment and the diversity of world cultures. With more than 500 original images, she has exhibited at more than fifty visual art shows and painted forty murals. She also is widely published. For many years, she has been an educator working with indigenous and minority populations. She has won many awards and grants for educational programs, organizational work and human-rights advocacy. She is a mother, grandmother and foster parent, with family in African American and Native American communities, and she has long-term friendships across the world. tonitruesdale.com

Nancy Vedder-Shults was named a Wisdom Keeper of the Goddess Spirituality Movement in 2013. She is the author of *The World Is Your Oracle: Divinatory Practices for Tapping Your Inner Wisdom and Getting the Answers You Need* (2017), an innovative book that presents forty multicultural techniques, of which one-third are visual, one-third are auditory and one-third are kinesthetic. Nancy writes for *SageWoman* magazine and *Feminism and Religion* and will soon blog for *Pagan Square*. She also recorded *Chants for the Queen Heaven*, a CD of goddess songs from around the world. WorldYourOracle.com

LIST OF ILLUSTRATIONS

1. 35,000-year-old female figure, Hohle Fels cave, southwestern   29
    Germany
2. Crouching stone fish figure from the Mesolithic site of   31
    Lepenski Vir
3. Female silhouettes, painted and incised   33
4. Silver seal of Lajja Gauri from Kashmir Smast   39
5. Perseus slaying winged Medusa   40
6. Gorgon pediment from Artemis Temple in Corfu   41
7. Kiltinan Sheela-na-gig from Fethard, County Tipperary, Ireland   42
8. Moate Sheela-na-gig behind Moate castle, County Westmeath,   42
    Ireland
9. Birth-giving woman from Malta, in a magical stance   43
10. Sign in front of Starbucks in Del Mar, California   44
11. My Mitoni ritual, Nyamping segment   62
12. Lurik cloth with dringin pattern   63
13. Lurik cloth with tumbar pecah pattern   63
14. *Recalling the Goddess Sri,* art installation at FCA Gallery,   68
    University of Wollongong
15. Detail of the goddess Sri and the rice cones offering in *Recalling*   68
    the Goddess Sri
16. Viewers of *Recalling the Goddess Sri*   69
17. Detail of Kamaratih and Kamajaya in *Recalling the Goddess Sri*   69
18. *Mitoni, Lurik and the Stitches of Lament,* art installation at FCA   70
    Gallery, University of Wollongong
19. *Mitoni, Lurik and the Stitches of Lament*   70
20. *Mitoni, Lurik and the Stitches of Lament*   70
21. *Mitoni, Lurik and the Stitches of Lament*   71
22. Man walking on his knees to the Lady of Guadalupe shrine,
    on pilgrimage   81
23. Mother goddess Coatlicue   83
24. Mother goddess Tonantzin   83
25. Nuestra Señora de Guadalupe [Our Lady of Guadalupe], also   86
    known as the Virgin of Guadalupe, shown in the Basilica of Our
    Lady of Guadalupe in México City

26. The source of the Osun River, Igede, Nigeria. 105
27. *Ose Sango* 106
28. "Unbelievable, Oshun Comes Out Live, Out of the River and 109
Speaks," *The People's Voice*
29. *Blessing from Iko I and II* 110, 111
30. Iyalaase Osun of Iragbiji, Nigeria. 114
31. *Grandmother's House* 116
32. *House Shrine* 117
33. *Basket-House-Village-Universe* 118
34. *Ancient Kitchen* 119
35. *Clay Prayers* 119
36. *Callileach* 120
37. *Sacred Writing* 121
38. *Daily Bread* 122
39. *N'Debele Woman* 123
40. *The Culture of Women* 124
41. *Feast Day* 124
42. *The Return* 124
43. "Stone Portalway and Earth Spiral Opening" dream montage 133
44. "Triangle Canyon of the Goddesses Dream" dream montage 137
45. "Traveling Tsunami Bear Dream" dream montage 138
46. *Self Portrait: Ancient Mother* (Lydia Ruyle) 151
47. Photograph of Mary B. Kelly 157
48. *Berehina, Ukranian Goddess of Vegetation* 158
49. *Dordona, Hungarian Goddess of Harvests* 159
50. *Guan Yin, Chinese Goddess of Mercy* 160
51. *Hecate, Triple Goddess of the Crossroads* 161
52. *Kali, Black Virgin series* 162
53. *Laima, Baltic Goddess of Spring and Renewal* 163
54. *Lucina, Swedish Goddess of Light* 164
55. *Oshun*, Black Virgin series 165
56. *Rozhanitza, Siberian Elk Goddess* 166
57. *Emergence* 175
58. *Where the Spirit Goes* 176
59. *La Entrada Conquistadores en El Nombre de Jesus Christom* 176
60. *With No Eyes My Hands Feel What I See* 177
61. *Beneath the Red There Were the Blues* 178
62. *My Cornmeal Bowl Full of Prayers* 178
63. *Aboriginal Daughter with Great White Mom and Dad* 179
64. *Aboriginal Son with Great White Father* 180

65. *A Pathway of our future . . .*   181
66. *The Naming Ceremony*   182
67. *Is it Just Makeup?*   182
68. *Just Because You Put Feathers in Your Hair Don't Make You*   183
     an Indian
69. *Pueblo Indian Harvest Dance*   184
70. *Who Made the Box?*   185
71. *The Blessing of the Animals*   185
72. *Mother Earth's Blessing*   186
73. *Yew Medusa*   190
74. *Black Medusa*   191
75. *Red Medusa*   192
76. *Raging Medusa*   192
77. Gorgoneion antefix, Etruscan or South Italian   195
78. Gorgoneion antefix roof tile, Greek   195
79. Gorgoneion antefix roof tile, Greek, South Italian, Tarentine   195
80. Medusa head antefix, Greek, South Italian   195
81. Medusa head antefix, Greek, South Italian   195
82. *Fish Goddess of Lepenski Vir*   201
83. *Kiev Medusa*   201
84. *Melusine*   202
85. *Oshun*   203
86. *Sedna*   203
87. *Nu Gua*   204
88. *Mami Wata*   205
89. *The Yurt: Fire Goddess and Water Goddess*   211
90. *She Calls to the Soul Seeds Dancing at the Edge of the*   213
     Universe
91. *Medusa Re-membered*   215
92. *Praying Mantis & Butterfly Goddess*   217
93. *Sherawali*   219
94. *Honoring Lydia: A Double Goddess Altar*   221
95. *Artemis Bee Labyrinth*   223
96. *I AM CRONE*   225
97. *The Masks of the Goddess*   227
98. *Wisdom Harvest*   229
99. *la golondrina ibon*   231
100. *A GRANDMOTHER'S LOVE*   233
101. *God Giving Birth*   251
102. *Goddess Head*   252

103. *Treasure Ship: Goddess of the Earth*   253
104. *Nuestra Madre Coatlicue [Our Mother Coatlicue]*   254
105. *Untitled (Guanaroca: First Woman), Esculturas Rupestres*   256
      [Ruprestrian Sculptures]
106. *Dancing*   272